# Robert Frost
## and
# Sidney Cox

*Forty Years of Friendship*

# Robert Frost and" Sidney Cox

*Forty Years of Friendship*

## William R. Evans

Foreword by James M. Cox

University Press of New England
Hanover, New Hampshire and London, England
1981

*University Press of New England*

SPONSORING INSTITUTIONS

Brandeis University

Brown University

Clark University

Dartmouth College

University of New Hampshire

University of Rhode Island

Tufts University

University of Vermont

Grateful acknowledgment is made to The Estate of Robert Frost, Alfred C. Edwards, Executor, for permission to publish in this edition the unpublished letters, poems, and introduction contained herein. Acknowledgment is also made to The Estate of Sidney Cox, Arthur M. Cox, Executor, for permission to publish the letters and journals by Sidney Cox contained herein.

Many of the letters of Robert Frost were previously published in *Selected Letters of Robert Frost* edited by Lawrance Thompson. Copyright © 1964 by Lawrance Thompson and Holt, Rinehart and Winston. Three of the letters first appeared in *Robert Frost: Poetry and Prose* edited by Edward Connery Lathem and Lawrance Thompson. Copyright © 1972 by Holt, Rinehart and Winston. The poems "To the Right Person," "Bond and Free," and "Nothing Gold Can Stay" are from *The Poetry of Robert Frost* edited by Edward Connery Lathem. Copyright 1916, 1923, 1947 © 1969 by Holt, Rinehart and Winston. Copyright 1944, 1951 by Robert Frost. Copyright © 1975 by Lesley Frost Ballantine. These are reprinted by permission of Holt, Rinehart and Winston, Publishers. Part of the section entitled "Barding Around" was published in different form as "Frost's Barding at Bates" in the *Dartmouth College Library Bulletin* 19 NS (April 1979).

To Eileen

# Contents

# Foreword
## *James M. Cox*

T HE READER of this collection of letters will see how stub-
bornly and adroitly Robert Frost could resist his friends'
efforts to write about him or publish his letters to them. Yet *In the
Clearing*, Frost's last book of poems—published in 1962, a year
before his death—contained the following strange dedication:

> *Dedication*
> Letters in prose to
> Louis Untermeyer, Sidney Cox, and John Bartlett
> for them to dispose of as they please;
> these to you in verse for keeps

The dedication is strange first of all because the "bequest" of the
letters is all but intruded into the conventional bequest of the volume of poems to its readers. Beyond that, there is the fact that
both Sidney Cox and John Bartlett had both been dead for some
years and could scarcely do with the letters as they pleased.

Even so, Frost's dedication made clear that he was no longer
withholding permission for the letters to be published. Two of the
collections—the Untermeyer collection edited by himself, and the
Bartlett collection edited by Bartlett's daughter Margaret Anderson—were published in the year of Frost's death. Now, eighteen
years later, we have this fine edition of the letters to Cox; and by
including all the surviving Cox letters to Frost, William Evans has
given us a full sense of the correspondence between the two men.

If Frost had found in John Bartlett a student who was going to
be a newspaper reporter and in Louis Untermeyer a poet who was

---

James M. Cox is professor of English at Dartmouth College. He is no relation to Sidney
Cox, and he joined the English Department faculty after Sidney Cox's death.

well on the way to becoming an anthologist, he found in Sidney
Cox a teacher who would remain a teacher. He deeply needed, and
he deeply used, all three correspondents. He needed Bartlett and
Cox to write to from England when he was framing his belief that
poetry was the sound of sense; he needed Untermeyer when he returned to America—needed him as a means of relation to the
whole community of modern poets and poetry. And of course
Frost used all three of his correspondents—used them to publicize
his poetry and to arrange lecture engagements for him.

This practical and calculating side of Frost can be made so visible that it obscures the great humanity shining through his correspondence. For all its extraordinary research and completeness,
Lawrance Thompson's biography has succeeded in darkening the
humane side of Frost's life with just such visibility. The letters in
this volume throw light on both sides of both men. They show
Frost's willingness to dominate Sidney Cox as much as they show
Cox's too willing subservience to Frost. Time and again the letters
show a Frost impatient with Cox's devotion or scornfully critical
of his behavior. Even in his wise advice, Frost often seems more
brusque than kind. There is no escape from this side of Frost any
more than there is escape from the possibility that Cox's devotion
to Frost may have crippled his creative force. His vision of Frost
blinded him to much of modern poetry.

Yet seeing this side of the relationship ought to make us see another side more clearly. When they met in 1911 both men were
teachers. One was at the threshold of leaving teaching to give all to
poetry. The other was at the point of giving his whole life to teaching. Small wonder that Frost began the whole relationship by
taunting Sidney Cox for being overserious to hurry home and
grade papers. The whole burden of grading youthful student writing was what Frost, the much older man, was getting out from under in order to nourish the poet in him forever young. Cox, the
young man, was at the point of relinquishing what Sherwood Anderson calls "the young thing" within him in order to be a teacher
utterly devoted to youth. If Frost felt in Cox (and the letters show
how much he felt it) the enthusiasm for literature that a teacher
must have at the base of his being, he found in Cox the embodi-

ment of the teacher he could never quite abandon in himself. What Cox found in Frost was both the poet and the poetry—the writer—he was all but abandoning in himself to discover and nourish in others.

Frost was of course the stronger of the two and outlived his younger friend. He knew his own tenacity for survival; he had to see the frailty of those who loved him both without and within his family. Seeing it was part of the hard strength that gave him a relation to the world with sinew enough to outlast the best, the very best people he could meet in life. Yet if he was hard, he was also true. How easy it would have been for him to escape from the relationship once he returned from England to success and the beginnings of fame. Who of us has not somehow left someone behind, or been left behind on so much less basis. These letters are themselves proof that neither man left the other. They show that Frost no more gave up being a teacher than Sidney Cox gave up being a student. If the true measure of Frost's teaching is to be found in the wisdom he imparted in these letters, the measure of Cox is that he both inspired and received it. Beyond Frost's scolding and gruff resistance and beyond Sidney Cox's adulation, there is a spirit of generosity, kindness, and loyalty. There is, in a word, friendship— a relationship possessing the strength of love and need to last for life.

# Preface

As a Dartmouth undergraduate I listened to Robert Frost read his poetry to an overflowing crowd in Webster Hall. Afterwards, I asked him to autograph my Modern Library edition of his poems, and he obliged, smiling. That was my only personal contact with Frost. Sidney Cox, who had died before I enrolled at Dartmouth, was for me a vague figure, sometimes recalled by my professors.

More than a decade after that poetry reading, I was again at Dartmouth on a research trip, and I asked Dean Edward Connery Lathem about Cox. Frost's dedication to *In the Clearing* had fired my curiosity, and I wanted to know more about this teacher, writer, and friend of Frost's. That initial conversation with Dean Lathem ultimately led to this book, and I am deeply grateful to him for sharing with me his memories and judgments and for making available to me the rich collection of Frost-Cox material in Dartmouth's Baker Library.

This collection represents some forty years of intimacy and records with seismographic intensity the direction and duration of the Frost-Cox friendship. In Frost's unpublished Introduction to Cox's posthumous book, *A Swinger of Birches*, Frost observed: "Our intimacy was a curious blend of differences that if properly handled might prove an almost literary curiosity." Like many of Frost's pronouncements, this one can be interpreted several ways. But the important word is *intimacy*—Frost was not given to superlatives.

What was it that made the two men intimates? Shared confidences; similar views on the importance of ideas and the compelling need to explore those ideas no matter what enemy territory they led to; a devotion to literature because of its power to illumine human experience, whether of terror or exultation; and a recognition by each man that the other was living out his creative potential—Frost, through his poetry, Cox, through his teaching. If Cox, reading Frost's poems in manuscript in Plymouth in 1911 when Frost was still apparently a ne'er-do-well, sensed the greatness in the poet, so Frost, in that unpublished Introduction written when he was an old man, tapped the achievement of Cox's life: "He was a great, triumphant teacher." Like any friendship of long duration, this one had its scars: the letters reveal the wounds. But the letters are also graced with forgiveness.

During the years I have worked on this book—shaping the biography of Sidney Cox was probably the most difficult part of the task—I have benefited from the generous help of a number of people. I am deeply grateful to the family of Sidney Cox, especially Barbara Cox Vallarino, who gave me access to family papers, letters, journals, photographs, and mementos; William Bronk, poet and close friend of Sidney Cox, deserves thanks for sharing with me his memories and reflections on Frost and Cox. Likewise, a debt is owed to many others who took the time to write long and always valuable letters to me about Cox; these correspondents are cited in the text and footnotes. I am especially grateful to them for their assistance. I wish to thank Professor Harry Schultz of Dartmouth and Mary Schultz, his wife, who helped me immeasurably in matters of Dartmouth life.

Librarians, too, have been helpful and patient in answering my queries. I wish to thank them all, especially Rena Rogge of Kean College of New Jersey, Kenneth Cramer of Dartmouth College, Mary Riley of Bates College, and Richard Goff Smith of the University of Illinois.

I am indebted to Kean College of New Jersey for released time for research and a semester's sabbatical, which enabled me to pursue this study.

My thanks also go to Hilary Horton, an inspiring copy editor.

To all these, and others whom I have not named here, I am grateful. But I am most grateful to the person to whom I have dedicated this book, my wife, Eileen Kennedy Evans. Without her care, love, help, and understanding, this book could not have been.

                                                        W.R.E.

*Union, New Jersey*
*October 1980*

# Editorial Principles

A SIZABLE NUMBER of Frost's letters to Cox have been published in *The Selected Letters of Robert Frost* (Lawrance Thompson, ed., New York: Holt, Rinehart and Winston, 1964). They are reprinted here for the convenience of the reader. I have gone back to the original manuscripts used in *Selected Letters* not only to correct the very few errors there, but also to supply sections of the letters omitted in that volume.

I have retained the original spelling and punctuation in the Frost-Cox letters, unhampered by *sic*s from me. Frost sometimes used the apostrophe in contractions and sometimes did not, especially with the word *don't*. Where no date or place is given in the letters, when possible I have supplied this information in brackets. ALS at the top of a letter designates an autograph letter, signed, following which are the number of pages of the original; ALU is an unsigned autograph letter; TLS designates a typed letter, signed.

In the "letter-journals" the lines of dashes do not signify omissions; they were made by Cox to indicate separate entries.

One basic text mentioned in this book several times is *The Poetry of Robert Frost* (Edward Connery Lathem, ed., New York: Holt, Rinehart and Winston, 1969), referred to hereafter only by its title.

## Nothing Gold Can Stay

Nature's first green is gold,
Her hardest hue to hold.
Her early leaf's a flower;
But only so an hour.
Then leaf subsides to leaf.
So Eden sank to grief,
So dawn goes down to day.
Nothing gold can stay.

PART ONE

# The Meeting

I 9 I I

*"Nature's First Green"*

*The complaint of everyone who writes anything . . .*
*that nothing he writes quite represents his*
*thought or his feeling.*

ROBERT FROST *to* SIDNEY COX
*26 December 1912*

TWO MEN—strangers to each other—sat among the lonely chairs at a Plymouth Normal School dance one fall evening in 1911. Looking on at the dancers, they began to chat idly. The older man, thirty-seven, was Robert Frost; the younger, twenty-two, was Sidney Cox. Both were teachers: Frost at the Normal School, Cox at the local high school. Frost's friend Ernest L. Silver, the principal of the New Hampshire State Normal School at Plymouth, had been newly appointed to the position and had brought Frost with him from Pinkerton Academy, at Derry.

To Frost, Cox seemed "teasably young"; maybe Cox's college-boy's assurance piqued him. The brand-new teacher regarded Frost as old and uncouth, someone who had accomplished little in life. Frost's suit was unpressed; his gray shirt unstarched; he sat with his legs crossed. To break away, Cox mentioned he had themes to correct. Frost, poking fun at the task, flippantly re-marked something like "Tear 'em up, toss 'em out the window." Angered, Cox got up and left. He felt Frost's speech, like his clothes, lacked elegance; and he didn't like his lack of conformity, his wild and earthy quality. Later Cox asked Ernest Silver was it because of alcohol Frost hadn't achieved much. The question was repeated to Frost, who, stirred to mischief by Cox and his seri-ousness, set out "to take him." Flattered by Frost's interest and charged by his ideas, Cox came round. In the one year at Plym-outh their friendship struck deep roots. Remembering their first meeting, Frost wrote some forty years later: "It wasn't the last time he had to make allowances for me."[1]

Cox was close to a truth when he judged Frost a near-failure. Others had felt that, like Frost's father, he had not lived up to his promise. Robert Frost had been born in San Francisco in 1874, the first child of Isabelle Moodie Frost, a Scottish schoolteacher, a de-vout Swedenborgian, who filled her son with tales of mythic he-roes and their undaunted valor. Frost's father, William Prescott Frost, born in Kingston, New Hampshire, was a Harvard gradu-ate, a handsome, impetuous, athletic journalist, interested in po-litical office, fond of gambling and whiskey. During William's drunken states his wife had to protect their son and daughter,

Jeanie, (born in 1876) against his violence. Like a wishbone pulled between his mother's gentleness and his father's harshness, Frost grew up overindulged by his mother, who sought comfort in mystical flights, but severely disciplined by his father, who, despite his own pursuit of pleasure, was puritanically strict with his children.

When Frost was eleven, his father died, and his mother brought the family East to Lawrence, Massachusetts, a mill town, to be near her husband's relatives. Close to poverty, she earned a living for her family by teaching in a public school nearby, at Salem, New Hampshire. An insecure, competitive, and slow-to-forgive adolescent, Frost entered high school at Lawrence, in 1888. Covering his diffidence with an arrogant manner, he attracted few friends, but he was determined to achieve recognition. He found he enjoyed his studies, especially history and classics, and through intellectual attainments he gained the respect of his schoolmates and compensated, to some extent, for his feeling of insecurity. He became a prominent member of the debating society, had his first poems published in the *High School Bulletin*, and in his senior year was named its chief editor. At his graduation, he was co-valedictorian with Elinor White, a highly intelligent, passionately idealistic girl, who shared his devotion to literature. Determined to earn her college degree, she put off his insistent demands that they marry. He enrolled at Dartmouth College but stayed less than a semester. Upset by Elinor's refusal to leave St. Lawrence University, he seriously considered throwing away his life in the Dismal Swamp of Virginia.

When Elinor White, against her father's wishes, finally consented to marry Frost, he had no reliable way of supporting her, and his health was plagued by a vague malaise. He had fitfully held a series of jobs: teaching a little; working as clerk and factory hand in the mills at Lawrence; serving as a reporter for two newspapers. At the time of his wedding, on December 19, 1895, he had returned to teaching in a public school, and Elinor Frost helped out as a teacher in the unprepossessing private school that Frost's mother managed at the Central Building in downtown Lawrence. Elinor became pregnant, and their first child, Elliott, was born in 1896. In the fall of 1897 Frost entered Harvard as a special student and did well there, earning scholastic honors. But in less than two years he dropped out again, suffering from financial and domestic worries, worn out by fatigue, and fearful that he had tuberculosis. A doctor informed him that he should find employment out-of-doors, that he should stay away from taxing sedentary work.

Frost's grandfather, a disciplinarian whom Frost bitterly resented—but who was kinder and more generous than Frost ever credited—set Frost up in business by buying him a poultry farm at Derry, New Hampshire. So Frost, who had kept chickens before, drifted into farming. He was helped by his botanizing friend, Carl Burell, who was adept at gardening and shared Frost's interest in both nature and poetry. But Frost hated getting up early, milking the cow, feeding the chickens, and collecting the eggs. More to his taste were roaming the fields and woods in search of wild flowers, reading a wide range of authors, and trying to shape words into poetry. But he had had only limited success in publishing his lyrics.

After almost six years of half-hearted farming and several rejection slips from editors, Frost returned to teaching, this time at the well-established Pinkerton Academy in Derry Village. For financial reasons, it was a necessary step. His family now, in 1906, included four children: Lesley, a daughter, seven; Carol, a son, four; Irma, three; and Marjorie, one—Elliott had died at three and a half.

Because he was daring, a relentless self-seeker, Frost brought creative and original methods to teaching. His quirkiness as well as his innovations—a heavy emphasis on writing and oral work, dramatic productions of Marlowe's *Doctor Faustus*, Milton's *Comus*, Sheridan's *The Rivals*, and Yeats's *The Land of Heart's Desire* and *Cathleen ni Houlihan*—gained him attention across the state. In his heart's core, he wanted to be a poet; but teaching provided him with a livelihood. It also provided a new sense of self-confidence for the man whose failures were darkened even further by his black moods, by his brooding over slights and rejections.

When Ernest Silver, the principal at Pinkerton Academy, was invited to head the Plymouth Normal School in 1911, he asked Frost to join the faculty there. The Normal School had an enrollment of about one hundred—all girls—and the one opening was in psychology and the history of education. The area of specialization did not matter to Silver: he wanted Frost for his stimulation, his ability to fire the minds of students. Frost saw Plymouth as a step upward, but one that did not satisfy his ultimate ambition. In 1911 he had published only a scattering of poems, in newspapers and magazines such as *The Independent*. Settling at Plymouth, the Frosts lived in a cottage near the imposing red-brick main building of the Normal School.

When Sidney Cox met Robert Frost at the Plymouth dance, Cox was a serious young man, an inexperienced first-year teacher. To prepare himself for his career, he had studied assiduously, lived frugally, and worked at humdrum jobs to pay his college expenses. His family was well connected, though of slender means: his ancestors on his mother's side included John Alden of the *Mayflower*; and among his relatives were distinguished college professors and ministers of prosperous congregations. His father, however, a high-principled Baptist minister, made only a modest living as the pastor of several middling congregations. He had married Elizabeth Hayes, member of a highly regarded family in Lewiston, Maine.

Elizabeth Hayes kept a journal, wrote long letters, saved boxes of correspondence, listed the books she read—and passed these habits on to her son. A prayerful Victorian woman, concerned with niceties and refinement, she had grown up in an atmosphere of considerable culture. Her father, Benjamin Francis Hayes, a doctor of divinity and a professor at Bates College in Lewiston, had served as acting president there in 1876. Her mother, Allie Cary Hayes, had had a fulfilling career as a teacher and had established Sunday-school classes for working girls, out of which grew the Lewiston Young Woman's Home and the Lewiston Women's Christian Association.

When Elizabeth Hayes was twenty-six, she received a letter from an acquaintance, a minister named Arthur Elmes Cox, who asked her permission to begin a correspondence, perhaps one that would lead to marriage. She knew him as a soft-spoken, neat, clear-thinking man, whose teachers spoke highly of him and his enthusiasm for Biblical scholarship. Born in 1858 in Buckinghamshire, England, he had emigrated to the United States when he was fourteen. Although she had liked his appearance, she had not thought romantically of him until he began his courtship. Undeterred by her initial hesitation, he pursued her diligently and successfully.

Two years later, in January 1888, Arthur Cox and Elizabeth Hayes were married in her family's home. After their brief wedding trip to Boston, Elizabeth Cox assumed her duties as a minister's wife in Limerick, Maine. Her husband's responsibilities were strenuous: he was the pastor of a scattered congregation and also the superintendent of schools. The pay was meager and his energies were taxed—he had to travel miles to visit his congregation and the district schools. On August 25, 1889, Sidney Cox was born; fifteen months later, his sister, Gertrude, was born. The children spent their early years in Limerick, but in 1902 Arthur Cox accepted the call, at a higher salary, to a Baptist church in Poland, New York.

At the time of the move, Sidney Cox was entering adolescence. He had been raised in a family in which the relationships were warm and close, tied by the vision of a God who was intimately present—the stern Sovereign of the New England Calvinists had by then become a loving Father. Arthur Cox's sermons, inspired by texts from the New Testament, applied these verses to the needs and decisions of everyday life. Sunday services were followed by Sunday school. Adolescents were baptized by immersion and encouraged to take the Temperance Pledge. The church worship was linked to suppers and to socials, Bible study and Christian Endeavor meetings, and a practical concern for the sick and the poor.

The children grew up well cared for in the penny-pinching household, and they saw their mother accept suffering bravely within the family as well as without. Soon after Gertrude's birth, Elizabeth Cox had a severe sacroiliac sprain, which necessitated long periods of rest and sometimes the use of a wheelchair. Sidney Cox felt that his father's talents went unrecognized: the cramped corners and small-town pastorates Arthur Cox was appointed to were no just reward for his intellectual powers, learning, and quiet zeal. Unlike his wife's relatives, he never received the call to prominent congregations in important cities.

Gertrude and Sidney Cox were encouraged to read, to study,

to write. Their parents gave them instruction in sex; their father explained that the pre-Flood books of the Bible were "fables," though nonetheless valuable for that. They were concerned and talked openly about Gertrude's menstrual difficulties.

The brother and sister attended high school in Poland, New York. After classes, Cox studied, worked at a part-time job— sometimes delivering newspapers, sometimes clerking in a drugstore—and then, after supper, he studied again. There was no time for sports: to attain his goal, he had to be single-minded. He wanted to enroll at Bates College, to prepare for a career as an English teacher.

Bates had been founded during the Civil War by Oren B. Cheney, a Dartmouth graduate and energetic minister who envisioned a college tied to the Baptist Church, where students from the farms of Maine and New Hampshire could receive a superior education. In 1907, when Sidney and Gertrude Cox enrolled in the freshman class, the family's personal associations with Bates were close. Their grandfather had been among the founding faculty and had taught with distinction modern languages, English, and apologetics. The president of Bates in 1907, George Colby Chase—an indefatigable fund raiser and strict administrator sensitive to the values of his Baptist board and alumni—was a family friend. He knew how intelligent, moral, hard-working, and self-directed young Sidney was. And he was always seeking strong candidates for his college, which in 1907 had 438 students, taught by nearly two dozen faculty members.

In weekly letters to his parents, Cox described with gusto his undergraduate life. He studied Latin, Greek, French, German, English, elocution, civics, algebra, trigonometry, chemistry, astronomy, philosophy, religion, history, and psychology. In four years he took sixty-three courses and received thirty-six A's, twenty-three B's, and four C's. To earn money, he collected bills for the Globe Steam Laundry; dusted the library shelves; and one summer worked as a nurse-orderly in a hospital. He and Gertrude were avid debaters, Sidney helping to defeat the visiting team from City College of New York; disappointed when he and his sister did not reach the finals in a statewide tournament, Sidney learned bitterly that hard work could not accomplish everything. He thought reading Goethe's *Faust* in the original was the greatest literary experience in his life. On one rare and wonderful occasion, he watched Bates defeat Bowdoin in a football game. He tried sports, but hand and eye wouldn't coordinate.

Cox agreed with President Chase's decision that a co-educational college like Bates should not sponsor a dance. Some Baptists were uneasy about young men and women studying together, and their uneasiness would have mounted to fear if they had heard students were dancing with each other. Cox described how when five girls were expelled because they had attended an off-campus dance, their angry fellow-students held a mass meeting, yelling, "Strike, strike." They jeered and roared at the faculty's decision, upset the office of English professor William Hartshorn, and finally were quelled by a diplomatic move on the president's part. The girls were readmitted, but Cox, who had sided with the faculty, felt the mob was childish, unjustified.

He went to Christian Endeavor meetings and Bible-study classes, and on one occasion preached at a nearby church. When a friend who had "known sin" needed a confidant and adviser, Cox on a long walk consoled him. He was less kind to an acquaintance whom he found drunk.

In these letters Cox is open, frank, self-possessed, and loving. The prose is accurate, honest, unconvoluted. Substitutes for long family conversations, the letters are full of questions. He inquires about his father's salary and what his parents think about Gertrude's recurring illnesses; she finally had to leave college at the end of her junior year, and, suffering from physical difficulties as well as neurasthenia, she rested at home. She did earn her degree, however, a year after her brother. The only anxiety the parents had about their son was that he would overwork himself.

Cox's parents encouraged him to become an English teacher. His mother knew his secret desire was to hold a chair of literature someday. His classmate and close friend, Ralph Dow, fooled by Cox's self-contained optimism, thought him too scientific, too speculative, too unemotional to be a good literature teacher. But his teachers gave him excellent letters of recommendation, which he copied for his parents to enjoy.

Commencement 1911 was a glorious day for Cox. He was

awarded honors in his triple major: philosophy, English, and history. His mother, in a wheelchair—the only family member who could be present—heard him deliver a speech entitled "Soul Architecture." God, the Master-Builder, said Cox, furnishes the materials; but the educator erects "the grand and beauteous structure of the soul." With the right kind of teaching, the regeneration of the world will be accomplished.[2]

Earnest, idealistic, and untried, Cox had begun in the spring of his senior year to search for a teaching position. He was delighted when he was hired by the Plymouth high school. As suggested by his college English adviser, he asked for the respectable salary of nine hundred dollars—and got it. The school ranked among the highest in the state, and the principal, a Bates graduate, knew the Hayes family. Classes started at 8:45 and ended at 4:15. Cox would be in the classroom all the time, except for three "free" periods a week, when he would handle the homeroom affairs. Plymouth, located in the foothills of the White Mountains, with a population of about three thousand, was a "pretty" county seat, with a public library, frequent concerts, and a good lecture series. The handsome school building, four years old, was near the Plymouth Normal School.[3]

Two significant events in the fall of 1911 helped to shape Cox's life: the launching of his career as a teacher and—ironically enough for a student who had opposed dancing—that meeting with Frost at a school dance. True, the meeting got off to an abortive start; but Frost, determined "to take" Cox, found ways of making their paths cross.

Frost, lonely for intellectual companionship in that small town, had probably heard about the bright young graduate from Bates who was teaching English at the high school. Needing a friend he could trust and "piqued" by Cox's prim serious manner (which might want taking down a peg or two), Frost wanted to see if Cox had anything to offer him. They began to play tennis and to tramp through the countryside together; and on these long walks Frost realized Cox and he shared a deep commitment to literature, a willingness to confront the ideas in a work of art, to battle them out question after question, to speculate on the philosophical issues evoked by a poem or a Shakespearean play. As much as Frost,

Cox was stirred to thought by literature. Cox, now launched on his own, was jettisoning his conventional notions of respectability and, probably incited by Frost, was beginning to probe the realities deeper than appearances. Cox profoundly admired the creator of a work of art, and so he was respectful—even reverent of—Frost's attempts to earn a place in that pantheon. In Cox, Frost found the listener he could talk to and tease, who was as eager to explore the country of the mind as he was the woods and waters around Plymouth.

Once during the winter, Cox remembered later, they found an aisle through snow-laden spruces. Once, while autumn leaves were falling, they crossed on the covered bridge spanning the Pemigewasset River and followed the road around Mount Prospect. Frost talked about a cosset lamb and baseball and words: an old-maid schoolteacher's mispronunciation of *lasciviousness;* the adverbs *slow* and *slowly*, both good, he thought; the refusal of language, like life itself, to be regulated and unified.

Perhaps he embroidered on his adventures to shock his young listener. He told Cox how, standing alone on the top of New Hampshire's Mount Lafayette, he had recited all of "Lycidas." He mentioned how in the flush of youth he had taken to heavy drink to see if it would inspire his poetry.

The pattern of Frost's conversation during these tramps was like the movement of his poetry: opening with the specific, the immediate, something close at hand, he would move to elliptical generalizations about poetry, about experience, about life. At the end, the pair would round off their "talks-walking" with glasses of white grape juice at the local drugstore or a leg-of-lamb dinner Elinor Frost had prepared.

Cox listened to Frost read Francis Thompson's "The Hound of Heaven," as well as Finley Peter Dunne's humorous essays on "Mr. Dooley," the Chicago saloon keeper. One night he heard him do Synge's *The Playboy of the Western World*, with full Irish accent, picked up from Frost's friend John Lynch. On another evening Frost read Shaw's *Major Barbara*.[4]

It was a heady year for the conventional Cox. He had embarked on his teaching career; he had made friends with a real poet, a man he could look up to, take direction from. During that year

Frost continued to write poetry and to teach. Innovative but lazy, with no formal training in education, Frost mocked traditional teaching methods and threw out the usual survey text. He had his students tap the original sources, the seminal minds: Pestalozzi, Rousseau, Plato. But sometimes he was capricious and lackluster: for days on end he would read to his bored audience *A Connecticut Yankee in King Arthur's Court*. At other times he wanted free moments to read, so he assigned themes written in class—which he collected but never bothered to correct.

At the end of the academic year, the two men reached important decisions. Cox, aware of the growing reputation for graduate work of the University of Illinois, had decided to study there for an advanced degree. Frost, gambling on his belief that a breakaway would provide him with the time and place for his writing, determined to leave the United States. Wavering at first between British Columbia and England, the farmer, teacher, and part-time poet chose to cross the ocean.

Cox's background, though enlightened, had been sheltered: the young man had walked the paths his parents and his own conscience had prescribed. Meeting Frost, he found the rebellious, the unknown. Not a drunk, as Cox first thought, Frost was a relentless seeker, unimpressed by externals; an uprooter, who questioned life, religion, writing: who balanced speculations playfully, ironically—and transformed them into poetry. Frost shook Cox out of his conventional attitudes, his acceptance of polite standards. He released a suppressed force in him, a force that would get the young man into trouble, but that would be the power that charged his teaching.

Reinforced by Frost's encouragement, flattered by Frost's attention, and buoyed by his own happy year as a teacher, Cox applied for and won a scholarship that would enable him to take his master's degree in English at Urbana. There, in one academic year, 1912–1913, he earned his M.A., submitting as his thesis "Carlyle's Influence on Kipling."

Cox's mentor Frost, who disparaged college and university professors, was not orthodox as an educator. If need be, he could continue to teach, but on his own terms and out of his own convictions. Class preparations, rigid schedules, homework assignments, grading the papers of students—whom he called theme-children, after Lamb's "dream-children"—all impeded his work as poet. Taking the money from the sale of the Derry farm, he and his family, late in the summer of 1912, went by train to Boston, boarded the S.S. *Parisian*, and set sail in August for Glasgow. Frost knew that his position at the Normal School would not be kept open for him, but he didn't care. He wanted to be "bound—away!"

## NOTES

1. Robert Frost, Introduction, *A Swinger of Birches*, by Sidney Cox (New York: New York University Press, 1957), p. viii; Sidney Cox, *Robert Frost: Original "Ordinary Man"* (New York: Henry Holt and Company, 1929), p. 10. Frost's flippant advice on theme correcting was a likely conjecture by the Dartmouth English professor Stearns Morse, who knew Frost and was a close friend of Cox's for many years. See Mayo Johnson, "The Life and Teachings of Sidney Cox" (Thesis, Dartmouth College, 1953), p. 3.

2. *The Bates Student* 39 (June 1911):230–33.

3. The biographical material on Sidney Cox and his family is based on his mother's, Elizabeth Cox's, unpublished journals, the unpublished letters—most of them undated—of Gertrude and Sidney Cox to their parents, and Elizabeth Cox's unpublished letters to her children. For the college years, there exist about two hundred letters.

4. Sidney Cox, "Robert Frost at Plymouth," *The New Hampshire Troubadour* 16 (November 1946):18–22; Lawrance Thompson, *Robert Frost: The Early Years, 1874–1915* (New York: Holt, Rinehart and Winston, 1966), pp. 369–76.

PART TWO

# "Bound–Away!"
## 1912–1915

*Come with rain, O loud Southwester!*
*Bring the singer, bring the nester;*
*Give the buried flower a dream;*
> *"To the Thawing Wind"*

COMPLETELY UNKNOWN and living near London in Beaconsfield, Robert Frost, about mid-October 1912, walked into the office of the publisher David Nutt in Bloomsbury. He showed his manuscript to a sad-looking woman dressed in mourning, the widow of Alfred Nutt, the publisher's son. In a French accent, she said she would represent the firm, and near the end of October, Frost heard the glad tidings. David Nutt would bring him out. About the first of April, 1913, *A Boy's Will* was published, complete with a gloss on all poems except two, a piece of his foolery, Frost claimed. At thirty-nine the sometime farmer, sometime teacher finally had his first volume in print.

Spurred by the recognition, which released dormant energies, Frost shaped monologues, dramatic dialogues, narratives—poems that caught the sounds of voices. From his readings aloud in the long evenings at Plymouth, he had come to realize how meaning could be communicated by the sound of a sentence. He gathered these poems for a second collection, which he called tentatively *Farm Servants and Other People*. Then, remembering the headline of an advertisement listing properties for sale he had seen in a Boston paper, he hit on a better title: *North of Boston*, his second book, was published by Nutt on May 15, 1914.

All of the poems in *A Boy's Will* were written in America. Most of those in the second collection, though having germinated at Derry and Plymouth, were written in England. *North of Boston* signaled a new style. Frost had found an authentic voice and mastered the subtle techniques by which the sound of a line determined its meaning. Whereas the lyrics and narratives of *A Boy's Will* reveal a sensitive response to nature and to self (and some of them, such as "Mowing," "October," "Reluctance," and "The Tuft of Flowers," are poems of beauty, moments of grace in a youthful collection), the volume is marred by archaisms ("fain to list") and falsely poetic contractions, such as *o'er* and *e'er*. One poem, a lament for a lost butterfly, Frost knew was immature but included for sentimental reasons.

*North of Boston*, by contrast, has poems of genius, the rich feast after years of preparation. Frost ranged in subject matter from the allegory on art in "The Mountain" to rural morality in "The Code." He moved from the wry humor of "Blueberries" and "A Hundred Collars" to the meditative lyricism of "After Apple-Picking" and "The Wood-Pile." In "The Black Cottage" he showed how the memory of a dead woman overpowers the house, the living. He probed the psychological tensions between husband and wife in "Home Burial" and "The Death of the Hired Man," between neighbor and neighbor in "Mending Wall." He laid out the faint battle lines between sanity and insanity in the narrator's mind in "A Servant to Servants."

For these poems, Frost found metaphors in a ladder pointing to heaven; in pine cones and apple trees divided by a stone wall; in the moonlight on Mary's lap, "harplike morning-glory strings"; in a child's tiny grave. Memorable lines shine out from the poems: "Something there is that doesn't love a wall"; "Good fences make good neighbors"; "the best way out is always through"; "Home is the place where, when you have to go there, they have to take you in"; and home is "Something you somehow haven't to deserve."

Some four months after Frost had left home, he wrote his first letter to Sidney Cox, the day after Christmas, 1912. He was answering a letter and postcard from Cox, who was studying at the University of Illinois and had fallen in love with Beth Howard, who refused to marry him because he "lacked self-confidence." Pouring no balm on the deeply felt grief, Frost outlined other failings of the young lover. But Elinor Frost consoled him: she wrote that she had never thought self-confidence an "endearing" quality. Cox continued his relationship with Beth Howard; and even two years later, as a high-school English teacher in Schenectady, New York, he would still become elated over "a wonderful letter from Her."

Frost's letters to Cox are full of the literary life in London. Implying an intimacy with "Yates" that he did not have, Frost displayed his literary acquaintances and disparaged rivals—such as "the sing-songing Alfie No-yes" (Noyes). Seeming to praise Yeats, whom he did regard as a great poet, Frost was, in actuality, fooling Cox and mocking this competitor by caricaturing Yeats's near-belief in fairies.

Cox filled his letters with comments on his reading and his thoughts on teaching grammar, rhetoric, and literature as an interpretation of life. Frost recognized Cox's talents and gave him a backhanded compliment: "You ought to be a tremendous force for something when the right touch releases you." The poet repeated Robert Bridges's "brave theory of rhythm"—then dismissed it. He knew Cox would listen—and be a proselytizer for—Frost's own ideas, his "Sound of Sense" theory.

By the spring of 1914 Frost knew the London literary world well enough to realize that his affinities lay with the rural, traditional Georgian poets Wilfrid Gibson and Lascelles Abercrombie, rather than with the urban modernists Pound and Yeats. Frost had enjoyed the garden and pear trees of his thatchless "Bungalow," but at the urging of friends who wanted him near them, he deserted suburban Beaconsfield for Gloucestershire. Retreating to the pastoral life meant no more convivial gossip at Harold Monro's Poetry Bookshop in Holborn, and no more theatergoing in the West End, where the Frosts had seen Harley Granville-Barker's tradition-breaking *A Midsummer Night's Dream*, full of modern sets and gilded fairies. Instead, there would be ruminative conversation around a cider barrel and long walks in the hedgerowed fields with his newfound friend Edward Thomas, whose poetic talents Frost recognized and encouraged. Ironically, Frost wrote to Cox: "Places are more to me in thought than in reality."

In need of funds for the move to the country, Frost tapped Cox for a loan of twenty-five to fifty dollars. The teacher's salary was modest—a recent fifty-dollar raise was far less than Cox had hoped for—and he couldn't afford to lend even twenty-five dollars, the sum having been earmarked for a badly needed new suit. But Frost accepted the refusal with equanimity. (When he sent Cox Ezra Pound's review of *A Boy's Will*, he took care to scratch out the part that implied he had inherited wealth.)

The peace at Frost's cottage, Little Iddens, in Gloucestershire was shattered when the Great War opened, August 1914. Jubilant, Frost wrote, "I like this war" to Cox, who realized its horrors and his own possible involvement. On second thought, Frost labeled the war an ill wind. Aware that it was making *North of Boston* small and irrelevant, he prepared uneasily to return home. He had gambled heavily, staking all his money from the sale of the farm on becoming a poet. He knew now he would have to earn a living: his days of being a full-time poet were ended. Short of money again, Frost borrowed the fare home from Abercrombie, John Haines, a Gloucester poet and barrister, and James Cruikshank Smith, a Scottish Shakespearean scholar, who was a warm friend.

Scanning the reviews of *North of Boston* to see what impression they would make in America, Frost was sensitive to every word. He now became horrified at Pound's blasts at the American editors who had shut their minds "against serious American writing" of the previous twenty years, for Frost knew he must not alienate these editors; he realized that Pound was drawing him into his own vendetta with American publishers.

Frost saw two possibilities for supporting himself in America: to return to farming, or—and this one was more inviting—to teach ideas at some small college. Cox could be useful in publicizing him. Sending the young teacher a list of favorable reviews, Frost asked his friend to pass the good news on to literature professors who might be interested. Cox was glad to do so.

The letters from this period reveal the streak of cruelty in Frost: the crude descriptions of W. H. Davies and his limp, the biting criticism of his rivals' poetry, even his friend Gibson's. And the absence of letters reveals Frost's weapon of not writing: "Please don't punish me by a very long silence," Cox begged. Cox wanted to be told what to do, how to help. After three years of friendship, Cox, though ordered to, still could not address Frost by his first name. He did not recognize Frost's mischievous irony. Frost had to tell Cox, "Don't take me too seriously," a warning Cox could not grasp.

There was little Cox had not revealed to Frost, from the ill-fated romance with Beth Howard to his plan of becoming a college professor. He wanted to pursue doctoral studies at Columbia University. Frost encouraged him; as a professor, Cox would be an even more helpful friend. Above all honest, Cox assumed that his friend was, too. But Frost had even fooled Pound (who, in his review of *A Boy's Will*, hailed the poet as being "without sham and affectation"). Cox never contradicted his master, and Frost relished a dis-

ciple. "You set me off," he told Cox, and in the letters Frost
showed off.

But if Frost was egotistical, overbearing, baiting of his Plymouth friend, he was also deeply loyal. Frost, the author of two volumes of poetry, acquainted with the important literary figures of
his day, and friend to several of them, had achieved recognition,
some fame, in England. Cox, an earnest, unknown schoolteacher
who spilled out his emotions in long letters, was a reliable, although sometimes irritating, correspondent. Frost could have
dropped his friend. But he valued the guilelessness, the sponta-
neity, the openness of Cox, who shared the poet's deep love of literature. And in Cox, Frost saw a man dedicated to teaching, who,
taking his own road, was teaching students literature the way
Frost felt it should be taught: as a creative power that illumined
life. Frost, flatteringly, almost truthfully, told Cox: "I write few
such long letters to anyone as I write to you."

[With Letter 1, Frost included, in his handwriting, the poem "In England." The poem was reproduced in facsimile in the catalogue of the exhibition "Fifty Years of Robert Frost," Dartmouth College Library, Hanover, New Hampshire, 1944.]
ALS, 2 pp.

## I.

26 December 1912   The Bung. Hole
Dear Sydney Cox:          Beaconsfield

I fully intended to write you some word that should reach you somewhere near Christmas time. You might need it to help you over the vacation and you might not. I knew you wouldn't be going down East this year. At any rate you would have time to read it if you didn't have time to answer it. But you have no idea of the way I mismanage myself since I broke loose and ceased to keep hours. It seems as if I did nothing but write and write and everything else I planned to do went where the Scotchman's saxpence went when *he* went to London. If you don't know that story you can ask me about it next time you see me.

You will accept I suppose a note that shall be no more than promissory of more to come. I write chiefly to assure you of our pleasure in your good letter as I should have written the minute I received the characteristic postal that came posting on its heels. It needed no apology. You were enthusiastic about your studies, matter-of-fact about your menial duties, a happy combination that strikes me as peculiarly American. What more could anyone ask in one off-hand letter? But if the letter was good enough for us, the postal was better. That rises to heights almost universal in that it voices the complaint of everyone who writes anything, viz., that nothing he writes quite represents his thought or his feeling. It is as hard to fill a vacuum with nothing as it is to fill a poem (for instance) with something. The best one can hope for is an approximation. Wilfrid Meynell calls his latest volume of poetry Verses and Reverses and owns in a preface that they are mostly reverses. There you have it. The veteran learns to value what he writes as little for graces of style as for spelling. What counts is the amount of the original intention that isnt turned back and lost in execution. Symonds says Dowson (the sad sinner) for once says everything in Cynara. I wonder what Dowson would say if he were alive as he might have been with a little less liquor and a little more of the water one sees so seldom over here—never a drop of it in lunch rooms, railroad stations, or streets.

There that's all I can give you now.

Of course Miss Howard must make us a visit if she is coming to England. Tell us more about her plans when you write next time. Mrs Frost says she will join me in my next letter.

R.F.

### In England

Alone in rain I sat today
On top of a gate beside the way,
And a bird came near with muted bill,
And a watery breeze keep blowing chill
From over the hill behind me.

I could not tell what in me stirred
To hill and gate and rain and bird,
Till lifting hair and bathing brow
The watery breeze came fresher now
From over the hill to remind me.

The bird was the kind that follows a ship,
The rain was salt upon my lip,
The hill was an undergoing wave,
And the gate on which I balanced brave
Was a great ships iron railing.

For the breeze was a watery English breeze
Always fresh from one of the seas,
And the country life the English lead
In beechen wood and clover mead
Is never far from sailing.

R.F.

ALS, 2 pp.

**2.**

2 May 1913

Dear Sydney Cox:                              The Bung Hole, Beaconsfield

It grows a long time since we heard from you and I begin to wonder whether or not you can have gone over to the enemy. There is the other possibility that you have been addressing letters as above and that the Eng. postman has failed to see the Am. joke. This, you must bear in mind is The Bungalow. It is only The Bung for short and Hole by discourtesy. You are not on terms to be calling it that. We who love it call it anything we please like the affectionate father in H G Wells' story who called his favorite daughter Maggots. We are all pretty much at home here by now. You ought to see us, theoretically up to our eyes in the flowers of an English spring. I could say actually if we were as our neighbors amateurs of gardening. I like that about the English—they all have time to dig in the ground for the unutilitarian flower. I mean the men. It marks the great difference between them and our men. I like flowers you know but I like em wild, and I am rather the exception than the rule in an American village. Far as I have walked in pursuit of the Cypripedium, I have never met another in the woods on the same quest.* Americans will dig for peas and beans and such like utilities but not if they know it for posies. I knew a man who was a byword in five townships for the flowers he tended with his own hand. Neighbors kept hens and let them run loose just to annoy him. I feel as if my education in useless things had been neglected when I see the way the front yards blossom down this road. But never mind; I have certain useless accomplishments to my credit. No one will charge me with having an eye single to the main chance. So I can afford perhaps to yield a little to others for one spring in the cultivation of one form of the beautiful. Next year I go in for daffodils.

I think I understood Yeats to say the other night that Tagore whose poetry is the latest big thing here, has been visiting your college at Urbana. I meant to ask Yeats more about it. I wonder if you met Tagore. Very likely I shall run across him before he goes back to Bengal. I was to have met him at Ernest Rhys', Sunday but decided in the end to take some other day for my call when I could have Rhys more to myself.† Tagore comes to Yeats here as the greatest English poet. How slowly but surely Yeats has eclipsed Kipling. I have seen it all happen with my own eyes. You would expect to see Tagore seeking Kipling for his Indian sympathies and interests. But no, he is drawn to Maeterlinck on the continent and to Yeats on these islands.

Sincerely yours<br>
Robert Frost

* *Cypripedium*: genus name for the wild lady's-slipper orchids Frost often searched for with the man who tended flowers, poet-friend Carl Burell, at Derry, New Hampshire. See my "A Literary Friendship: Robert Frost and Carl Burell" in *Frost: Centennial Essays*, ed. Jac Tharpe (Jackson: University Press of Mississippi, 1974).
†Ernest Rhys (1859–1946): British author, anthologist, and editor of Everyman's Library.

[With Letter 3, Frost included three poems in his handwriting. Two of them, "A Misgiving" and "Good Hours," are essentially the same as in *The Poetry of Robert Frost*, and so are not included. The third poem, "Bond and Free," differs considerably from the final version in the Lathem edition.]

ALS, 3 pp.

## 3.

10 July 1913    Beaconsfield<br>
The Bungalow

Dear Cox:

I get your story and I am sorry for you. The only thing I don't understand is the philosophical not to say meek way in which you take your luck. You attribute it to your lack of self confidence. What would that mean I wonder. Are you any less sure of yourself than are others of your age? And is it in religion or in business or in politics or in society or in love? One thing I know: you will not be any more sure for a while after an experience like this. I don't like it for you.

If you want my opinion, I think it all comes of your overhauling your character too much in the hearing of others. You give your case away as Tennyson did his when he confessed that wherever he wrote King Arthur he had in mind Prince Albert. He spoiled the Idyls for the present generation (I mean our own) and perhaps for all generations to come. And yet the poems are neither better nor worse for the confession. You *must not* disillusion your admirers with the tale of your sources and processes. That is the gospel according to me. Not that I bother much to live up to it.

And if you want my opinion, there is one other thing that enhances your effect of extreme youth. You are too much given to being edified—benefited, improved by everybody that comes along, including me. You must learn to take other people less uncritically and yourself more uncritically. You are all eaten up by the inroads of your own conscience.

To get back to your trouble. I can't account for the calm you preserve except on the assumption that you hope there is still hope. Be frank about that. If it is anything to you, or can result in anything, for us to meet Miss Howard, Mrs Frost and I will be glad to have her out to see us in August. But if the affair is closed I am afraid I should only be awkward in meeting her. What should I say. I am not good at talking about everything but what is in the back of my mind. But you shall decide. Do you have something like a real wish that we should talk with her—for some secret reason that you may not want to own to even to yourself? Let me know soon. I will scold you more in my next letter.

Sincerely yours
Robert Frost

This is best.

## Bond and Free

Oh, Love has earth to which she clings,
And circling arms and hills about,
Walls within walls, to keep fear out;
But Thought has need of no such things;
For Thought has a pair of dauntless wings.

Oh, Love has left on lawn and lea
Her print in many a flowery place,
From straining in the earth's embrace;
And such is Love, and glad to be!
But Thought has kicked her ankles free.

Thought cleaves the interstellar gloom,
And sits in Sirius all night long,
And comes at daybreak, winging strong,
With the smell of burning on every plume;
While Love has slept in a little room.

Robert Frost

Plymouth N.H.

[This undated letter in Elinor Frost's handwriting was probably included in the envelope with Letter 3.]

ALS, 6 pp.

## 4.

[Beaconsfield

Dear Mr. Cox:　　　　　　　　　　　10 July 1913]

I think its very sociable for you to wish to hear from me, also, and I am very glad to write. I should have done so before, but I have been very busy, as usual. Over here I have a smaller house to take care of than in Plymouth, and in other ways my housework is easier, but I am teaching the children myself, and of course that takes time. We cannot afford to send them to good private schools, and it is quite out of the question to send them to the free County Council schools, for it would be too awful to take them home speaking Cockney English, wouldn't it? Either kind of school would be bad for our children, for one kind would influence them to look down on a certain part of humanity, and the other to look up to the other part of humanity. I think our American school system very much superior to anything there is in England.

The children are all very well now and are growing so fast that I begin to feel very small myself. I think they will all be taller than I am. They do not like England as well as America, though London seems a wonderful and fascinating place to them. Sometimes I have wished that we had taken lodgings in the city itself instead of a house so far out, as the life there would have been more exciting for us all, but of course it is much better for the children's health out here. London is a foggy, smoky place. Beaconsfield is a pretty town, and there are delightful walks in all directions, across smooth fields separated by hedge-rows, and through stretches of beautiful old beech woods. All through May and June we have had charming weather, and the country has seemed very lovely after the many weeks of gloomy skies during the winter. The birds which we have never seen before, the skylark, the cuckoo, and the English blackbird, have been very entertaining to us.

I am glad that you have enjoyed your work at college so much this year; judging from what you tell us of it, it must have been very interesting. You speak of having heard a course of lectures by a Professor Polla[r]d—oddly enough, we met his wife at a tea in London just before they sailed for America.* The English have such a wrong idea of America, but you couldn't expect anything else from the sort of American news that gets printed in the papers here; anything vulgar and sensational about us is welcomed, and only confirms what they had already thought of us.

And so Miss Howard is coming abroad this summer—I felt very sorry to hear the news in your last letter, for I saw plainly last year how happy you were in your affection for her. I do not count self-confidence as one of the endearing qualities of our natures, and perhaps she will come to feel differently about it after a time.

I am sorry you are not near enough to us to come and see us this summer. We seem so far away from home and friends.

With all good wishes, I am

Sincerely your friend,
Elinor M. Frost

* Albert Frederick Pollard (1869–1948): professor of English history at the University of London and fellow of All Souls College, Oxford; gave ten lectures in May 1913 at the University of Illinois, Urbana.

ALS, 6 pp.

## 5.

Beaconsfield
The Bungalow
Dear Cox:                              [c. 15 September 1913]
Suppose I put off scolding you the rest till another time and allow myself the freedom in pencil of saying anything that comes

into my head. I wonder if there is anything in particular you would like to know about how life goes over here and I wonder if I am mind-reader enough to guess what it would be.

There is Yates you spoke of as being rated by the departmental professor considerably below that good boy from Oxford, the sing-songing (as distinguished from song-singing) Alfie No-yes. Do you want to hear what I think of him? If you are where you can lay hands on the Oxford Book of Victorian Verse I can talk to you from that. It gives Noyes plenty of space to show his paces. "When spring comes back to England" is a pleasant enough lilt—the children like it—very likely it is the best thing Noyes has done. But no one would say that it was stirring. The second poem with the tiresome "mon bel ami" refrain expects you to be moved at the thought that Venus has settled down to suckle John Bull's baby by an English hearth. The thought is not stirring: the note is not deep enough to be stirring. Swinging is not stirring, you know. Neither is swelling necessarily stirring. The poem in which he gets Francis Thompson "purpureally enwound" swells, but who cares a pin. I wish I knew what you thought he had written that got below the surface of things. I believe he has preached a little—is preaching now on the subject of peace. I recall a poem beginning, Beyond beyond and yet again beyond! What went ye forth to seek oh foolish fond. That strikes a note. ("Foolish fond" is rather awful.) I doubt if there is very much to him however. He is nothing for the American people to rage over. His attractive manners and his press agent have given you an exaggerated idea of his importance.*

Yates' lines

> "For the good are always the merry
>   Save by an evil chance,"

are worth all of Noyes put together.

"Who dreamed that beauty passes like a dream?" That line fairly weeps defiance to the unideal, if you will understand what I mean by that. The Rose of the World, The Fiddler of Dooney, The Lake Isle of Innisfree, Down by the Sally Gardens, The Song of the Wandering Aengus, the Song of the Sad Shepherd—those are all poems. One is sure of them. They make the sense of beauty ache.

"Then nowise worship dusty deeds."

Such an untameable spirit of poetry speaks there. You must really read Yates. He is not always good. Not many of his longer things are more than interesting. But the Land of Hearts Desire is lovely and so is On Shadowy Waters in poetry and Cathleen Ni Hoolihan in prose.

Some one the other day was deriving all the Masefield and Gibson sort of thing from one line of Yates' Land of Hearts Desire,

"The butter's at your elbow, Father Hart."

Oh Yates has undoubtedly been the man of the last twenty years in English poetry. I won't say that he is quite great judged either by the way he takes himself as an artist or by the work he has done. I am afraid he has come just short of being. The thing you mention has been against him. I shouldn't care so much—I shouldn't care at all, if it hadn't touched and tainted his poetry. Let him be as affected as he pleases if he will only write well. But you cant be affected and write entirely well.

You'll be thinking this is an essay on something. Lets be personal for a change.

I had a chance to see and hear the other night how perilously near Yates comes to believing in fairies. He told with the strangest accent of wistful half belief of the leppercaun (spell it) two old folks he visited had had in a cage on the wall. The little fellow was fine and sleek when they trapped him, but he pined in captivity until they had to let him go. All the time they had him another leppercaun hung about the house mourning (in silence) for him. And when the old folks out of pity let him go the two fairies hurried off hand in hand down the glen. Yates I could see, was in a state of mind to resent being asked pointblank what he thought of such a story. And it wouldn't have been best for anyone to go on the assumption that he told it to be amusing. My Catholic friend Liebich tells me he for his part didn't know but that everybody had some sort of belief in fairies. He said it was something like the belief in the communion of saints.

There's a good story I had pretty directly from Mrs Sharp about how she was out with her husband (Fiona Macleod) walking somewhat ahead of him in an English lane one day when she saw something childlike with a goat's legs scuttle into the woods. She stood still with astonishment. Her husband came up. "William, what do you think?—a faun! I saw him."

"It's nothing," said William without coming to a standstill, "such creatures are all about this part of the country."[†]

We are just back from a two week's journey in Scotland. We went up the coast to Dundee by boat and from there by train to Kingsbarns a little old town close to St. Andrews. We saw some sights inevitably though we were not out sight-seeing. The best of the adventure was the time in Kingsbarns where tourists and summer boarders never come. The common people in the south of England I don't like to have around me. They don't know how to meet you man to man. The people in the north are more like Americans. I wonder whether they made Burns' poems or Burns' poems made them. And there are stone walls (dry stone dykes) in the north: I liked those. My mother was from Edinburgh. I used to hear her speak of the Castle and Arthur's Seat, more when I was young than in later years. I had some interest in seeing those places. The children saw the Black Watch march into the Castle with a band of bagpipes.

The trouble with this sort of composition is that one could go on with it forever. I have told you enough to show you what we are doing with ourselves. If I haven't—well today we walked to Jordans and stood between Penn's grave and the graves of his five little children. It is not far to go. We have done the walk before. We mean to get down to church there some day. The meeting house is much as it was in Penn's day. Only the money-changers have got a foothold in it—I mean the sellers of picture postcards to the fugitive American. I don't know who is to blame for this, the Englishman or the American. People here blame the latter. Etc etc etc etc

You may do anything you can to give the boys of Poland a better chance for all I care. I am not always a doubter. Have me in mind five or six years from now when results begin to show. You must work off your enthusiasm in any way you can.

Tell us about the new job. You will soon be drowning your cares in unlimited theme-correcting. Mortify the flesh, old man. Suffer. My soul, how you like it.

Sincerely yours
Robert Frost

* Alfred Noyes (1880–1958): patriotic writer of simple, rollicking verse. Best known for "The Highwayman" and "The Barrel-Organ." The first poem cited is entitled, "The World's May Queen"; the second, "Our Lady of the Sea"; the third, "On the Death of Francis Thompson." The fourth poem, beginning "Beyond, beyond and yet again beyond," is "Art, the Herald," from Noyes's *Collected Poems* (1913).

†William Sharp (1855–1905): Scottish poet and man of letters; compiled with his wife an anthology of Celtic poems. His best work appeared under the pseudonym Fiona Macleod.

ALS, 1 p.

# 6.

Beaconsfield
The bung-hole-still.

Dear Cox                [c. 8 November 1913]

You must send me these two reviews back if you will. Not that I want them to treasure; I am not given to laying up for myself treasures of that kind. But I may want them to impress one more person with before I get through. On second thought, I will consent to spare the one from *The Academy* on condition that you send it to the professor who found my quality so indefinable.* (Don't get mad! it has never entered my head but that he meant to be nice: thank you for showing him the book.)

We have just had Guy Fawkes Gun Powder Plot Day which for squibs or firecrackers is to our Fourth-of-July as water is to wine or as poor damp pop-corn is to good pop-corn. I saw nobody hanged in effigy—not even Lloyd George, though he must have been hanged many times over.

Yours
R.F.

Have I sent you David Nutt's Catalogue?

* An anonymous, highly laudatory review of *A Boy's Will* appeared in *The Academy* on September 20, 1913. Favorable reviews also appeared in *The Times Literary Supplement* (April 10, 1913), *The English Review* (June 1913), *Poetry and Drama* (June 1913), and *The Dial* (September 16, 1913).

ALS, 3 pp.

7.

Beaconsfield
The Bungalow
Dear Cox:                          [c. 26 November 1913]

The next thing to do is to get married and, as the hero of one of the eclogues in "North of Boston" says, "forget considerations." Go out of yourself some fine morning and by way of celebration lick something if it is no more formidable than the Peace Movement. You do right to damn grammar: you might be excused if you damned rhetoric and in fact everything else in and out of books but the spirit, which is good because it is the only good that we can't talk or write or even think about. No don't damn the spirit.

You will be all right (Do the theme-children—Charles Lamb had dream-children—do the theme-children still want to spell it alright?) You ought to be a tremendous force for something when the right touch releases you. A belief in fairies may be just the thing. What are they but the Irresponsibilities, and a precious source of inspiration midway between heaven and hell. We haven't always to be either good or bad you know. Or rather you don't know, but a lady has been sent to tell you. There are whole days when the fairies and a belief in them will justify you in being gay, nothing but gay.

I preach. But this is the last time. You will not need to be preached to any more. Not even by your own conscience! Give yourself a chance. The world is ourn.

Let's hear a little more about it at your leisure. I feel sort of half introduced to someone. Take your time. As it comes natural.

Mrs Frost and I were at a play on Saturday in which we were asked point blank to profess our faith not only in fairies, but in devils and black art as well. So I suppose I shall have to. Do I, then? I do, as they say in the marriage ceremony. Only I shall have to be allowed to define in what sense. But that is another story and a lifelong one.

I'm glad for you. So also is Mrs Frost. She wants me to tell you that specially from her. It is not the first time we have had to be

glad for a friend in need lately. First there was John [Bartlett] of
Vancouver.* Then it was Wilfrid Gibson and now it is you. Well
well. Be young, mes enfants.

Ever yours

Robert Frost.

I am writing this without having read your Japanese letter.†

---

* John Bartlett (1892–1947): a student of Frost's at Pinkerton and a close friend all his
life. See Margaret Bartlett Anderson, *Robert Frost and John Bartlett: The Record of a
Friendship* (New York: Holt, Rinehart and Winston, 1963).

† The letter may be from Cox's Japanese friend, Rio, whom Cox had met at Bates.

ALS, 4 pp.

## 8.

19 January 1914    Beaconsfield

Dear Cox                The Bungalow

Absolve me of trying to make you think of me as hobnobbing
with the great over here and I am ready to begin my *very* short
talks based on Quiller-Couch. I'm far from important enough for
the likes of the Poet Laureate to have sought me out. I'm simply
going to tell you about him because I happen to have eaten at the
same table with him by an accident. I was visiting Lawrence Binyon (see anthology) when Bridges turned up.* I have a right to tell
you how the king looked to the cat that looked at him.

He's a fine old boy with the highest opinion—of his poetry you
thought I was going to say—perhaps of his poetry, but much more
particularly of his opinions. He rides two hobbies tandem, his theory that syllables in English have fixed quantity that cannot be dis-
regarded in reading verse, and his theory that with forty or fifty or
sixty characters he can capture and hold for all time the sounds of
speech. One theory is as bad as the other and I think owing to
much the same fallacy. The living part of a poem is the intonation
entangled somehow in the syntax, idiom and meaning of a sentence. It is only there for those who have heard it previously in
conversation. It is not for us in any Greek or Latin poem because
our ears have not been filled with the tones of Greek and Roman
talk. It is the most volatile and at the same time important part of
poetry. It goes and the language becomes a dead language, the po-

etry dead poetry. With it go the accents, the stresses, the delays that are not the property of vowels and syllables but that are shifted at will with the sense. Vowels have length there is no denying. But the accent of sense supercedes all other accent, overrides and sweeps it away. I will find you the word "come" variously used in various passages as a whole, half, third, fourth, fifth, and sixth note. It is as long as the sense makes it. When men no longer know the intonations on which we string our words they will fall back on what I may call the absolute length of our syllables which is the length we would give them in passages that meant nothing. The psychologist can actually measure this with a what-do-you-call-it. English poetry would then be read as Latin poetry is now read and as of course Latin poetry was never read by Romans. Bridges would like it read so now for the sake of scientific exactness. Because our poetry must sometime be as dead as our language must, Bridges would like it treated as if it were dead already.

I say you cant read a single good sentence with the salt in it unless you have previously heard it spoken. Neither can you with the help of all the characters and diacritical marks pronounce a single word unless you have previously heard it actually pronounced. Words exist in the mouth not in books. You can't fix them and you dont want to fix them. You want them to adapt their sounds to persons and places and times. You want them to change and be different. I shall be sorry when everybody is so public-schooled that nobody will dare to say Haow for What. It pleases me to contemplate the word Sosieti that the reformers sport on their door plate in a street in London. The two i's are bad enough. But the o is what I love. Which o is that if we must be exact.

Bridges wants to fix the vocables here and now because he sees signs of their deteriorating. He thinks they exist in print for people. He thinks they are of the eye. Foolish old man is all I say. How much better that he should write good poetry if he hasn't passed his time. He has been a real poet, though you never would judge it from a thing in the Dec. Poetry and Drama in which he takes the unsentimental view of teachers that they cram us with dead dry stuff like the dead flies on the window sill.

You will have to import your own books I'm afraid, unless Sherman French & Co of Boston would get them for you. Books and postage in the awful quantity you mention would cost you four American dollars. You mustn't get one book more than you honestly feel that you can dispose of. No silly promises are binding.

Yours<br>R Frost

Make you a present of all the words I have misspelled in this letter. They'll do you good if they correct a little your tendency to think as a teacher that everything must be correct.

---

*Laurence Binyon (1869–1943): lyric poet and an official in the British Museum; his best-known poem is "For the Fallen."

ALS, 2 pp.

## 9.

3 March 1914    Beaconsfield

Dear Cox                            The Bungalow

Would you or would you not lend me a matter of twenty-five or fifty dollars (if fifty is too much, twenty five) to help me out of a tight place? I am making a change which will cost a little and for various reasons it has to come just when I am out of money. I might have to keep you waiting till I get my allowance in July and then again if returns from certain things come in I may be able to repay you at once. I have several things out which will appear in magazines if they can be got in before my book appears. If not I lose on them. Mrs Nutt is against me in the matter of my selling to the magazines. She seems jealous of my getting cold cash for anything that in book form is so unprofitable. She seems to, I say. I don't know quite what to make of her. She is friendly enough except when we are on the subject of magazines and American publishers. She acts as if she thought I was up to something. Last time I saw her she told me frankly she thought I had no right under my contract to traffic in my poetry before I brought it to her. This is embarrassing.

Don't hesitate to refuse me the loan if you must: I had rather ask a favor like this of you and John [Bartlett] than anyone else. I ought to be able to go to the trustees of my grandfather's estate, but they have always been chiefly trustees of his hostility to my poetry.

You will be amused to hear that the Edinburgh English Society will give a whole evening to a new American poet named Me, this month. Too bad my book isnt out to take advantage of the local interest that may stir up.

Now you be perfectly honest.

Yours ever and whether or no,
Robert Frost

ALS, 4 pp.

10.

The Bungalow
26 March 1914    Beaconsfield
Dear Sidney                     (This being my birthday.)
(I think it should be first names between us by this when it is already first names between me and my later-found friends in England.)

I have no friend here like Wilfrid Gibson whom I am going to join in Gloucestershire next week. We bid a long farewell to London to be near him and Lascelles Abercrombie. The cottage is already found for us. Iddens it is called—in Ledington Ledbury. You must address us there from now on. I don't know, but I suppose we shall sleep under thatch. Those other poets do.

I was worried about the money to make the move, but we shall pull through all right. You shall have your suit of clothes and know at the same time that we are not in straights.

We shall make a week of it in London before we drink silence and hide ourselves in cloud. I sold some poetry to Poetry and Drama and I propose to take it out in room rent in the upper floors of the Poetry Shop in Devonshire St Theobalds Road London W.C. if you know where that is. I may have told you about it. It sells nothing but poetry. The fellow that runs it and edits the quarterly I speak of is a poet and all about him are the poets my friends and enemies.* Gibson had a room there for a year before he married the proprietor's secretary. Epstein, the futurist sculptor, the New York Polish Jew, whose mind runs strangely on the subject of generation, whose work is such a stumbling block to the staid and Victorianly but who in spite of all is reckoned one of the greatest living geniuses, will be across the hall from us. All the poets will be in and out there. It will be something that Lesley of the children will be sure to remember.

We mean to do the city for the youngsters as much as I am capable of doing a city or anything else. There must be a great deal to see in London if one will look for it. There is the Tower and—well there simply must be something else. I must get a guide book.

I really do take an interest in the historical places. I didn't fail to notice that I passed the scenes of two battles—Evesham and Worcester—when I was travelling the other day. But I dont know what I would have done if I had been set down in either of them. It thrilled me enough merely to see the names on the stations. I got as much out of seeing Dunfermline town from the train as from straggling around Edinburgh Castle for a day. The best thing in Edinburgh Castle was the Black Watch on parade. Places are more to me in thought than in reality. People are the other way about. (Probably not so—I am just talking.)

I ought not to be talking. I have really too much else to do till we get away. I meant this to be but a short letter to make you easy on my score. I shall write you more at length when we are nearer the Severn Sea (see in Anthology the really good poem by Davidson. Poor Davidson.)†

Yours ever

R.F.

* Harold Monro (1879–1932): poet and founder of *The Poetry Review*; founded and ran the Poetry Bookshop in London, 1913–1932.

† John Davidson (1857–1909): pessimistic Scottish poet. The son of a minister, he went to London in 1889 and, neglected, lived in extreme poverty until he drowned himself. Frost is probably referring to Davidson's poem "A Runnable Stag."

ALS, 8 pp.

11.

18 May 1914   Little Iddens   Ledington

Dear Cox:                 Ledbury

I have taken particular pains to write the address legibly and do you take notice. We are actually in Gloucestershire but near the line and our postoffice is at Ledbury in Herefordshire. This is a great change from Beaconsfield which was merely suburban. We are now in the country, the cider country, where we have to keep a barrel of cider for our visitors and our hired help or we will have no visitors nor hired help. So we are in the way of adding drink to cigarette smoking in the record of our sins. Even Elinor gets drawn in since the only kind of ladies we know over here are all smokers. I think the only house I visited where the cigarettes weren't passed around was Ernest Rhys'. I never thought of that till this moment. I don't know why it was, probably because Rhys himself isn't a smoker. His son is though.

Let's see—you say be personal. I wish I knew what you meant by personal. I thought I was egotistically so in telling you of my encounter with the greatest poet (titular) in England. I believe I told you what I told Bridges about the science of verse, matter that is of the highest importance and not yet to be found in book form on earth. The novelty if you didn't miss it was the definition of a sentence which is calculated to revolutionize the teaching of literary composition in the next twenty years.

My late encounter with the man who considers himself the second greatest poet in England and heir apparent to the Laureateship was of another description. He is the Davies (W.H.) of the Victorian Anthol.* I saw something of him in London—once, as I think I told you, at a dinner in Soho where he made an exhibition of himself. He is the unsophisticated nature poet of the day—absolutely uncritical untechnical untheoretical. He has the honor of having a pension from the British government. Society runs after him. He sells upward of 100£ worth of small poems in a year. His success seems to have hurt him a little and its not strange that it has when you consider his origin. Six years he tramped in America till he fell under a freight car and lost a leg. Then he came home and stumped about selling shoe strings and penny rhyme sheets. Then my friend Adcock discovered him and the rest has followed—recognition from Shaw, Conrad and everyone else that counts. The poems in the Anthol are a fair sample of what he can do. No one at the present time can get those flashes in a line as he can. His note is Elizabethan. No one doubts that he is a very considerable poet, in spite of several faults and flaws everywhere. But his conceit is enough to make you misjudge him—simply assinine. We have had a good deal of him at the house for the last week and the things he has said for us to remember him by! He entirely disgusted the Gibsons with whom he was visiting. His is the kind of egotism another man's egotism can't put up with. He was going from here to be with Conrad. He said that would be pleasant because Conrad knew his work *thoroughly*. After waiting long enough to obscure the point we asked him if he knew Conrad's work *thoroughly*. Oh no—was it good? We told him yes. He was glad we liked it.

He set about encouraging Lesley to write about nature. It would be good practice for a child. He admitted that he had used it up as copy. Lesley is old enough to have to struggle to keep a straight face in such circumstances. There now, he said, see that little bird, that little green one, I wonder what kind he is. Says Lesley It's a sparrow and it isn't green, is it? And Davies stumped into the house. He doesn't really know nature at all. He has lately been telling the British public that the American Robin isn't red breasted and it has no note that he ever heard.

I suppose he is the most naively wicked person that walks, or should I say limps? He always makes me think of Ferguson's Scorney Bull (in The Vengence of the Welshmen of Tirawley.)— he's that lewd and lame.[†] His private life is public property, so he makes no bones of speaking in any company of the women he spends his money on. They are cheaper than in America and I don't suppose his tastes are up to the most expensive ones here: the one of his fortnight before coming down to the country cost him thirty shillings. The strange thing is he is humanly fond of his creatures and takes their side against the respectable kind. I believe he has written a simple-hearted book about them in which they are rather finely discriminated—the golden girls he has met. He's a little weathered man with none of the personal charm of the lady-killer remember. Yet Bernard Shaw considers that he has made himself an authority on the ladies (daughters of Lilith) our society builds on, but prefers to know nothing about. I have no doubt he knows much more about them than about birds, cows and flowers. He really cares little for nature except as most other people do in books. He asked me confidentially before he left why I had been so foolish as to get so far from London.

If this isn't being personal, let me try what I can say in a few words about where we are. The important thing to us is that we are near Gibson; we are far from any town. We are on a lane where no automobiles come. We can go almost anywhere we wish on wavering footpaths through the fields. The fields are so small and the trees so numerous along the hedges that, as my friend Thomas says in the loveliest book on spring in England, you might think from a little distance that the country was solid woods.[‡]

You mustnt mind if I write and never look back. I write few such long letters to anyone as I write to you. I have to save myself for other things. Elinor and the children wish to be remembered. Lesley will hardly be one of the children much longer. She's as tall as her mother and reads a decent paragraph of Caesar off without looking up more than a couple of words. Sometimes too she does a paragraph of English writing I admire.

Here's hoping the best for you next year. Did you get the raise you asked for?

Yours ever

R.F.

Later. My book seems to be out, though I haven't seen it yet. I have had these slips from the publisher. Perhaps you could send them where they would do some good.

We expect to see Miss Grace McQuenten of Plymouth N.H. and the Emerson School of Oratory over here in a week or two. I don't suppose you knew her—she was in Plymouth so little while you were there. She lived on the slope street that ran down to Coffee's Ice Cream Soda Fountain. You and I are far from there.

* William Henry Davies (1871–1940): Welsh-born, one of the Georgians; a hobo-peddler until over thirty.
†Samuel Ferguson (1810–1886): Irish poet, author of the ballad "The Welshmen of Tirawley." In it "Scorney Bull" is Scorna Boy, a "bailiff, lewd and lame," who is killed by the Lynotts after he has lasciviously drawn a young maid to him.
‡Edward Thomas (1878–1917): reviewer, essayist, and finally poet; Frost's closest friend in England. Frost pointed out to Thomas the poetic qualities of his prose work *In Pursuit of Spring*, and thus encouraged, Thomas began to write poetry of a high order.

ALS, 3 pp.

## 12.

My dear Mr. Frost,                    30 May 1914   Schenectady

I dassn't call you first names—yet—though I'm mighty pleased that you have abandoned the mister for me.

It's a dreadfully long time since I wrote to you though it's not at all that I was willing to let it be. I suspect you can guess that much of the time lately I've been nothing worth expressing. Some of the time my chief end has been to keep occupied—though, of course, I've done that no better than usual. When my Mother or Gertrude write that they are sorry I "suffer" it doesn't seem that that word fits at all. I merely hornify—not that I am getting hardened, either.

In connection with that, some good friends of mine might rise to confute that statement if they knew that I had kept the mosquitoes away while I sympathized with "Joseph Vance," lying in the woods today, with two good pipefuls of Old English Curve Cut.* But that would be because they judge men by manuals.

The serenity that seemed to caress me as I looked and listened in the woods this afternoon was not due merely to the combination of tobacco and the minor melody that nature made—nor to that with the genial inspiration of the sad strong spirit of De Morgan, but a little, too, to the fact that a few days ago I had a wonderful letter from Her, who has been gone two weeks to Waterville Maine to cope with the awkwardness and homeliness of a graduating class anxious for an impressive commencement. If I am to write you what feels to me like a real letter I must thus bring in my closest concern. Beth and I have not seen much of each other lately. We both say that it is best that we should not marry. But we both wish that it were enough so that we should feel it right. That must be Lithuanian to you. I trust that it doesn't seem maudlin. I mean that she has times of liking me much; but that she, being she, does not care enough. How few women there are who have the power of enduring with a smile unceasing non-fruition which is required to give up love and house because their dream has not come true! But I told you she believed in fairies.

Several times I have looked into Academy and the English Nation for a notice of your new book. It isn't out yet, is it? The last time I looked I found an essay that I liked very much by Galsworthy on "The Plain Man." That and one on "Facts" are all I know him by; but I like him. Have you met him?

At Easter I had a wonderful time visiting my friend Ralph Dow and his wife and baby. He and I found ourselves much closer together than when we graduated from college. He is a rare fellow. I'd like to bring him to you some time. He married at the time of graduation to keep an early promise; and now he pays. Evelyn, his wife, is the kind of woman a man feels toward as he does toward a sweet little girl. She cannot go with him where the real ark of the covenant is kept. But he is a fond and most considerate husband, and he delights in his work, even though she cannot appreciate his best efforts; and look forward to companionship from his adorable little girl.

I am to return to Schenectady next year with only fifty dollars—all anyone gets—increase in salary. I hope it won't be too many years before I can get back to University; for while I believe I am learning now, certainly I cannot be my best as a teacher of boys and girls most of whom have a hereditary, and acquired indisposition to use their minds except as warehouses for properly folded, wrapped and ticketed bolts of information.

This summer I am to be in Poland, and I shall read as much as possible, from my twenty new volumes of Everyman's ranging from Plato to De Quincey, and Walt Whitman.

A few days ago I had from the library a volume of Alfred Noyes. A lot seemed rather good to me but I could not get enthusiastic over; and I must confess there was some I could scarcely understand. I wonder if this is possible:      "And every pang of every grief
                                    That ruled my heart an hour

Gave new splendor to the leaf
New glory to the flower    Isn't that
the optimism of saying what you'd like to have be, is? Anyway I
don't believe in his religion of a universe. Pan lives and laughs in it
all. But only the Most High—Most Beautiful, Most Perfect—is
God.

I heard Eugene V. Debs from amidst an audience of half-think-
ing "working people" whom he told they were thinkers. He is a
skilful orator of the "boundless prairie, and leagues of shining
rails," and resplendently majestic type—a sincere and earnest man
of intellect. But he woefully lacks Matthew Arnold's kind of culture. I'd like to know what your impressions of British Socialism
are. I think you'd be interested in Arturo Giovannitti's "Arrows in
the Gale"—poems.[†] I liked them well enough to give the book to
Beth.

My affectionate best wishes to you and Mrs Frost, and to the
generation following.

Yours,
Sidney.

---

[*] *Joseph Vance: An Ill-Written Autobiography* (1906): an extremely popular autobiographical novel by William De Morgan (1839–1917), an English artist and retired man-
ufacturer of tiles and pottery.

[†] Arturo Giovannitti (1884–1959): Italian-born American poet (*Arrows in the Gale*,
1914) and social crusader, jailed during the Lawrence, Massachusetts, textile strike in
1912.

ALS, 3 pp.

## 13.

20 August 1914    Little Iddens
Dear Cox                    Ledington    Ledbury

You must think I have been and gone to war for the country that
has made me a poet. My obligation is not quite as deep as that. If I
were younger now and not the father of four—well all I say is,
American or no American, I might decide that I ought to fight the
Germans simply because I know I should be afraid to.

The war is an ill wind to me. It ends for the time being the
thought of publishing any more books. Our game is up. There will

really be genuine suffering among the younger writers. My friends have all been notified by the editors they live on that there will be no more space for special articles and reviews till the war is over. De la Mare (greatest of living poets) has just lost twelve or fifteen hundred a year by being dropped by the publisher he read MS for.

So we may be coming home if we can find the fare or a job to pay the fare after we get there.

I don't mean to complain. I like the war and the idea of abolishing Prussia, if there is any such thing.

The book was lucky in one respect. It may not have had time to sell much; at least it had made its mark with the reviewers. I give you a list of the chief articles about it in case you should care to look them up. No book of verse has had as much space given it for a good while.

| | | |
|---|---|---|
| Eng Nation | June 13 | 3 Cols |
| Outlook | June 27 | 3 Cols |
| Pell Mell Gazette | June 20 | |
| Egoist | July 1 | Col |
| Times | July 2 | |
| Bookman | July | Col |
| News & Leader | July 22 | Col |
| Eng Review | Aug | Page |
| New Weekly | Aug 8 | Col |

They have all been ridiculously favorable. The Times has talked of the book three times. I understand that there has been an article in the Boston Transcript based on the Nation article.* *And* the Plymouth (N.H.) Public Library has bought me. And I have had a letter from Stowe Vermont which showed that the book had penetrated to that village behind a mountain.†

I will send you a book as soon as ever I can afford to and with it one or two of the reviews you might not be able to see easily. Will you be good enough to send them along to some professor of literary inclination?

We are here or in this neighborhood till we sail for home. Probably that means for some time. We are going to share house with the Abercrombies for the winter to cut down expenses for both families. Abercrombie is a poet too. See your Anthology. Our address then will be (you can write to me there in answer to this): The Gallows, Ryton, Dymock, Gloucestershire.

I have talked enough about myself for your purposes and mine. Lets hear about you.

Yours ever

Frost.

*The "Listener" column of the *Transcript* had used material based on Lascelles Abercrombie's "A New Voice" in the English *Nation*, June 13, 1914.

†Mrs. Henry Holt had sent Frost an appreciative note from Stowe; and Henry Holt became Frost's publisher in 1915.

A L S, 9 pp.

# 14.

Dear Mr. Frost,              24 August 1914   Poland, New York

I am hoping that "North of Boston" which I failed to find at Brentano's will reach me from David Nutt ere long. Meanwhile I am so shocked at myself for waking about five o'clock in the morning that I've decided to let it break the spell the desire to accomplish much reading has held over me all the summer and write a letter.

I suppose you understand the singular retiscence I have about writing to my bosom friends now that my exuberant confidings have been shown to be mere gushes of evanescent joy. At least you will not attribute my tardy correspondence to waning affection, or more sacred interests. Will you?

Both the name and description of Little Iddens sound inviting to me; and I am indulging a vain wish that during these last days of my vacation I might call upon you.

If I did I know a great many interesting things I should want to get you to talk about. But first I should have to make an ignominious confession—that despite the fact of my being impressed (all-too-faintly it appears) by the new theory evoked from you in your talk with the laureate, I did *not* fix it distinctly. Moreover I have lost or mislaid beyond finding that letter alone of all you have written to me. Won't you please tell it to me again. All the evidence to the contrary notwithstanding I am very interested. The other day I saw a reference to Bridges' theory about the danger of deterioration in the pronunciation of English and I thought I had an answer ready myself. Possibly in that a vaporous memory of what you wrote might have been traced.

I have read the lyrics of Davies in the Oxford book several times, and I enjoyed the fresh way in which he put old thoughts in singing lines. But he does not open my eyes or kindle my heart as the poets I like best do. One would suppose that the unique past he rises from would have stamped into his personality diverse and sharp *particulars* of life and the world so that he would scorn to make use of types and classes like "birds" and cows and sheep. However he must be a very interesting man to become acquainted with even if his life does lack the sweetness of his verses.

I read the few things I come across by Wilfred Gibson with avidity. A long poem called "Wheels" in the Independent of July 6 seems very wonderful to me. It impressed me as more tremendous than any of the songs by him in the Oxford book. I think my friend Dow subscribed for that periodical publication of poems by him and another writer. Dow also had "A Boy's Will" sent for by the public library of New Bedford—where he is teaching history in the High School.

One of the men over there that I am becoming very much interested in is H.G. Wells. I shall be very glad if you can tell me anything about him. We four in this family enjoyed his Kipps a good deal this summer. And the finest thing this war has called forth, so far as I know, is an appeal to America by him, published in some of our newspapers.

I wonder what *you* are thinking about the war! Will it alter the color scheme of maps? Will it be a death-blow to the militarist movement? But you don't need to be quizzed. One fact apparent already is that Alfred Noyes at least exaggerated when he declared that there would be no romance—no magnificent deeds of valor in a modern war. What does he think of the storming of hill forts with a nearby machine-gun incessantly pouring shot into the unchecked columns climbing a narrow path? And what does he say to women repulsing an assault on fortifications by pouring boiling water? And I thought he prophesied that hand-to-hand combats were never to happen again. But if war is not less glorious, it seems to be more gruesome. And there seems to be no village in any country removed sufficiently to be immune from its oppressive consequences.

No, I did not get my raise at Schenectady. Perhaps I did not deserve it. However I am for several reasons regretful that I must return thither for only fifty dollars more than last year. The one thing that prevented me from securing an attractive college position, which I went to New York to interview the President about, was my determination to resume graduate study after two more years of teaching. *Now* I am going to bend all my exertions in the direction of Columbia for *one* year from this fall. In the meantime, however, I am interested in taking up a second year's work in Dorp—the Dutch name for Schenectady—though I can't expect it to be easy to play my part wisely outside of school.

This summer I've tried to get in a lick of sadly needed reading, and I've had a fine time with many interestng talks at home, as well as a few warm arguments. At present I am giving most of my spare time to Lockwood's [Lockhart's] Life of Scott, which the editorial preface declares is counted by the high critics foremost not to say first among biographies. Do you consider it so? It strikes me as dealing almost exclusively with "the outward shows of things"—journeys, purchases, feasts, sports and the external facts of producing books. By inference one comes at the real Scott, I suppose. Certainly, if so, he was an entertainer not a prophet; a right royal good fellow but not a man of sympathetic understanding. It was refreshing to me yesterday to turn to DeQuincey's Reminiscences of Coleridge, where [there] is an *interpretation* of facts, and a style of flexibility, and elegance not derived from the observance of rules. I suppose the Panders of Lockwood would say a biographer is the more praise-worthy who presents comprehensively the facts and leaves the evaluating of them to the student. But I object still that I want to know something more about his home relations than that he was a devoted husband and an affectionate and ambitious father, and a magnanimous master. *Why* was he a Tory? *How* did he happen to remain verbally—at least—orthodox in religion? *Why* did he tamely submit to the arbitrary class distinction which separated him from his first love? An acquaintance with his temperament furnishes, they will say, an answer to these queries. But I say give me Carlyle's manner of revealing personality. And yet—perhaps Carlyle's implies more—what I dislike—a distrust of the insight of any but the heroes, among whom of course he was.

Please tell me something of your fortunes with the critics and the public—also the publishers.

I wish I could say in words how much I like your letters. Please don't punish me by a very long silence. Please give my greetings to Mrs. Frost and Lesley and the children.

Yours sincerely,<br>Sidney Cox

ALS, 1 p.

## 15.

[Little Iddens

Dear Cox                                      c. 25 August 1914]

I should take it kindly if you would pass these along. Anything you can do for me just at this time will be a double service. My only hope is that some interest will be taken in the book in America: here none can be from now on: people are too deeply concerned about the war. Did I ask you if you would try to find an article about this Nation article in The Boston Transcript. It must have appeared in late June or early July. I should like to see a copy of it very much.

Luck to you in every way<br>R.F.

ALS, 4 pp.

## 16.

Ryton   Dymock   Gloucestershire

Dear Cox                              [17 September 1914]

You wont catch me complaining of any war—much less of a great war like this that we wage on both sides like mystics for a reason beyond reason. Some philosopher has spoken for the Germans: "The hour of obedience has come"—the hour of the triumph of German obedience, religious and secular, the hour for the rest of the world to learn to obey. Just so we thought the Germans thought. Therefore we go out to kill them. I wish we might lose none of our own in the struggle but Norman Angell, David Starr Jordan, Andrew Carnegie, Alfred Noyes and the Peace-editor of The Independent.* No I love this war regardless of what it does to me personally. That, I fear, is going to be a good deal, though nothing of course in comparison with what it will do to thousands of Englishmen. It ends my little literary game—that's all. No more books from anybody for the present. And the fact seems to be that it needed just one more book to clinch my business. As it is I am caught betwixt and between. No need to go into it. Enough to say that if I spend money here another year I spend it for nothing. I shall just have to try to get home and live to write another day. I have two fervent hopes. One is that the Germans may not sow the Western Ocean with mines before I cross with the family and the other is that I may find something to do to make up for lost money when I get across.

I havent read Lockhart and I dont think I should much care for him from what you say. Not that I ask for analysis. I am in love with the kind of books that get along without it. But I have little interest in Scott—the Scott at least that Lockhart seems to have seen, the gentleman the goodfellow the entertainer the knight (was it) of Abbottsford (I once lived for a year in a barn of a hotel of that name in San Francisco.)

There are many answers to old Bridges. I dont know the one I had in mind when I wrote to you. I can always find something to say against anything my nature rises up against. And what my nature doesnt object to I dont try to find anything to say against. That is my rule. I never entertain arguments pro and con, or rather I do, but not on the same subject. I am not a lawyer. I may have all the arguments in favor of what I favor but it doesnt even worry me because I dont know one argument on the other side. I am not a German: a German you know may be defined as a person who doesn't dare not to be thorough. Really arguments don't matter. The only thing that counts is what you cant help feeling.

Who wants to fix the present sounds of words? Who by any diacritic device could fix them on paper if he wanted to? No one in God's world can pronounce a word that he hasn't heard. No one can pronounce a word unless he can pronounce the whole language to which it belongs.

The fellow I'm living with at present is the last poet in your Victorian Anthology. If you want to see him to better advantage you must look him up in the Georgian Anthology where he shows well in a long poem called "The Sale of St Thomas." Or if I can find it I will send you some time the copy of New Numbers containing his "End of the World" a play about to be produced in several places—Birmingham next week, Bristol soon, and Chicago some time this winter. He is one of the four treated in an article in the Nineteenth Century lately—Gibson, Masefield, Davies and Abercrombie. I've told you about Davies. Did I tell you he was down here with us and one night the Gibsons limped him over on his wooden leg three miles in the rain from their house to Abercrombies? They hurried poor Davies till the sweat broke out all over him. It was partly out of spite. They had been having a bad time together as rivals in poetry. To make it full and running over for Davies they told him he ought to be proud because he was going to see the greatest poet in England. "Huh," says Davies, when he arrives in the dooryard dead beat, "good thing it's the greatest poet in England." He said it bitterly, but the Gibsons taking him at his word hurried in to tell Abercrombie that by consent of Davies he was the greatest poet in England. But that's what Davies thinks he is himself. And that is what Gibson, or Gibson's wife, thinks Gibson is. (Gibson and Davies both make more out of their poetry than Abercrombie. Davies sells well here and Gibson in America.)

Abercrombie has written a good deal of prose for a living. You ought to be able to find something of his in your library—his "Thomas Hardy" his "Epic" or his "Speculative Dialogues."

We are in another old house, this time under a very ancient thatch: the bottom layer of straw is rye—perhaps put on two or three hundred years ago. We are away in the country where you wouldn't think we would have any part in the excitement of war. But we haven't escaped being taken for spies. As writers we are a little mysterious to the peasant kind. They have had the police busy about us—about Abercrombie, too, in spite of the fact that he is well connected in the "county." They confused me in some way with a Dutchman we had with us, a Van Doorn with an accent and a long black beard. They suspected Abercrombie because a year ago he entertained a strange artist lady who goes about the country on her hands and knees because she's paralyzed or thinks she is. Sometimes she rides in a pony cart. She has to be lifted in and out of that. She gets anybody to pick her up off the ground. She is all wasted to nothing. But as the country folk remember her she might well have been a German officer in disguise.

This is supplementary to that other letter with the reviews. I shall write again soon and send you if you will let me some of David Nutts folders advertising my book.

Elinor joins me in sending regards—best.

Yours ever<br>R.F.

* Sir Norman Angell (1874–1967): English author and lecturer, who held that it is the vanquished who really win a war. David Starr Jordan (1851–1931): American biologist and educator. The "Peace-editor" is minister, Orientalist, and editor William Hayes Ward (1835–1916), whose sister, Susan Hayes Ward, was literary editor of *The Independent*.

ALS, 2 pp.

## 17.

October 1914   The Gallows

Dear Cox           Ryton  Dymock  Gloucestershire

It warms me cockles to see you so enthusiastic over my book. Three or four more such friends and I should be a made man. You have done so much more than you ought already that you wont object to doing a good deal more for me. So I send you with the book certain circulars to scatter. To be most effective they should go to people who care especially for you or for me or for poetry. But if you like you may give them to some boy to distribute on the street corner when the mills are emptying at night. Or flutter them yourself from the tail end of an electric [trolley car]. Don't count on doing too much execution with them. Not everyone will find them persuasive and not everyone will like the book as well as you would like to have him. A good many simple souls, educated or uneducated, will miss the "poeticisms" by which they are accustomed to know poetry when they see it.

Sometime we *must* discuss that minister [in "The Black Cottage"] and his creed. I make it a rule not to take any "character's" side in anything I write. So I am not bound to defend the minister you understand.

We grow more and more concerned for our future. The prose I sometimes talk of writing for bread and butter would simply bring me nothing now if I wrote it. I may have to go home soon. The difficulty there is that the expense of getting home would leave me under the necessity of getting a job for a while till I got on my feet again. I should awfully like a quiet job in a small college where I should be allowed to teach something a little new on the technique of writing and where I should have some honor* for what I suppose myself to have done in poetry. Well, but I mustnt dream.

Sincerely yours<br>Robert Frost

*Just a little little bit.

ALS, I p.

## 18.

The Gallows<br>Ryton   Dymock   Gloucestershire

Dear Cox                       [c. 1 November 1914]

This is only to say that Henry Holt will supply the book in America. Will you write that on any circulars you have still to send out?

They say the germans have made the whole Atlantic unsafe. This raises questions for me.

    1) Do I dare to go home now?

    2) Won't it be more dangerous to go every day we delay?

    3) Won't it be impossible to get money across to live on pretty soon?

    4) Do I dare to stay?

Perhaps you think I am joking. I am never so serious as when I am.

If you never hear from me again, write Henry Holt and Co Publishers New York, on the circulars and let it go at that.

Yours ever

Robert Frost

You got the book I sent?

ALS, 5 pp.

## 19.

December 1914   [The Gallows]

Dear Cox                    Ryton   Dymock   Gloucestershire

I am glad you are going into it with me and one or two others. [Edward] Thomas thinks he will write a book on what my new definition of the sentence means for literary criticism. If I didn't drop into poetry every time I sat down to write I should be tempted to do a book on what it means for education. It may take some time to make people see—they are so accustomed to look at the sentence as a grammatical cluster of words. The question is where to begin the assault on their prejudice. For my part I have about decided to begin by demonstrating by examples that the sentence as a sound in itself apart from the word sounds is no mere figure of speech. I shall show the sentence sound saying all that the sentence conveys with little or no help from the meaning of the words. I shall show the sentence sound opposing the sense of the words as in irony. And so till I establish the distinction between the grammatical sentence and the vital sentence. The grammatical sentence is merely accessory to the other and chiefly valuable as furnishing a clue to the other. You recognize the sentence sound in this: *You*, you——! It is so strong that if you hear it as I do you have to pronounce the two you's differently. Just so many sentence sounds belong to man as just so many vocal runs belong to one kind of bird. We come into the world with them and create none of them. What we feel as creation is only selection and grouping. We summon them from Heaven knows where under excitement with the audile [audial] imagination. And unless we are in an imaginative mood it is no use trying to make them, they will not rise. We can only write the dreary kind of grammatical prose known as professorial. Because that is to be seen at its worst in translations especially from the classics. Thomas thinks he will take up the theme apropos of Somebody's scholarly translation of Horace or Catullus some day when such a book comes his way for review.

I throw all this out as it comes to me to show you where we are at present. Use anything you please.* I am only too glad of your help. We will shake the old unity-emphasis-and-coherence Rhetoric to its foundations.

A word more. We value the seeing eye already. Time we said something about the hearing ear—the ear that calls up vivid sentence forms.

We write of things we see and we write in accents we hear. Thus we gather both our material and our technique with the imagination from life: and our technique becomes as much material as material itself.

All sorts of things must occur to you. Blaze away at them. But expect to have to be patient. There are a lot of completely educated people in the world and of course they will resent being asked to learn anything new.

You aren't influenced by that Beauty is Truth claptrap. In poetry and under emotion every word used is "moved" a little or much—moved from its old place, heightened, made, made new. See what Keats did to the word "alien" in the ode. But as he made it special in that place he made it his—and his only in that place. He could never have used it again with just that turn. It takes the little one horse poets to do that. I am probably the only Am poet who haven't used it after him. No if I want to deal with the word I must sink back to its common usage at Castle Garden.† I want the unmade words to work with, not the familiar made ones that everybody exclaims Poetry! at. Of course the great fight of any poet is against the people who want him to write in a special language that has gradually separated from spoken language by this "making" process. His pleasure must always be to make his own words as he goes and never to depend for effect on words already made even if they be his own.

Enough of that. I dont blame your good friend. Nor do I blame the poor educated girl who thought the little book was difficult. The "contents" notes were a piece of fooling on my part. They were not necessary and not very good.[‡]

I'd like to thank specially the fellow who picked out Mowing. I guess there is no doubt that is the best poem in Book I. We all think so over here. Thank Hatch for me too.[§] Don't forget.

And thank yourself for all you are doing for me. I need it in this game.

I should like a good talk or three with you. On the war if you choose. On anything. You are going to do a lot all round I know. Your opinions are worth listening to because you mean to put them into action—if for no other reason. But there is no other reason as important. What a man will put into effect at any cost of time, money, life, or lives is what is sacred and what counts. As I get older I dont want to hear about much else.

I have nearly written myself tired for tonight.

Write often and keep my courage up.

Yours ever
R.F.

Get rid of that Mr. on my name next letter or take the consequences.

---

* Cox, preparing his first article for scholarly publication, had probably asked Frost for a response to his ideas. The article, "A Plea for a More Direct Method in Teaching English," was published in *The English Journal*, May 1915.

[†]Castle Garden, famous first as an amusement hall in New York City, was from 1855 to 1892 the immigration station, before the opening of the station on Ellis Island.

[‡]Frost is probably referring to the glosses in the table of contents for *A Boy's Will*.

[§]Probably Clarence Hatch, a former student of Cox's.

[Frost, in including with Letter 20 the Pound review of *A Boy's Will* in *Poetry* (May 1913), scratched out these lines in it: "It [the poem "In Neglect"] is to his wife, written when his grandfather and his uncle had disinherited him of a comfortable fortune and left him in poverty because he was a useless poet instead of a money-getter." Frost gave this reason for his scratchings out: "I have scraped out some personalities (very private) which are not only in bad taste but also inaccurate." Where Pound wrote that Frost had been "scorned by 'the great American editors,'" Frost added a footnote: "The author's surmise—inference from my sad look." Pound commented that Frost's book had "a number of infelicities," and

Frost added a second footnote: "This is the superior person who objected to Trial by Existence."]

ALS, 10 pp.

## 20.

2 January 1915 [The Gallows]
Dear Cox                    Ryton    Dymock    Gloucestershire

Be sure to send your article as soon as you have it. I see you really doing something in the next few years to break into the worst system of teaching that ever endangered a nations literature. You speak of Columbia. That reminds me of the article on American literature by a Columbian, George Woodbury [Woodberry], in the Encyclopaedia Britannica. I wish you would read it or the last part of it just to see that we are not alone in thinking that nothing literary can come from the present ways of the professionally literary in American universities. It is much the same in the Scottish. Everything is research for the sake of erudition. No one is taught to value himself for nice perception and cultivated taste. Knowledge knowledge. Why literature is the next thing to religion in which as you know or believe an ounce of faith is worth all the theology ever written. Sight and insight, give us those. I like the good old English way of muddling along in these things that we cant reduce to a science anyway such as literature love religion and friendship. People make their great strides in understanding literature at most unexpected times. I never caught another man's emotion in it more than when someone drew his finger over some seven lines of blank verse—beginning carefully and ending carefully—and said simply "From there to—there." He knew and I knew. We said no more. I don't see how you are going to teach the stuff except with some such light touch. And you cant afford to treat it all alike, I mean with equal German thoroughness and reverence if thoroughness is reverence. It is only a moment here and a moment there that the greatest writer has. Some cognizance of the fact must be taken in your teaching.

Well I didnt intend to be running on like this so soon again but somehow you set me off. I have my work to think of too—though I dont get on with it to speak of in these unsettled times. The war has been a terrible detriment to pleasant thinking in spite of all I can do to approve of it philosophically. I don't know whether I like it or not. I don't think I have any right to like it when I am not called on to die in it. At the same time it seems almost cowardly not to approve of it on general principles simply because it is not my funeral. It seems little minded. There we will leave it. I hate it for those whose hearts are not in it and I fear they must be many, though perhaps not so many as it is the fashion to make them out, nor so many as they were in Nelson's navy for example where more than half the sailors, some say, were "pressed" that is to say, kidnapped. One of the most earthly wise of our time thinks the common soldiers do actually know what they are fighting for and he has said so in the only good war poem I have seen. (Thomas Hardy's my man.) There are many possibilities. The soldier may know. He may not know as in Southey's After Blenheim. He may be at fault for not knowing, deficient in national imagination. He may be the larger for not knowing: he may have been a fool always when he thought he knew, playing into the hands of captains and kings. It may be as the Syndicalists hold that his interest is no longer in nations (never was in fact) but in the federation of industrial groups without masters.* This must be a slippery piece of paper—I run to length so easily on it.

There are about half a dozen things I wanted to say to you before ringing off—business things.

The first is that you mustnt take me so seriously. You may be just as friendly as you like. I shall need your good opinion of my books in the fight that is ahead for them in my own country.

That brings me to my second. I fear I am going to suffer a good deal at home by the support of Pound. This is a generous person who is doing his best to put me in the wrong light by his reviews of me: You will see the blow he has dealt me in Poetry (Chicago) for December, and yet it is with such good intention I suppose I shall have to thank him for it. I don't know about that—I may when I get round to it. The harm he does lies in this: he made up his mind in the short time I was friends with him (we quarreled in six weeks) to add me to his party of American literary refugees in London. Nothing could be more unfair, nothing better calculated to make me an exile for life. Another such review as the one in Poetry and I shan't be admitted at Ellis Island. This is no joke.

Since the article was published I have been insulted and snubbed by two American editors I counted on as good friends. I dont repine and I am willing to wait for justice. But I do want someone to know that I am not a refugee and I am not in any way disloyal. My publishing a book in England was as it happened. Several editors in America had treated me very well, particularly those of The Companion, The Forum and The Independent. It was not in anger that I came to England and there was no shaking of dust off my feet. Pound is trying to drag me into his ridiculous row with everybody over there. I feel sorry for him for by this time he has nearly every man's hand against him on both continents and I wouldn't want to hurt him. But I feel sorry for myself too. You can imagine the hot patriot I will have become by the time I get home. And then to be shut out! I dont see that it is possible to do anything publicly to dissociate myself from Pound but do you think it would be a discreet thing for you to say a word to Sherman or perhaps (what do you think?) even write a short letter to the Sun or The Times or both saying that you have reason to know that I would have no pleasure in that part of Pound's article in Poetry that represented me as an American literary refugee in London with a grievance against Amer editors.† The article was very generous. Pound was a generous person who had gone out of his way to do me several favors, for which you supposed me grateful. But you knew I had favors to thank American editors for, too. A good deal of my first book (in fact one third) had been published in American magazines—the three I have named (you could name them.) My publishing over here was as it happened. I had come across to write rather than to publish. And it was too bad to use a tolerably good book in honest verse forms to grind axes on. Books have enough to contend against anyway.

You could say something like that to Sherman if you thought he would be likely to have been offended by the article in Poetry. Many have seen it and been offended. Do as you please. I leave the Sun and Times to your discretion. Sometimes it is better not to take arms against such misfortunes.

I am not quite heart broken over the way it has gone in this matter. I have done what I have done and I believe I have made place enough for myself to be sure of a hearing for anything else I do. I ask no more. I should like now to go to a small college with the chance of teaching a few ideas or barring that I shall get me to a farm where between milking one cow and another I shall write Books III, IV, & V and perhaps draw a few people about me in time in a sort of summer literary camp. We will talk of this some day.

Do you suppose it might be worth my while to sing myself to McCracken?[§] I am half inclined to try.

Write when you aren't too busy. I haven't heard what proportion of good boys you have had to work with where you are.

Yours ever
R.F.

P.S.

We won't stir the Pound matter up I think. You can take what I have written as so much entertainment. If ever anyone gives you the chance in public or otherwhere—well you have the facts and you can use them. Pound sought me in every instance. He *asked* for the poem he speaks of ["The Death of the Hired Man"] and then failed to sell it. It was even worse than that. I had demanded the poem back when I learned the name of the magazine [*Smart Set*] he was offering it to but he went ahead in spite of me. And there began our quarrel. I thought never to see him again. But when Book II came out he asked me for "copies" (plural) for review in such a way that I couldn't refuse to meet what looked like generosity half way. It wouldn't do to go into this, but what I have written in the body of the letter you could use should I be attacked when Holt sends out copies for review. Of course it is quite possible that I exaggerate the importance of Pound's article. Let's hope so.

We think of home all the time.

---

* Syndicalists: anarchistlike labor unionists who founded the Industrial Workers of the World (I.W.W.), and who advocated revolutionary action to replace existing governments with a reorganized society.

† Stuart P. Sherman (1881–1926): literary critic and English professor at Illinois, where he was Cox's teacher. Attacked formalism of graduate education in English in the *Nation* article. Carried on a controversy with H. L. Mencken for nearly ten years. Became editor of *The New York Herald-Tribune*'s "Books" section (1924–1926). Remained a friend of Cox's; Cox wrote the unpublished article "The Humanism of Stuart Sherman."

‡ Henry Noble MacCracken (1880–1970): English-literature scholar and president of Vassar College, 1915–1946.

A L S, 4 pp.

## 21.

2 February 1915
Dear Cox                    Herefordshire [Little Iddens]

No more letters here please. We sail for home by the St Paul from Liverpool Feb 13. If you want to be first to welcome us you can drop us a line on that c/o the American Line, New York. I should think it might reach us. Be sure to name the boat and her date of sailing. I shall enquire for a letter.

You and I wont believe that Gibsons is a better kind of poetry than mine. Solway Ford is one of his best. It is a good poem. But it is oh terribly made up. You know very well that at most all he had to go on was some tale he had heard of a man who had gone mad from fear and another of a man who had been pinned and over-taken by the tide in Solway. I am even inclined to think he invented the latter. It hardly sounds plausible. The details of what he asks you to believe his hallucinations were are poetical, but not very convincing. And then look at the way the sentences run on. They are not sentences at all in my sense of the word. The sentence is everything—the sentence well imagined. See the beautiful sentences in a thing like Wordsworth's To Sleep or Herrick's To Daffodils.

Remember, a certain fixed number of sentences (sentence sounds) belong to the human throat just as a certain fixed number of vocal runs belong to the throat of a given kind of bird. These are fixed I say. Imagination can not create them. It can only call them up. It can only call them up for those who write with their ear on the speaking voice. We will prove it out of the Golden Treasury some day.

Current Opinion was kind. I have to thank you for *so* much notice in America. There was a grudging note that I suppose didn't escape you. Never mind. The book is epoch making. I dont ask anyone to say so. All I ask now is to be allowed to live.

You have been splendid. Poetry needs just the kind of help you are giving me.

I wish you and your friend could be in places near me next summer.

I do this in a hurry. Don't expect to hear again till I send you a card from the boat.

Bluffers are the curse. I sometimes have my doubts of all the High Schools together. Your German friend is probably a sceptic as regards the higher education of the masses. I am not really with him! at the same time—

Yours ever
Frost

Words are only valuable in writing as they serve to indicate particular sentence sounds. I must say some things over and over. I must be a little extravagant too.

For goodbye The Nation named N.O.B. among the four best books of verse for 1914 and Viola Meynell used the Pasture poem to introduce her latest novel Columbine. I wish Sheffauer might have seen N.O.B. It seems more in his line than Book I.*

---

* "Sheffauer": Robert Haven Schauffler (1879–1964), anthologist, biographer, poet. Wrote sympathetically of American immigrants, corresponded with Cox, and was disliked by Frost, who dismissed him as "a treacherous second-rate mind." See Letter 25.

## PART THREE

# Franconia: Frost and Cox
## 1915–1916

❧❧❧❧

*A word more to you my son.*
ROBERT FROST *to* SIDNEY COX
*22 March 1915*

# Homecoming

## MARCH – JULY 1915

WINTER 1915 Robert Frost returned home from England. Disembarking from the S.S. *St. Paul* in New York after a potentially dangerous crossing, owing to German submarines, he spotted on a newsstand near Grand Central Station *The New Republic* of February 20, 1915. Flipping it open, he found Amy Lowell's long and favorable review of *North of Boston*. "He [Frost] goes his own way, regardless of anyone else's rules," Lowell wrote, "and the result is a book of unusual power and sincerity."[1] In New York Frost was pleased that his publisher, Henry Holt and Company, was ready "to be a father" to him. Then in Boston he met, as he put it, his ancient enemy, Ellery Sedgwick, who had rejected poem after poem for *The Atlantic Monthly*. Now the editor greeted Frost with warmth. Amy Lowell invited him to her mansion, Sevenels, in Brookline, receiving him in a chandelier-lit oak-paneled library, which held her Keats manuscripts. And Frost's goings about were recorded by a chatty journalist, Sylvester Baxter, who wrote the "Talk of the Town" column for *The Boston Herald*. Baxter puffed the poet, listed the celebrations in his honor, the prominent literati he had met, and then declared Frost "a most agreeable personality—'one of the most loveable men in the world.'"[2]

Frost's success in Boston may have assuaged his troubled ego, but it did little to fill his wallet. Short of money, he could not go to Schenectady, New York, to visit Sidney Cox. Apologizing, he cited the narrator's lines in Browning's "Up at a Villa—Down in the City": "Had I but plenty of money, money enough and to spare / The house for me, no doubt, were a house in the city square." The house had to be in the country.

Renting rooms as a temporary base for his family at the Bethlehem, New Hampshire, farm of their Irish friends, the Lynches,

Frost set out on his search for a house among the little towns in the White Mountains. Finally, in April, he found a house on the side of Iron Mine Hill, outside of Franconia but within walking distance of the village center. In June the family moved into what came to be called the Frost Place, a small farm with a barn, pasture, woods, and a fine view of the mountains. From the porch or from the window of the second-floor bedroom, Frost could look out on majestic Mount Lafayette.

Cox, in Schenectady, was disappointed that Frost did not visit, but he had reason to be elated. His first published article, "A Plea for a More Direct Method in Teaching English," had appeared in *The English Journal* of May 1915. The article is awkwardly written, its structure muddied by long references to Locke and anti-utilitarianism. But Cox's argument breaks through: beyond teaching mere form, rigid rules of grammar and rhetoric, the teacher should lead the ordinary person to think; the goal of education is "to develop in every boy and girl an understanding truly adorned with a beautiful and fine temper." Concerned with values, Cox asserted: "A moral imperative presses upon the real lover of truth to get his full meaning precisely expressed."[3] This consuming love of truth would thread Cox's teaching. His unconventional approach to teaching had been fired by Frost's influence; but the moral fervor was Cox's own.

In a vague, unenthusiastic way, Frost approved of the "Plea"; but more to the point, he was "aching" to talk with his friend. "I want to see you intirely," he wrote, and invited Cox to the casual hospitality in Franconia. Exuberantly, Cox accepted, and planned a walking trip from Schenectady to the White Mountains—the train to be taken only when absolutely necessary. His companion would be Alex Bloch, an unmarried German schoolteacher a few years older than Cox. Bloch was an experienced hiker, and a likable, intelligent friend.

NOTES

1. Pages 81–82.      2. 9 March 1915, p. 9.      3. Pages 306–7.

ALS, 3 pp.

## 22.

[Lawrence, Massachusetts
Dear Cox                              c. 2 March 1915]

Your letter was the first thing I read in America. In fact I read it before I was in America that's to say before I passed quarantine. You are always encouraging.

I wish I could afford to visit you at Schenectady and see you first and then anyone else you cared to bring along.

I ran spank on to your Schauffler (pronounced Shoffler) in New York and made him a friend. I think we can like each other despite the irreconcilability of what we write. You must meet him.

You know that the Holts have my book out. Pretty cover. But the best of the Holts is that they are going to be a father to me.

Did you see what Amy Lowell had to say in The New Republic for Feb. 20. She will pervert me a little to her theory, but never mind.

I am on the way to Bethlehem New Hampshire. Write to me there in care of John Lynch. I wish we might be near you in the summer somehow. More of my plans when I know more of them myself.

Allers yours
R.F.


ALS, 2 pp.

## 23.

13 March 1915
Dear Cox                              Littleton N H [Bethlehem]

Write to me as soon as you can to say you got my letter from New York and understood my reasons for not going to Schenectady. I was aching to see you and almost hoped you would propose coming to us. You have a salary and can go and come as you please. When I got to Lawrence where I could ask for money (and might or might not get it) I had less than fifty cents left in my

pocket. You can read Browning's Up at the Villa for a proper statement of why a man of my means might live in the country. As a
matter of fact I like the country and might live there all the time of
choice. At the present moment however I must live there of necessity. I am not rich enough to live even for a few weeks in the style
you suggested in Schenectady.

I didn't get through New York and Boston without more attention than you may think I deserve from my fellow countrymen.
The Holts are splendid. If you want to see what happened in
Boston, look me up in the Boston Herald for Tuesday March 9
under the heading Talk of the Town. A number of my old editorial
enemies actually asked me for poems. Let us weep before it is too
late.

Yours ever<br>
R.F.

Address
R.F.D. No 5
c/o John Lynch
Littleton
N.H.

ALS, 2 pp.

## 24.

22 March 1915

Dear Cox          Littleton N.H. [Bethlehem] R.F.D. No 5

Of course you wouldn't be anything so petty as miffed. But you
might be honestly hurt or disappointed if you weren't given thoroughly to understand.

Dont worry too much about my money difficulties. Some time I
will tell you exactly how it is I can be down to my last shilling and
yet in no immediate danger of coming on the town. I am always
more or less in trouble but it wont be for five years or so that I'll be
in jail or the poorhouse. My only hope in those days will be my
children or such of them as think well of me—don't judge me too
hardly for having written poetry. There's Marj—she told Mrs
Lynch, I'm told, that I was a good one to write poetry and to bring

up children. She's very likely wrong, but as long as she believes what she says—

And a word more to you my son. You are to dispense with further talk of disparity between us. I have never had such thoughts and I dislike having them thrust upon me.

Thus shamelessly I send you the Herald scrap. If the fellow who wrote it seems to know more of my goings and comings than he could without complicity of mine, the reason is because he is a lovely old boy and quite took possession of me while I was in Boston. When he wasn't actually with me like Mary's lamb he was keeping track of me by telephone. I believe he is doing for me on principle. He's got me on his conscience. The Ellery Sedgwick of the piece is mine ancient enemy the editor of The Atlantic.

Yours ever

Robert Frost

ALS, 4 pp.

## 25.

16 May 1915

Dear Cox                    Littleton N.H. [Bethlehem]

Jessie B. was all right. I ask no more than temperate praise from any of them. Temperate praise in the long run will help me most. And do you remember that when you get your chance to write of me as you know me. Don't let your admiration run away with you. Consider appearances in public. Make the most of the advantage of having known me personally to correct any lies about me that may be current. But don't overdo the praise.

The only nastiness in Jessie B's article is the first part where she speaks of the English reviews as fulsome. There she speaks dishonestly out of complete ignorance—out of some sort of malice or envy I should infer. Her anthology with the silly name made a very bad miss in England.*

She has no right to imply of course that I desired or sought a British-made reputation. You know that it simply came to me after I had nearly given up any reputation at all. That you may have a chance to tell 'em some day.

Jessie B. has a right to think what she pleases of Book I. I know pretty well what she thinks and why she thinks it.

You musnt judge of how things are going with me by the limited number of papers you see. Already I have had in America more notice than any American poet in many years. I mean public notice. Privately I have been overwhelmed with the friendship of Howells, George Palmer, Mrs Marks, Alice Brown, Basil King, E.A. Robinson, Mrs T.B. Aldrich and any number of others you might or might not know.[†] I tell you this to set your mind at rest. I dont like to see you so troubled about me when I am the envied of all my fellow craftsmen.

One of my best friends is young Louis Untermeyer. Shauffler didnt pan out very well. He showed jealousy of my British made reputation. I suspect you didn't tell me all he said in his letter to you. I found him a treacherous second-rate mind.

So rest easy. Take life easy as the leaves grow on the tree. When you see your chance do what you can for me. There are several false impressions at large that I should like to see nailed.

Since you are not going to college next year perhaps you will feel that you can afford a visit to us in the summer. We hope to be settled on a farm of our own before long. We have found what we want in Franconia.

The summer-camp scheme will have to wait a while.

Be good.

R.F.

---

[*] Jessie Belle Rittenhouse (1869–1948): poet, critic, anthologist, a founder of the Poetry Society of America. Her review of *North of Boston* appeared in *The New York Times*, May 16, 1915. The anthology Frost mentions is probably *The Little Book of Modern Verse: A Selection from the Work of Contemporaneous American Poets* (1913).

[†] All Boston-Cambridge literati. William Dean Howells (1837–1920): novelist, critic, editor; George Herbert Palmer (1842–1933): Harvard professor; Mrs. L. S. Marks (Josephine Preston Peabody) (1874–1922): poet, playwright; Alice Brown (1857–1948): novelist, playwright, poet, short-story writer; Basil King (1859–1928): novelist; Edwin Arlington Robinson (1869–1935): poet; Mrs. T. B. Aldrich (d. 1927): widow of writer and editor Thomas Bailey Aldrich (1836–1907).

ALS, 4 pp.

## 26.

Dear Cox:                          24 June 1915    Franconia N.H.

Thanks for your article. It's the right stuff. I wonder how far you would dare to go in describing your directer method in teaching English. You are much safer in a paper like yours than you would be in one like the first in your magazine for instance. It takes an awful courage to come right out and tell the way you do it in so many words. Chandler's device is dead deadly wrong. And so is that of the lady who writes on An Evolution of English Teaching.*

I'm blessed if I dont believe sometimes that the whole subject of English was better neglected and left outside the curriculum. School is for boning and not for luxuriating. We dont want much school even when we are young, that is to say, we want a great deal more of life than of school. And there is no use in this attempt to make school an image of life. It should be thought of as a thing that belongs to the alphabet and notation. It came into life with these. Life must be kept up at a great rate in order to absorb any considerable amount of either one or the other. Both are nonsense unless they mix well with experience. They are the past and the future and the distant, and the problem is to bring them to bear a little on the present and the near, to make them make some difference even the slightest. Too much time spent on them is either an injury to the infant or a waste of time on the infant that refuses to be injured. Literature—I dont know where literature comes in, if it comes in at all. It is ever so much more of life anyway than of school. It is almost too emotional for school handling, almost too insubordinate and unconventional. The one thing that it is bound to be is what it is not told to be. Mind I do not say what it is told not to be, though there might be reason for its being that.

I write as I feel tonight. Some of what I say is true. Run it all through a DeLaval separator.

I am up to my eyes in milk and suchlike farm produce. Hence this Georgic figure. And I'm too tired to be awake writiñg.

Hammer away at them. You are going to do a lot. You have the energy and you have the other things.

Yours ever

Robert Frost

Have you any way of finding out for me the correct spelling of the name of some professor of English in University of Penn. who seems to sign himself Cornelius Weygant. Print it out for me.[†]

---

*The first article in *The English Journal* of May 1915 is Frank W. Chandler's "A Creative Approach to the Study of Literature." His "device" urges contact, "touch," with literature, rather than facts about it. The other article is Mary Percival's "An Evolution of Oral Composition," stressing lists of topics for students to speak on, including "Noyes as a Patriotic Poet."

[†]Cornelius Weygandt (1871–1957) visited Frost in Franconia and was host to him in Philadelphia.

ALS, 3 pp.

## 27.

Dear Cox:                    20 July 1915    Franconia N.H.

I want to see you intirely and I wonder if we can't arrange it in spite of the devil. Let me tell you first how we are fixed. We are not really in possession here yet. We are still without our furniture and sleeping cramped in borrowed beds. There has been some difficulty about the title to the place which has kept us from going ahead very far with our plans. But it might be that I could find you a room with some farmer near us and for meals you could picnic with us. That seems an inhospitable sort of invitation and if you care to wait a year you can have a better one—if we are all alive and not worse off then than we are now. What say you?

Some of the rest of them have been reprinting me without money and without price. I imagine it is good advertising. They may teach me a thing or two, as for instance how to drop g's from words ending in ing. The parodies in the New York papers all rebuke me for not dropping the g. I can stand being parodied in the same way I can stand being pirated. But I hate being instructed— at my age.

A place I passed at night alone something like twenty years ago made In a Vale then and there in my head and I wrote it down with few changes the next morning.

You have been a good friend to the books. You must twit your Illinois professor with the Garnett article in The Atlantic for August.* The Nation is nonsense. Its bragging advertisement is everywhere.

I may see you, then, when you are on your walk. I am just out of Franconia—just off the Easton road at the first bridge you come to.

Yours ever<br>R.F.

* Edward Garnett (1868–1937): critic, biographer, essayist, whose "A New American Poet" appeared in *The Atlantic Monthly* of August 1915. Later, in Letters 28 and 31, Cox confuses Edward Garnett with Garnett's father, Richard (1835–1906): poet, publishers' reader, Chief Keeper of Printed Books at the British Museum.

# The First Walking Trip

## JULY–AUGUST 1915

THE LAST WEEK IN JULY 1915, Sidney Cox and Alex Bloch set out on the First Walking Trip. Cox kept what he called his "little diary," writing down notes in a small financial ledger sprinkled with lesson-plan reminders. He recorded prices, observations, and conversations. Then, in long "letter-journals" to his parents and his sister, Gertrude, he copied out most of the notes from his diary. The letter-journals of the First Walking Trip are reprinted here. Much later in life, Cox looked back at the letter-journals for his study of Frost, *A Swinger of Birches*; but the portraits and observations in the later book are softened, sometimes bowdlerized, perhaps because Frost and Joseph Warren Beach, another visitor to Franconia who appears in the book, were still living. The letter-journals are full of frank youthful judgments. Nothing is cleaned up.

In his letters, Cox says he feels guilty that he isn't home to help his family move again. His father had accepted a call to the modest Baptist church in a booming area, Johnston City, Illinois. (The move proved unsuccessful: Arthur Cox stayed there only a year, because the congregation complained he spoke too softly.) Still emotionally dependent on his parents, Cox justifies his using *darned* in a letter. Though his mother had asked him not to, he had taken to smoking a pipe. He wrote in his journal but not to his family that once he and Frost were drinking "imitation champagne," and when Cox told the poet he was a teetotaler, Frost said he could do more good by showing people how to drink without overdoing it, than by leaving it alone altogether. Frost was not much in earnest, Cox thought.

On July 25 the two walkers boarded the train at Schenectady, and late in the afternoon they arrived at Rutland, Vermont. They headed east, crossing the hemlock-bordered Quechee Gorge, its green waters jetting over the rapids; and then north, up hill and down, to Hanover. Tired, they spent the night in an ugly bedroom of a tavern outside Lyme, New Hampshire. For the next five days, except for an occasional short train ride, they hiked. They saw hillside farms with Jersey cattle, blue harebells sparkling on fields, and mountain peaks. They bought beans, a can opener, a spoon, bread, and cookies for forty-two cents. Cox had his shoes repaired for five cents, his hair cut for a quarter, and his suit pressed for seventy-five cents. They hitched a ride from a good-natured though sick farmer, who gave them helpful directions and a lot of refreshing cold water. They met some of Cox's former pupils, one of them now a fine young man, a Dartmouth freshman. They were served breakfast by a beautiful girl with brown eyes; they swam in the Baker River; they heard a splendid band concert.

On July 31, helped by a generous man with a Pierce-Arrow, they found the "little dingy white house as yet unsettled." The Frosts were not yet unpacked; furniture was scanty; and the small farmhouse was tight for the family of growing children—Lesley, the eldest, was sixteen; Frost's son, Carol, was thirteen, a year older than Irma; Marjorie was ten. But the hospitality, though unsystematic, was unbounded.

There was one flaw: another guest, a tall, thin, sandy-haired, timid yet opinionated man, who did not believe in God. Joseph Warren Beach held a Ph.D. and was an English professor at the University of Minnesota. Jealousy ran through Cox. Beach had achieved what he could only dream about.

Cox and Alex Bloch explored the villages and towns around Franconia, climbed the mountains and hills. But the intoxicating moments were the evenings when Frost and Cox—the master and the disciple—resumed their conversations about duty and sacrifice, God and man, poets and poetry. Frost read aloud to his guests. One night it was Walter de la Mare's "The Listeners," which he thought "the greatest poem in English in recent years."

Another evening, something unusual happened. Frost was reading his own poems, "The Death of the Hired Man," "After Apple-Picking," "The Mountain," "The Generations of Men," and then hesitated before doing the next one, "Home Burial." He said he was afraid he "should excite himself overmuch" in reading it. Finally, he read it, "with strong feeling but did not try fully to play the parts. He said the four 'don'ts' were the supreme thing in it." Cox did not know then that Frost would rarely give that poem in his public readings; and he was apparently unaware of the probable reasons for Frost's hesitation. The poem was too close to home, bringing back memories of the death at three and a half of his firstborn child, Elliott, at the Powder House Hill farm, some fifteen years before. "Home Burial" (the very title has a double meaning) evoked too strongly the differing ways Frost and his wife, Elinor, responded to Elliott's death. He covered his pain with talking, she with silence.

ALS, 11 pp.

## 28.

Dear Gertrude,                                    8 August [1915]

Got back last night. I feel like saying things that would sound too much like the Y.M. & Y.W.C.A. delegates back from the big conventions.

The two weeks have been rich in three of—say four of—the greatest kinds of experience life affords: physical exhiliration excited by successful use of legs and lungs; varied and uninterrupted reaching into and drawing from Nature; brief but interesting contacts with people chiefly likeable; and intimate associations with the very finest people in true friendship.

I wish I could talk to you about my trip and about Alex Bloch and Mr. and Mrs. Frost and Leslie and Carol and Erma and Marjorie for hours.

As it is, I find it hard to know what to leave out.

From Plymouth we took the train to within six miles of Franconia. But our efforts to find him led us two miles and back out of our way. About six o'clock a week ago last night on the brow of a hill we came upon the little grayish house with a gable projecting to form the piazza roof. Mr. Frost was sitting there on a packing box talking with a dapper English professor with a little red moustache.* He limped down to meet us, and soon we forgot ourselves in the continuation of their talk about American poets.

I am ashamed to confess that at first I was a shade disappointed. He had not shaved for days; he wore no tie; his suit was formless, his pants, that is, for his workman's shirt was not partly hidden by a coat; his hair was rumpled; his hands were brown and rather hairy and his foot which was lame from a rusty nail was shod with a big rubber. But his complete indifference to his physical appearance soon brought me to a sense of the shallowness of my observation. And by his talk and the gentle way he took the irritating showiness of the professor's talk about literary celebrities (?) here in America my old unquallified admiration was restored. He was not anxious to establish his own value in the eyes of any of us. But soon the strength and insight and humor and originality of him began to impress us inevitably. The other man, Doctor Beach, had arrived only ten minutes before us.

By and by Mrs. Frost came out and my heart leaped. She was cordial without the least embarrassment or affectation. Soon she went back and the conversation went on until Alex and I began to wonder if any plan was to be made about supper. But at length Mrs. F. returned and called us all in assuring us that we made no trouble.

Part of us had our drinking water in cups; the tea was poured from a measure for milk, and the soup which I think was the staple was served from an earthen mixing bowl with a large spoon instead of a ladle. It was simply explained to us that part of their goods had not yet been brought up; but there were no apologies. And everybody ignored the visions of furniture stacked in disorderly heaps in adjoining rooms, and a door off its hinges leaning against the wall.

During supper and after we had left two of the children to attend to the dishes. Mr. Beach disgusted Mr. Bloch and me by doing a lion's share of the talking. But he did not trouble Mr. Frost. The latter was in no sense dominated by him, even to appearance, but he recognized without anything but an inward smile that, as he said when we protested to him the next day, "his tongue was hung in the middle."

After we had left the table Mrs. Frost suggested gently but without a hint of timidity that he had better milk the two cows. But he chose to continue the talk.

At length he, or more likely, Mrs. Frost brought up the question which had seemed important to Alex and me—how we should be disposed of. Mr. F. spoke of the tent at the back of the house; but we saw it would take time and trouble to get that ready in the dark. And so finally we went and telephoned at the next farmhouse for a room and breakfast at an inn for summer boarders in Franconia. Dr. Beach assured us *we* should not want to go to the grand Forest Hill House to which he had been recommended.

By ten o'clock we had had a lot of delightful talk in which *I*, I must confess, had not been free from an anxious desire to convince the Ph.D. that I and my friend amounted to something, too. But we had all been drawn near together, and perhaps I was the only one silly enough—no Dr. B. was too—to be impressed by the nonchalance with which all the family accomodated themselves to the fact that there were not enough comfortable chairs to go 'round.

At ten we started down the hill and Mr. Frost went with us about three quarters of a mile to the edge of the town. Then he limped back to milk and we walked on feeling that Mr. Beach was a little patronizing and a trifle superficial in his talk about socialism.

At the inn a pleasant, proper little old lady unlocked the door for us, showed us where to wash, and then led us to a comfortable, fresh-smelling large room with two beds. We found three New York teachers, and a man and woman from Mississippi at the table. They were all pleasant and we, particularly Alex, I guess;— for he seemed a bit more alive to the interesting things all through the trip than I—were taken with the Southern accent of the two near us.

When we got back opposite the superb range of Mountains, of which Lafayette is the highest, which Mr. Frosts little farm faces, we sat under an apple tree in the yard. Soon Mr. Frost came down to greet us. He told us Mr. Beach, whom he "did not know from Adam" was going to stay a few days, and advised us to take our trips to the Profile and Flume, and to Mt. Washington while he was there.

It was quarter of ten then and we sat down on camp chairs in the tent to talk until Mr. Beach came. Mr. Frost was in the midst of one of the significant little stories which he tells in an off-hand way, full of queer forceful phrases from the country people's vocabulary when the clever professor entered and took out cigarettes, saying "Ah! a little anecdote!" with a rising inflexion on the final word.

Presently we set sail for the Old Man of the Mountain. I'll go on from there in my letter to Father and Mother.

I did not send a card to Frances tho I did to Ralph and Elvira, Harold and Helen, Mr. Dewey, Mrs. Schermerhorn, Mr. & Mrs. J.W.B. and Mr. Utter at Poland. Should I have?

I am going to send you that little book "Light in the East."[†] Before I went away I showed it to Miss French with a remark about the similarity of the things in it to things in the bible. She said she did not think it very like. Its sayings she pronounced abstract, in contrast to the dynamic concreteness of such things as the story of the Good Samaritan. And I guess she's right.

"Special cases" Mr. Frost insists are the important element in thinking. He despises mere speculation.

Sometime I want to talk to you a lot about Mr. Frosts theories about poetry. Meanwhile, if you want me to I'll try to write something. And if possible, after you get a little settled in Johnston City I wish you would get the *Atlantic Monthly* for August and read Mr. Frost's three poems, and also the article in which Richard [Edward] Garnet, who seems to be a critic on a par with Stopford Brooke and the best I have read, says that a piece in "Home Burial" "for tragic intensity is unequalled in American poetry."‡ There is a story in that number, too, by Ann Sedgwick who, I judge from an article in an earlier number on Am. fiction by the same man, which Mr. F. read aloud is one of the foremost of Am. prose writers.

I was very glad to get your letter. You made me feel your self. And Ich liebe dich mehr als ever. Our month at home was *good* in the sense of Genesis 2.

Yours,

Sidney

---

* Joseph Warren Beach (1880–1957): influential teacher and critic at the University of Minnesota; author of *The Concept of Nature in Nineteenth-Century Poetry* (1936).
† *Light in the East* (1900), by Bishop James Mills Thoburn (1836–1922).
‡ See footnote to Letter 27, p. 73.
§ Anne Sedgwick (1873–1935): author of nineteen books, including *A Childhood in Brittany Eighty Years Ago* (1918).

ALS, 17 pp.

## 29.

Dear Father and Mother,                                  8 August [1915]

I hope the goods have come, and in good condition. But even so, I suppose you must see a harder task ahead of you than a mountain to climb would figure. If I could be there to help you settle I'd gladly risk my examination in the History of Education.

But since I cannot go home after the finest of trips it is good I can come to so congenial a place as this is.

What I said about Alex Bloch was more than made good, much more, by my two weeks of continuous intimacy. Both Mr. and Mrs. Frost, and all the children, too, showed that they liked him very much. And the liking was mutual. To me he kept exclaiming when we were on our two trips from Franconia, and every night after we had got into our beds in the tent, about what a fine man Mr. Frost is, and how lovely Mrs. Frost is, and what fine children they were. He told them it had been the best vacation he had ever had, and that he liked America better.

It is no wonder. Their hospitality was so unaffected, so evidently, as he said, "from the heart." Mr. Frost told him at the first that he was his enemy. But as he said day-before-yesterday when we left, he showed all the time it made no difference with individuals, if the individual was a decent man.

I suppose it would not avail to try to describe the children to you individually, though each has marked individuality. I should try if I could be with you. I was struck by the fact that each of the three girls parts her hair and combs it back, even Leslie who is, or might be, almost a young lady. Of externals the whole family is indifferent; and yet one would go far to seek such attractive faces because of the vigor and sweetness of character showing through and the frequent smile of sensitive humor.

If I were Edward's grandmother I think I should be uneasy in a few years unless I could introduce him to the family. Possibly Leslie would be too intellectual for him ever to care for except as a foeman worthy of his steel. Bosh!

Alex and I agreed that the conversations at table and afterward were interesting and rich to a degree surpassing any that we had ever listened to. That was an advantage that offset the disadvantage during the first four days in which we made Franconia headquarters, of the presence of an exceedingly well-read, and very "advanced" young professor of literature, who seemed to be making a summer tour to the homes of men and women distinguished in American literature. His knowledge would have been quite dazzling but that it seemed like a fire-fly in full-moon-light.

Our first day there we walked five miles to see the Profile. We shouted and took a picture or two across Echo Lake, stood and admired the poise and serene benevolent strength of the Great Stone Face. (As we were doing so I mentioned Hawthorne's story to Alex, and one of two ladies who were walking up said "That's it, Nathaniel Hawthorne," and thanked me). [I] found and talked with two of my brightest Plymouth boys who are working at the Profile House garage; and then started on for the Flume 6 miles further. There were dark clouds in the sky, but we walked briskly along singing. Soon it began to spit rain, and after we were well away from all possible shelter but the trees to rain hard. When it pelted we tried standing under a tree but lightning drove us out. We had all the effect of a cold shower bath despite our clothes. I enjoyed it from the first; but Alex wanted to stand and wait for it to let up. It persisted; so we decided to walk on by that time saturated with water as to trousers and shirts and soggling in our shoes at every tread. When an auto ("on toe") came along Alex started singing "How dry I am," and we did that for more than a dozen during the five and a half miles of rain.

When we reached the Flume the rain had nearly ceased. We bought some sweet chocolate bars and went ahead. By the time we were between the cliffs the sun was out so that snap-shots were possible.

Father, do you remember the old dame you piloted up there? I thought of our trip then, and liked this one better. I felt free to say to myself what bad taste and what queer lack of sensitive harmony with you or even me made her presence necessary.

We got back before a fine but almost rudely simple supper.

To condense, since I've spent all the forenoon, and all the evening to 10:08 on letters to Ralph and Gertrude and this, in which I'm trying not to duplicate anything, I will resume the extracts from the little diary, expanding when necessary.

### Evening

Mr. Beach remains. From Jane Austen and Meredith through the reading (aloud by Mr. F.) of 2 of Walter de la Mare's, one of Fletcher's, and some (more) to the theory of poetry with an announcement of Mr. F's protest against "poetic flummery."

Mr. Beach fears he will arouse antagonism and thinks his awfully severe standards of criticism leave no support for Am. poets save Emerson, Whitman & Poe (?) with some of Whittier.

(It surprised me that) Dr. B. & Mrs. Frost consider Longfellow great!

Prof. B. thinks Shakespeare differed from modern dramatists in the fact that "there were no ideas in his plays"! I protest & Mr. Frost supports me. I state the idea in the Merchant of Venice and Mr. F. in Julius Caesar.

Mr. Frost says difference lies in the fact that S. never, save in one, started with a formula (that is as in a geometric proof with a theorem) first, but that he *felt* a meaning in the situation [and] as he wrote the essence idea was developed in his mind often to a formula. (As in Merchant of V. "All that glitters is not gold.") Modern dramatists like Ibsen, at his worst, and Shaw, always, start formula first & as a consequence situation and characters are "warped, warped, warped" (viz. Ibsen's "Master Builder") (which I have never read, like so many poems, plays & books talked of there, but shall want to.)

Mr. Bloch & Mr. F. had good talk on *the* war, and war on way back from escorting Dr. Beach to town. Mr. F. believes that human nature in society makes a certain amount of war inevitable, and that no matter how gifted the man he can do nothing nobler than to go to war for his country. That war brings out much that is fine in man, tends to recall society from sordid materialism and now as always has genuine glory in it. One day he and Mr. B. made a survey of history together & concluded that there is, despite the pacifists no evidence of the passing of war. And that evidence is equally opposed to the theory of Norman Angell that the vanquished always wins. However he sees a possibility of a world federation and police which may limit war, and would be glad to see it.

## Aug. 2

Started for Mt. Washington got breakfast (a very good one for 30¢ at a boarding house). Rained, and we went and sat on steps of Dow Academy. About eleven bought fruit and candy and returned to house. Made lemonade, after watching the children play croquet in barn. (Carrol had invented blocks to stick wickets into.) Long talk P.M. about poetry, the Independent which, though Ward the editor is a friend of Mr. F. has recently refused some of his poems. Soon after they accepted with fulsome praise some of his friend Gibson's, to whom Mr. F. had recommended the periodical, and then returned some more of Mr. F's saying that G. had anticipated his vein. That was just before the English critics gave him full recognition. This month he has three poems in the Atlantic, one of which their office politely returned 6 months ago., the theory of progress. Mr. F's assurance of an even general level in matters of fine thought and feeling throughout history.

(Ask me sometime to tell you about Mr. Frost's passport experience, and about Mr. F. and the gamekeeper.)

Went swimming. Mr. Frost told very interestingly of a narrow escape from drowning while in Scotland. A current near the shore resisted his utmost efforts to get in. A man on shore reached him a hand and saved him.

At supper immortality which not only Mrs. but Mr. F. firmly holds "with an almost physical certainty."

The nonsense of "logical systems" of thought. The determined character of most of our thinking. All things in the universe related. The shaping of our thought depends mainly on what we start with, and what we take next.

Mr. Frost likes to sing old ballads like "The raggle-taggle gypsies," which he supposes must be the source of Browning's "The Flight of the Dutchess."

He thinks he has been most influenced in his writing by the Russian, Turgeneiff, Benjamin Franklin and Wordsworth, through the great admiration he has for them.

The social order based on sacrifices (made by the individual) on the various planes of selfishness. For the family we make sacrifices on all, save that highest plane of the spirit on which no sacrifices could be made. For the state we sacrifice on a lower plane of more material things. And in intercourse we sacrifice a selfish desire on one plane to gain on a higher. For example, he said that in a discussion he sometimes relinquished a victory he saw possible for the satisfaction of knowing he had an advantage he would not take. That is very frank self-description. But the truth holds good in social renunciations that have a nobler seeming. And I think it is a very profound and beautiful thought that, tho as Dr. Beach and the socialists maintain, even the puritan who refrains from specific proscribed sins to save his soul is selfish, and all others when analyzed; yet these are several planes of selfishness.

— —— — —— — —— — —— — —— — ——

After supper we had some fine reading in modern poetry—never his own.

He warns against too much specialization. Says hyperbolically, that the colleges are "hopeless."

In poetry the words must always be inevitable, never used because they are fine.

— —— — —— — —— — —— — —— — ——

That takes me in my diary to August third. I hope even those disjointed jottings will enable you to form by piecing, some conception of the joys of my visit—the rich spiritual feast. At any rate, unless it bores you, my time is well spent; because the recollections I have are so good.

It leaves out the strong, sweet, laughing, earnest, sympathetic, scrupulously honest, frank and hearty yet always controlled spirit of the man. Every thing he says comes from deep within him specially for him or them he talks with. Nothing he says is learned or even merely reasoned. It is experienced and felt. He does not use the word love with flippant frequency but love fills and overflows him. It never gushes. He did not in all the time I was there make a single friendly speech to me. And I am afraid I missed it, especially when he divided his attention so equally between Alex and me at parting. But I see that his is the admirable way.

Besides I was to *bring* Alex, and he was to be sure to come *with* me. Moreover he did say, by the way, once, "Old friends are best." And on the back of his photograph he wrote before handing it to me, "Your old friend R.F."

Good-night. Be frank with me. Has my enthusiasm outrun discretion in this letter? If my conscience, which I am too absurdly conscious of, says not, tomorrow or next day I'll transcribe part or so of the fourteen pages remaining in my diary.

He dislikes adjectives; and I notice that in speaking of him I employ a string of them and nothing more.

I am hoping for news and more news especially about how you all feel spiritually even more than physically.

Your loving son,
Sidney

ALS, 14 pp.

## 30.

[Postmarked 27 August 1915,
Schenectady]

Dear Father and Mother and Gertrude,          18 August [1915]

I'd like to be with you tonight. It wouldn't matter where I had to sleep.

The last three days I've read very slowly with frequent more and less valuable pauses nearly all the time. Of course I've had some fine talks with the Misses Comstock and with Mr. Bloch. And yesterday I forced myself into a walk that proved highly interesting. I pulled apart about a dozen flowers. And best of all I found a man tending an engine by a reservoir in process of building. He was very approachable, and I found he was fine stuff.

Here are some questions I am eager for answers to:

Do you have electric lights? Do you have a lawn? How near the street? Color of the house? Any bay windows? What sort of outlook? What sort of basement? A hose? A place for a garden? Enough windows? An attic? How about piazzas?

Does Johnston City impress you as small? Is it, then, a mining town? Coal? Are there many darkies? Immigrants? What are the prospects about a maid? What sort of streets, especially yours? I suppose mail is not delivered?

Have you discovered any finer people? Is there any intellectual life in the town? Is there a library? Many young people? Is that Mrs. Jones the only one who has been in to see you much? What sort of neighbors on the *other* side and across the street?

Do you have times of feeling terribly out of your element? Homesick? And what have you heard from Poland?

The Comstock sisters are much interested. Miss Lucy came to me one morning after talk the evening before about you and your new environment to say, She had been thinking that in spite of the lack of people of your ilk, Father, who could enter into your interests you would have a splendid chance to exert an influence toward finer things in all directions.

And she spoke of how being in your home, Mother, and seeing your napkins and dainty ways would make your callers form more refined standards.

Now, to resume my story of the Mount Washington trip:

We got drinks of water at the Base and hastened on chosing the railroad track for shortness. And we walked as fast as we could go. Soon it got dark so that we could see only a few feet in advance whether there was a path at either side or not. We took turns leading. Every once in a while we slumped down the sloping cinder bank. And much of the time we had to walk between the rails stopping now on, now between, and now heel on and toe three inches below in the cinders between. Frequently we came to small bridges. But we tried not to slacken our pace, Mr. Bloch being best at holding to it. My shoes were lighter than his hiking boots, and my feet got sore.

After a while we began to look longingly as we rounded each curve for the lights of The Mount Washington House. As we continued to be disappointed Alex who had said at the top of the mountain that we must say we would make the train, and not consider failure possible, began to lose hope.

But we did not slacken our stride. Some large animal jumped up from behind a bush and scampered to the thicket, crashing branches. We thought it was a deer.

At last lights appeared and then an illumination from many windows. It seemed the glory of a palace to us. But we had still a mile to go; and we heard locomotive whistles.

Suddenly we came to a longer bridge. Part way across Alex stopped and warned me to look and step cautiously. There was a gap nearly three feet wide. I congratulated myself upon being over it. But he by that time recalled the treacherous bridge we had walked over securely at noon. There were several more wide spaces which we could barely see.

We got over the bridge and I began to look eagerly for the chapel tower from which ran a path. After long minutes we came to it and it was a relief to tread firm ground.

But when it turned slightly from the tracks Alex took to the ties again. I protested vainly and felt mad. Soon we were within sight of the station. Alex began to run. I felt more like limping—one of my ankles had been a trifle swollen for a few days. But I ran saying I thought we had time. He would not risk it.

In two or three minutes we were on the train having made the six and a half miles in an hour and twenty-three minutes. The strain started in less than one more. And while Alex was taking many draughts of water I went to sleep.

Too soon we were in Bethlehem; but we were much refreshed. And some bars of chocolate by way of evening meal helped.

Then we commenced our last lap of six and a half miles all down hill. We took the short cut as in coming up. A man overtook us in a Ford and gave us a lift for a quarter of a mile or so. After we had passed several farms I began to expect to reach the long precipitous mile into Franconia. We got into woods which made it so dark that we could not see each other side by side nor whether our next step was low or high. There were small stones in our shoes. I thought a nail was making a socket for itself in the ball of my foot.

Presently we emerged into a clearing and found we had a long stretch of winding gradual descent before we came to the steep. Alex had foretold it.

Then came the hill where the necessity was for holding back and not being unbalanced by rolling stones. The lights of Franconia far off through the woods pleased us.

Finally we were under them, and then past, and on our last mile. There we passed a man strangely muffled about the face. We discussed our suspicion. Alex said he disliked to meet a man at night when he was alone.

When we gained the brow of Mr. Frost's hill there was no dog to alarm the household, and all the lights were out. We stole into the kitchen for water. And then climbed into beds right gratefully, glad that we were back for what the next day might contain.

— — — — — — — — — — — —

Mr. Frost called our attention to a book by a Harvard professor of philosophy whom he recently met, which he thinks contains a valuable message for our day: *The Meaning of God in Human Experience*, William Ernest Hocking.*

Aug. 4 (From diary)

Late breakfast. Dr. Beach came up. Walked to garden—(at a distance)—and hoed a few rows, Mr. Bloch, Carroll and I, after talking a while.

Late dinner, more talk. Alex & Mr. F. & I go down town in rain while Mr. Beach sleeps in tent. Alex and I bought fruit and candy for Household.

The shouting deaf storekeeper and an inquisitive Frenchman who asked bluntly, "Who are those fellows" displeased Mr. Frost.

After supper he read "The Death of the Hired Man," "After Apple-Picking," "The Mountain," "The Generations of Men," and "Home Burial."

He hesitated before beginning the last for fear he should excite himself overmuch. He read with strong feeling but did not try fully to play the parts. He said the four "don'ts" were the supreme thing in it.

In "The Death of the Hired Man" he spoke of the passage about "part of a moon" and the . . . about a cloud, but he said that though they were more like older poetry he thought some of the less noticed things were more important (viz):

The way in which the sentences suggest the tones in such passages as that in which she tries to get Warren to lower his voice; & the one in which Warren says he tells him (the hired man) "he'll have to then."

And the neat colloquial sentences like the one about "Young Wilson's college boy's assurance piqued him."

— — — — — — — — — — — —

Mr. F. thinks that though the intensity is highest in "Home Burial" possibly "The Death etc." will be as highly regarded for some of the simpler things in it.

He spoke of the latter as a little drama in which the gradual change in Warren is shown. It has four distinctly drawn characters. It has climax and surprise; and it perfectly observes all the old unities.

— — — — — — — — — — — —

Mr. F. insists that Yankees are still the leaven of America. That Yankee characteristics and ideals will continue to be the Am. characteristics & ideals.

He also objects to the critics who say that he is the poet of a degenerating civilization.

— — — — — — — — — — — —

He thinks that to have geniuses and powerful men a people

must have many children of which a certain small proportion will be exceptional.

He even said that if a bright man & woman had ten children & a dull man & woman had the same number the dull family was as likely to contain the genius.

Every poem of Mr. F.'s is based on an actual experience. Alex and I are now sleeping in one of the tents that was in the background of "A Servant to Servants."

Some of the people have seen themselves in the poems.

He alters combinations and puts names and places together differently as convenience suggests. For example in "The Mountain" the mountain's name comes from another place & the town was not Lunenburg but one in Vt. near Lake Willoughby. Mr. F. says the "The M" is purely descriptive. (I had remarked that someone to whom I had read it wondered about "the meaning.")

In "After Apple Picking" are: the intoxication of extreme exhaustion, and "after-images," those of the apples "stem end and blossom end" probably due to an injury to the retina (caused by constant fixing of the eyes upon them. The feeling of the ladder rungs is another after-image.)

— — — — — — — — — — — —

Dr. Beach asked for autograph copies of the two books as well as a photograph and bade good-bye, Mr. F. walking a long way down the hill with him.

He, himself, is a poet in a small way (as he took pains to inform us all the first day) as well as a prof. of lit. in the Univ. of Minn. He has a yellow streak & a trifle too much dignity. And he seems well satisfied with not believing anything.

— — — — — — — — — — — —

Mr. Frost declares that the shrewd and pithy epigrams come from the people. A poet, he says, should note them (but not make a collection as Synge does) and catch the spirit of them so that instead of collecting them as Synge does he will remember them at the appropriate time & can make some himself such that no reader can tell which are his and which are remembered.

— — — — — — — — — — — —

And thus endeth the next-to-the-last extract. The part about our Mt. Washington trip is from memory—vivid enough, still, at least.

The night referred to above Alex told me he was proud of me because in my arguing that American and Yankee were no longer synonomous I stated my argument fully instead of acquiessing, which he said was my usual practice.

Another time he told me that I argued too much. Which is true & after all does not contradict the above.

After the first night of Mr. F's reading he spoke strongly in appreciation of it, and then said that I should never be able to read so well.

Another time when I made some remark about unsettled or changing views—I forget what it was like—he said "that is because you have not found yourself yet."

These things I say as much to let you see me through his eyes as to show you a phase of him. He criticized me little, and was a good companion all along. At times he was irritated, I could see, by my lack of foresight.

I have been disappointed at seeing relatively little of him since we got back. He is very humble and he does not hesitate to tell of his own weaknesses and boyish traits similar to mine—once in a while. And yet I think I detect a feeling in him of a defect in kinship between us. He is a far more independent thinker than I.

I must go to bed. I hope for a letter tomorrow. Wish I could hear a little twice a week. So far I have no diversions. But I'm not unhappy.

Lovingly,
Sidney

---

*William Ernest Hocking (1873–1966): Idealist; emphasized the religious aspects of philosophy.

ALS, 7 pp.

# 31.

Dear Folks,                                    25 August [1915]
   This has been a good quiet birthday. It was a pleasure to write
the long letter to you. And now I want to say when the feeling has
just come to me that I think somehow the tie present expressed
just what you meant it to. Anyway it pleased me much to get it.
   And I like it! It is very good looking. And it shows not only taste
on your part but a fine sense of what my taste is, too.

                                               26 August
   By persistence I have accomplished my stent of 150 pages in
Boswell. And before I go out for the evening to the home of the
manual training man in H.S., with the Comstocks and Alex I will
make another extract from my diary.

                                               5 August
   This Franconia Range across from the house and tent would
furnish a splendid subject for a series of studies by a great sober
landscape artist. This morning when first I sat up in bed only the
lower parts were visible (on account of the fog) behind and above
the nearer firs and spruces, a few birches and beeches too. But now
one higher mountain is obstructed by so fleecy a mass that now
and then large areas stand out clearly.
   The dragon has been out through the gap since yesterday and its
smoky breath still conceals the higher mountain top. The dragon
is a dense cloud that frequently crawls through a gap in the ridge
between Mount Lafayette and another next it, and lies along the
ridge with its head to the north.

——  —  —  —  —  —  —  —  —  —  —  —

   Walk with Mr. Frost and Alex into Mr. F's fir woods, and splendid talk. The necessity of a man's resisting his emotions. The importance of avoiding specialization.
   A real man gets some enjoyment from the tragedies in his own
inner life; but he does not *pretend* to like them because he really
suffers.
   Reason is the part of our mind useful to keep us from falling
into holes. Simple desires like the desire of a man on an ice floe to

get home are the truly moving forces in our lives. The marooned man would feel a desire, not the elements such as food, shelter, fire, wife, but an unanalyzed *desire to get home.* He would not go straight because his reason would counsel him to note current, winds, and rifts in the ice.

— — — — — — — — — — — —

(Later in the house, Mrs. F. present.)
No good women teachers. Schools nearly all bad. His children will get more harm than the good of learning what $7 \times 6$ is when they go to school here at Dow Academy next year unless he and Mrs. Frost have strength enough to counterbalance the bad effect.

— — — — — — — — — — — —

A year off by himself (with only a few books, no duties, no regular plan of life, no companions and only such part days of work for neighbors as would be needful to fill his lonely pantry) should be included in a young man's education, as it always has been with the prophets. (That was a startling idea to me tho Alex said he had wished to do that. I was astonished to find a similar one expressed by Hall in his book on Educational Problems.)* Mr. Frost had 3 months when he was 18 years old in a house by himself on Ossipee Mountain; and he and his wife had seven years with no (nearby) friends after he was married.

— — — — — — — — — — — —

Eve.
R.F. would not consent to our going down to Franconia with our suit-case. Instead we had a talk & he read some more poems from Book 2. From "Building [Mending] Wall" he illustrated a large variety of sentence tones. Great restraint in reading.

In the afternoon he had read Richard [Edward] Garnett's article (in the *Atlantic* I think for last *December*) on "Some Remarks on Eng. and Am. Fiction" which we all enjoyed. (The best thing I've seen or heard on modern American prose. Don't forget to read his article in the Aug. *Atlantic* on "A New American Poet.")

He talked about his contract with Mrs. Nutt his publisher for 5 books & the fact that he had received not a cent from her for either of the two already published. 'Twas apparently a light matter to him.

— — — — — — — — — — — —

Thank you very much Gertrude for the superfine handkerchief and the pencil case. Just came Aug. 27, and I'm all the more pleased. I wore the tie last night, Mother, and liked it. Schonen Dank.

Lovingly,
Sidney

Left blank by mistake.

I have a few interesting jottings about our return trip which I'll give next time. I guess we aren't going to have war with Germany after all. Are you disappointed, Father?

You are not to suppose that my manner of speech has become vulgarized because I half-used in a recent letter a word often associated with profanity. You know "damned" is a perfectly good word if its meaning is what you really desire to express. Nevertheless I don't use it more than two or three times a year.

*G. Stanley Hall (1844–1924): psychologist, philosopher, educator. First president of Clark University, first president of the American Psychological Association, author of *Educational Problems* (1911).

# Barding Around

IN CONVERSATIONS after supper at the Franconia farm during Cox's visit, the young man was consulted by Frost on the poet's plan for earning money in a relatively unpainful way. The plan—Frost called it "barding around"—involved reading to college audiences or literary groups his own poetry, commenting on it, and giving some of his highly individualistic opinions on art and life. In the back of his mind, Frost thought the readings would publicize his poetry and strengthen his ties with critics and literary groups—and maybe help him achieve his hope of "teaching ideas" at a college.

The previous May Frost had spoken at an afternoon meeting of the Authors' Club in Boston on his sound-of-sense theory, and he had, he thought, bumbled in reading a few poems. But things went better that evening, when he made a public appearance at Tufts University; in fact, from that reading came an invitation to do four others, at fifty dollars each—if he would give a free one to the boys at the Browne and Nichols School in Cambridge. It was clear to Frost that the bardings could be a source of income.

Elinor Frost was not happy with the plan. She would be left alone with the children and the farm chores; and the readings would deprive her husband of time to write poetry. After Frost began the readings, upon his returns home he would be greeted by Elinor's silence, a particularly damaging punishment: "Anybody's silence always works like madness in my brain," the poet told Cox. The summer of 1915 Elinor Frost was again pregnant, and she suffered a miscarriage the following November. She was nonetheless cordial to her husband's visitors, including Sidney Cox, even though Frost was then thinking of using Cox as an intermediary to get a reading engagement at Bates College.

Frost used the young teacher's connection with the president of his alma mater, George C. Chase, to secure the engagement. The poet issued the orders; Cox followed them. President Chase had the reputation of being "fanatically frugal," so much so that in his fund-raising travels he slept on a cot in the office of a local alumnus rather than pay for a hotel room; he used a wheelbarrow, instead of hiring a porter, to carry his luggage to the train station.[1]

The bargaining began. Frost was wily, but so was the cagey, pennywise president of Bates. Chase's first letter to Frost is missing, but Frost's answer to it, on October 12, 1915, and his paraphrase of Chase's letter of November 1 make Chase's response evident. Chase had probably pointed out to Frost, who had asked for seventy-five dollars, that Alfred Noyes had spoken at the college for less than fifty. The mention of the rival poet, the "sing-songing Alfie No-yes," stirred Frost to anger—and he let Cox know it.

After intricate negotiations, Frost did speak in the new chapel at Bates on March 13, 1916. William Hartshorn, Cox's former English professor, opened the grand event by saying that the audience, including many outsiders, wanted "to see a real poet, and to notice how he differs from the ordinary human being." To the *Bates Student* reporter, Frost seemed plain and ordinary enough. He read his own poems, beginning with "The Christmas Tree" (published as "Christmas Trees" in *Mountain Interval*, November 1916) and ending with "The Road Not Taken," also in *Mountain Interval*. Commenting on his poems, Frost expanded on his sound-of-sense theory: "Any sentence that does not give two ideas, that does not have a double meaning, fails to appeal to the imagination, and is not poetry." But what won the audience, the reporter observes, was Frost's sense of humor in such poems as "Brown's Descent" and "The Code."[2]

Cox could not be at the Bates reading, but he was at the one the poet had given in Schenectady, New York, a month before. Cox had persuaded the Women's Evening Missionary Society of the First Presbyterian Church in that city to substitute Frost for their annual Scotch Night. Nearly four hundred people—"The best-known people of Schenectady . . . best known that is from the standpoint of appreciation of the finer things," according to the *Union-Star*—crowded into the church.[3] The Missionary Society women sold candy before and after the barding. Two members of the congregation sang solos to piano accompaniment. After the gala preliminaries, Dr. A. Russell Stevenson, the pastor, introduced Frost.

Gauging his audience carefully, Frost assessed how much—or how little—of his theory a general audience could comprehend. He made sure they understood his "New Sound in Poetry," the title of his commentary, by clinching his points with examples that must have drawn a laugh from his hearers. They recognized, for instance, the tone in which you get rid of an unwanted dog. The audience found the evening thoroughly enjoyable, though perhaps they were as unknowledgeable as the *Union-Star* reporter, who compared Frost to James Whitcomb Riley and praised him for not looking like a poet: "He does not affect the sport shirt and flowing tie. Nor does he wear his hair over his shoulders."[4]

In the long letter Cox wrote to his family on February 19, he recreates the evening so vividly, cramming the depiction with details, that this is the best account of both the content and the flavor of an early Frost barding-around. As he describes his hero's triumph, Cox is naive, ingenuous, filled with exuberance and emotion; he tells his family "it *was* one of the happiest evenings" of his life. Frost, shaping poems that lit up life's terrors, daring metrical risks with sound, was also cannily shaping his public mask, the cracker-barrel philosopher. He knew that if his readings helped him to win popularity and fame, his books would sell more copies, making it possible for him to support his family as a full-time poet. But in 1916 this way of earning a living was still hit-or-miss. Despite his success in Schenectady, Frost netted only fifty dollars that evening. (Cox probably did not tell him that the take for the Women's Evening Missionary Society was 170 dollars, possibly even more.)

NOTES

1. "Harry Rowe Remembers," *Bates College Bulletin*, February 1977, p. 2.
2. *The Bates Student*, 16 March 1916, p. 1.
3. *Union-Star*, 18 February 1916, p. 4.
4. Ibid.

ALS, 2 pp.

## 32.

Dear Cox                30 August 1915    Franconia   N.H.

I will write you a better letter than this in requital of all the lovely things you have been saying of me and Bloch has been trying to say. Bloch mustn't try too hard to be adequate. We liked him and we saw that he didn't dislike us. So a good deal goes without saying.

But as I was about to say this letter is chiefly designed to deal with the business you have so gloriously stirred up for me. Money! You can thank Chase for his interest and make the tentative proposal as coming from yourself (or from me if you think best) that I should have seventy-five dollars and pay my own expenses. You could put it as a question if you were speaking for yourself. You manage it as seems wise. If you think seventy-five too much and want me to go for less either for my sake or your own make it fifty and expenses.

I think of you when I look into the tent.

The last state of the one who speaks in the Ode to Duty is no better than the first.*

I will write. Be good.
Ever yours
R.F.

*Wordsworth's speaker in the "Ode to Duty" still remains, to Frost, a "bondsman" at the end of the poem, even though to a higher power than "uncharted freedom."

ALS, 2 pp.

## 33.

Dear Cox:                27 September 1915   Franconia N.H.

This is just to say that I am off for New York City on pressing business with my publishers—and will there be any hope of catching a glimpse of you down there? I shall be in town from Tuesday morning (the 28th) till Thursday night—possibly Friday night. You could drop me a line in care of Henry Holt & Co (*not to be forwarded*).

I shall lavish thanks on you if I see you for your good offices with President Chase. I suppose that is a sure go. I have heard nothing from Lewiston.

Your story which is none of my business I have never the less read. I like it a lot. Elinor will tell you what she thinks of it when she is the least bit stronger. You saw the state of health she was in. I suspect you scared her a good deal by throwing yourself so completely on her judgement. The story is done without nonsense. I am afraid the ordinariness of the young man is just a little ordinary for me. Your style shoots straighter and straighter. Permit me to say so much.

Remember me to our friend Bloch.

Yours ever<br>R.F.

ALS, 2 pp.

# 34.

President George C. Chase
Bates College
Lewiston, Maine

Dear Sir:                          12 October 1915    Franconia N.H.

Thank you for your friendly but very perplexing letter.

Perhaps you are in a position to divide two hundred dollars by five so as to give me for my share the fifty which is the least I am getting anywhere for an evening lecture. Modesty forbids my doing it. I might lead you to expect too much of my performance as a lecturer. You understand I am not regularly in the lecture field. I shall go where I go this winter chiefly as the author of my books and the exponent of one or two ideas not entirely old on the sound of poetry. I am really a person of very small pretension such as you may not care to spend fifty dollars on. You must take my dear

Sidney's word for nothing: he is my devoted friend. I say all this frankly to my own hurt, and every word of it goes against me, because I shall be sorry to miss the chance of meeting you all at Bates. It is the college people, and not least the undergraduates, that I like to think I make my appeal to. Practically all my engagements for the winter are at colleges.

Very truly yours
Robert Frost

ALS, 4 pp.

## 35.

Dear Cox                    1 November 1915   Franconia N.H.

You won't forgive me I fear for having been a trifle humorous in my answer to your President's proposal. I wasn't really very bad but after what he promised I couldn't resist the temptation to let him know that I thought his come-down a little absurd. He even had the nerve to send me a marked catalogue to call my attention to the fact that he had had Alfie No-yes in his course, which was rather like hurting my feelings because he knows and I know he never had Alfie for lessnahunderd. All I said was "Perhaps you would be in a position to divide two hundred dollars by five so as to give me fifty for my share. Modesty forbids my doing it." It finished him. But never mind. I dont care if you wont. I'm just as grateful to you for having tried to get me the chance at Bates. What counts is your friendly concern for me. That much more than the money.

I'm off to Boston for a few days soon and if nothing slips up should reap a couple of hundred on the trip. This all grows out of a little talk and reading I gave free for nothing at the Browne & Nichols School in Cambridge in the spring. You will be glad to hear this much good news.

I had a good letter from Dow urging me to urge myself on some New Bedford man who could give me a lecture. I'd like to go to New Bedford if it were only to meet Dow whom I missed last summer. But I dont see much hope where I have to begin by telling people who I am and what in my own opinion I have done.

Schenectady sounds better. Wouldnt it be fun if I could see you for a day in your Dutch-named big American town?

Remember me to Bloch and be strong against the day of wrath.

Yours always<br>R.F.

[Handwritten letter, 2 pp., probably in the hand of George C. Chase's secretary. On this letter Frost appended a note to Cox, who is presumably the one who added "Rec'd day following other letter."]

## 36.

Mr. Robert Frost
Franconia, N.H.

Dear Sir:                    1 November 1915    Lewiston, Maine

I was away from home when your letter reached Lewiston. I am taking my first opportunity for replying. We should feel ourselves highly favored in being permitted to announce a lecture from you in our college course.

As I wrote you, we are obliged very carefully to count the cost of each lecture. We shall be glad to assure you the price you name (fifty dollars) which I understand covers all expenses on our part. And we shall anticipate the pleasure of entertaining you in my own home.

I cannot at this writing give you a date in March or name a date for your consideration, but will do this very soon.

I have been much interested in "North of Boston" and hope, before you come to us, to familiarize myself somewhat with your other poetical works.

Sincerely yours,<br>George C. Chase<br>E.C.

Dear Cox

Just like me to think I had offended by my fooling. Anybody's silence always works like madness in my brain. Damme!

R.F.

ALS, 17 pp.

## 37.

[Schenectady]

Dear Folks,                                    19 February [1916]

Mother, I am glad you were able to write even a little after what the chiropractor did to you. Hereafter he and others like him must be told so that they can't fail to understand. I don't like to think of that happening to you.

It is nice to hear of your meeting people of your kind. And it is encouraging to hear of good times and invitations. I wish I could come to you on a sound wave to-day (at 183,000 miles a second) and tell you about Mr. Frost and the debate. But I'd rather take Mr. Frost to you. He would delight you all.

The audience was large—nearly four hundred. And they were with Mr. Frost all the time. They *liked* him. Many warm things have been said.

He read several poems both new ones, and poems from the books. His voice is full and sweet. And his perfect sincerity and restraint showed in the reading. Then he talked so simply and clearly about his vital theory that many of the people must have got it.

A poet, he says, is one who goes about looking and listening. Not in books, but in life. Sound is the main thing in poetry. And the good poet takes in the auditory images of human speech. Then, when he writes, he summons the appropriate sound images.

A live sentence conveys meaning not only by its component words but by its whole tone. And a good writer catches both. He cannot make new sound images. He merely summons the appropriate ones. For there is a fixed number of tones. Humans have more sound combinations than a cat-bird or a robin. But their number is limited.

To illustrate the difference between dead and live sentences he gave us these: Is supper ready? (dead); Have I asked you once, is supper ready?; Have I asked you twice is supper ready? (alive.)

Then he gave us examples that he gave children at a school a friend of his, Mrs. Hocking, wife of a Harvard Philosophy professor, has founded.

"The dog has come into the room."

"I will put the dog out."

"He will come back again."

Those are dead. These are alive:

"There's that dog."

"Out you brute!"

"Here he comes, right back."

I am not sure of that last one. But I think you will observe that he is right in saying that the tone is down there in black and white.

Wordsworth, he says, caught the sound images. And Milton, especially in "Lycidas." But Shakespeare is supreme.

He said if we let *playwright* represent the bad writer of plays, and dramatist the good writer of plays, the playwright was the one who had to teach the actors how to speak the lines. And the dramatist was the one who could go off and die and actors would get the tones just right.

He admitted there were cases of ambiguity about the sound images, but convinced us that they were not more numerous than those of ambiguity about visual images.

He called our attention to the tendency of all lesser poets, especially modern ones, to employ only the sound images already well established in books. But he made us believe that many fresh ones are to be found in conversation and that they are beautiful because they express varieties of human feeling. Which, he said, is the main thing.

For instance in poetry we have two prominent O's, the O of grandeur, and the O of (something like) disappointment. Shakespeare, for instance, has another, where, in *Hamlet*, the hero is gently and affectionately turning off the praise of Horatio. He says, "O, my dear friend," the O of deprecation. There are many more O's not used.

He did not speak of it. But he has used several such. For instance, in "Home Burial," where he has the woman in her horror at her husband's callousness say, "Oh, oh, oh, oh," etc.*

Miss Frances Whipple and others have expressed special appreciation of his sincerity. And that is the *great* thing supreme in him I think. He is far and away the most perfectly sincere man I know.

It was thrilling to me to see the glow of joy and admiration on the faces of people here—including Miss Jessie French—whom I have come to like very, very much, as they gathered around to be introduced.

Several of the college professors were hearty in appreciation—not excepting Prof. Hale.† And practical, scientific men and workers understood and liked him, too.

After it was all over and Mr. Frost had gone to bed, Alex and I came in here and had a feast of rejoicing. We both felt that it was one of the happiest evenings of our lives.

It was some satisfaction to know that the collection was $170 or more, that it was the best evening the society had ever had at their entertainment and that Mr. Frost got, all too little, fifty dollars.

His having been in this house will make us all sweeter, more genuine and more devout. All his conversation was interesting to the n[th], I might say if he did not make me despise myself for too much vehemence, too little restraint. And one thing, of the most interesting, was the emphasis he put upon the fundamental importance of faith. He showed simply and clearly that morality, science and art all rest upon belief—a belief that we cannot get back of nor defend.

And in speaking of a new book on philosophy by Balfour of the English admiralty, (which he is going to review) he said that philosophers are now the most fervidly religious men. It seems as if they are saying to the church, "Here, you can have back much of what you gave back last century. You needn't have given it up at all." The book is "Theism and Humanism."‡ Another that he commends is "The Meaning of God in Human Experience" by his friend, William Ernest Hocking of Harvard.

He said that the finest thing in nineteenth century thought is the fervid faith of the best scientists in the Truth they thought they were getting in their science, and which they really were seeking.

But he says such evolutionary speculation as that which one writer or philosopher exemplified in his theory that religion sprang from corpse worship is clap-trap. He said in his youth he fought his mother about beliefs which seemed antagonistic to evolution, but he discovered after a little that it was so easy and so cheap to account for everything by calling it an evolution from or vestige of an earlier or primitive means of survival that he recognized the invalidity of such pressing thought to logical conclusions. (It is so easy and so dangerous, he says, to follow thought in logical lines instead of taking the truth which fact reveals. Doing so is the bane not only of philosophy and science but of all art, even the art of conversation. *Aristotle* said it was folly to press principles to their logical limit, as I was delighted to find in Burke this year.) He gave an example of the evolutionary reasoning. He knew a man who had a habit as he walked rapidly along, of whirling suddenly completely around. A pettifogger at evolution could easily say his ancestors had developed that reaction in days when braves stabbed in the back.

And Mr. Frost told us about a great French scientist recently dead who exploded one of the extreme notions of evolution by his study of wasps.[5] One species stings caterpillars in *nine* separate nerve ganglia and wraps the victim up for the young wasps to eat in the spring. The caterpillar is paralyzed. Motion is impossible. But the wasp larvae (?) have *fresh* meat when they begin to eat. For a wasp to learn by chance those nine separate points to sting would require millions of trials. And each time until it was learned the failure to sting one would result in decayed caterpillar, and death of the young wasps. The species could not have survived during the learning process. Of course an advocate of unlimited confidence in chance evolution could destroy the contention that this shows something mysterious—something like design. But the French scientist did convince other scientists by the thoroughness and accuracy of his life-long investigations that the survival of lucky accidental variations (and mutations, too, I think) does not account for all the marvels of nature.

One of the notable things about Mr. Frost is the care he takes to guard against misapprehension. He says he does with people something like what he does when he wants to put a screw into a place close to an old screw hole—plugs up the old hole. If he did not they would confuse his thought with—let it break over into some trite old thought they had learned from their fathers or from a book.

He is spontaneous. He never gives praise when it is sought. He likes nothing because it is highly esteemed. He does not gush over anything or anybody. Show him a picture of a dear relative, and he will not try to say something nice about it. (A good deal like Uncle Edward in that as in much else.) He does not hesitate to expose defects and reveal folly in notions and in people. But he is invariably kind. And his dry humor saves all the delicate situations as well as glorifies the pleasant ones.

I wonder at the accuracy and range and newness of his knowledge. He could interest a man of any trade or profession in talk about the man's work, and tell him new things about it, too. And never offend the man. He can, as I saw yesterday, talk with a pigheaded man and make him modify his views and open his mind without knowing it.

I learned a lot of new interesting facts about his life this time. He thinks he has learned more from doing things than from the school and university. Yet he is more than a peer of the university professor on his own ground. That I say.

But he does not hesitate to talk about himself. He slides down in a big chair and half closes his eyes and wonders and thinks and feels, slowly, aloud, in a low, soft but always masculine voice. And he himself is not infrequently the theme when alone with friends. But, as Miss Comstock agrees, no one would ever think of accusing him of being swelled-headed or vain. He is very sensitive. And at first a public lecture used to do him up so that he would be sick in bed.

His talk justifies his theory about live sentences. It is full of astonishingly apt locutions, and yet a superficial person might think it commonplace for a genius. He is the sort of person that fools like the reporter who wrote of the lecture in the *Union-Star* compared to James Whitcomb Riley. And more intellectual surface-lookers think he is Whitmanesque. But he is the profoundest, shrewdest of thinkers, and he is not like anybody.

He is no extremist. He shows the habit of thought which I told you Uncle Frank described so well. In fact I defy any honest man to classify him as any kind of an ist or ite. It is hideous libel to say that he belongs to a school.

As I think he might say is true of all real, material things, he must be shorn of some of his most essential characteristics before he can be put into any pigeon-hole. He is a man. He is Robert Frost.

Webster debating club won the debate on the question "Resolved that New York State should adopt the Short Ballot," not withstanding that they upheld the negative. All the practical statesmen and all the political economists were against them. They won on honest, straight argument, knowledge of the problem, and forceful, well-directed rebuttal. Hale, the grandson of Edward Everett Hale, a gawky youngster of fourteen was best of all in rebuttal. He won spurs worthy of his ancestry. His father is no slouch of a literary man, though some people think he is a slouch in dress.

The decision was two to one in our favor, made independently in sealed envelopes. It should have been unanimous; for the affirmative lacked facts and resorted more than once or twice to despicable shyster tricks. I was proud of my boys. I really quite love them. We have been team-mates rather than director and workers, and a hundred hours or more of hard thinking together is as good as a bushel of salt consumed to make good humans friends. I do not intend you to think that I failed to be master, in a sense, all the time. But we ate apples and crackers at our meetings and I did not have to fear for my dignity.

Please send this letter around to all the clan, not excepting Cary and Frank. For if it's not the most interesting letter I ever wrote it's not for the want of the most interesting subject, Mr. Frost.

Lovingly,
Sidney.

---

* Cox mistakenly cites four *ohs* instead of the four *don'ts*.

†Edward Everett Hale, Jr. (1863–1932): son of the author of *The Man Without a Country* and professor of English language and literature at Union College, Schenectady.

‡Arthur James Balfour (1848–1930): English philosopher and statesman. Prime minister (1902–1905), foreign secretary (1916–1919), and author of *Theism and Humanism* (1915). Was devoted to the cause of international peace.

§Jean Henri Fabre (1823–1915): author of *The Hunting Wasps* (1915).

# The Second Walking Trip

## JULY–AUGUST 1916

ARRIVING IN THE RAIN at the Frost Place—after being bitten by bedbugs at their lodgings the night before—Sidney Cox and Alex Bloch were hospitably welcomed on August 9, 1916, by the poet and his family. Since the young men's last visit, the preceding summer, Frost, at the request of his publisher, had been preparing a third book of poems, called *Mountain Interval;* it was published later that year. Some of the poems in that collection—which included "The Road Not Taken," "An Old Man's Winter Night," "The Oven Bird," "The Hill Wife," "'Out, Out——,'" "Snow," and "Birches"—he read aloud to Cox and Bloch, and commented on them.

When the friends arrived, Stark Young, the writer, translator, and English professor at Amherst, was a guest. Young had brought with him an important message: President Alexander Meiklejohn, the proponent of the humanistic "Amherst Idea," was inviting Frost to join the faculty at the college for one semester, beginning in January 1917, at the generous salary of 2,000 dollars. (Frost would replace a professor who was to leave for Boston to serve in the state legislature.) Given free rein to teach on his own terms and out of his convictions, Frost would be assigned a seminar on the appreciation and writing of poetry, as well as courses in pre-Shakespearean drama and freshman composition. Although Frost felt uncomfortable in the professorial role, he accepted Meiklejohn's offer. The bardings around would not pay all the bills.

Cox again kept a diary, but this year he did not write long "letter-journals" home. His family at the time was moving from Johnston City, Illinois, to New Hampton, New Hampshire, where his father had accepted a new pastorate. Cox therefore saved his news about this Second Walking Trip to give to his relatives in person. He kept daily notes in a small loose-leaf diary, jotting down quotations, paraphrases, and observations in an elliptical style. (The material that follows is taken from the diary.)

The second day of the walking-trip vacation was spent climbing nearby Mount Lafayette. Frost and Stark Young dropped out a fifth of the way up, but Cox and Alex Bloch reached the summit and exulted there, in a "very full physical happiness." That evening the guests listened to "Mr. F." read his poems. The two young men were disappointed with "The Bonfire," but were delighted with Frost's comments. Frost was best satisfied when a poem came to him "whole," the way "Home Burial," "The Fear," and "The Bonfire" had done. He asserted that "the artist must not select a universal and then find particulars to fit it," but rather must keep the particular, or the "objective," and make "the meaning stand out a little by his representation of the fact." Frost then observed, "No real experience comes to you when you can take the sting out of it."

Cox later explained more fully Frost's emphasis on the "particular," in an August 27, 1916, letter to his friend Alice Ray, who had asked him about "'Out, Out——.'"

About "Out, Out." It must have been a real incident. Mr. Frost says he never invents. He merely selects. I know how you feel about the last line. ["... And they, since they / Were not the one dead, turned to their affairs."] But that isn't Mr. Frost. That's life. I don't know anyone who has more of the right sort of tenderness than Mr. Frost. It shows in the line 'Call it a day I wish they might have said.' You say 'I like it and still I don't.' That's exactly how I feel about life. And Mr. Frost says—finely, I think—that all art must be 'a part for the whole'; particulars from actual observance or experience which have tremendously interested the artist presented in such a way that the meaning which he sees in them will be a little emphasized—and yet with such 'gloating over the particular' that it may seem to some that he is interested mainly or even solely by the particulars.

"An enemy," writes Cox, "instead of calling him a dangerous radical might accuse him of having dug out old Greek and Roman eclogues and idylls and imitated them." On second thought, Cox reports, Frost explained that his poems were not imitations, but "comparable" to the works of the ancients. His narrative "The Bonfire," which was to appear in *Mountain Interval,* "had the lip,

bulge, and base of a Grecian vase." Miss Jeanette Marks, a professor of English at Mount Holyoke College, called him "'pro-
toplasmic'—that implies lack of form." But he cared about form.
There was nobody going who had as much of it as he: not substance fitted to a form, but substance taking a form. Frost could
draw the design of some of them. "Pattern is the essential thing in
poetry. Yet one can not fit substance to pattern."

Throughout the week-long visit, Frost and Cox uncovered,
often late at night, their deepest feelings about God. To Frost, God
"is that which a man is sure cares, and will save him, no matter
how many times or how completely he has failed." "Religion has
to do with the immortality of the soul and the confident relationship of man to God," not, as Cox suggested, devotion to things
spiritual. Ranging wide and probing deep in his evening monologues, Frost listed the order of "given" things: "religion, virtue,
beauty, property, and crimes." "They grade into each other and de-
compose into each other." "Religion could not be arrived at through
philosophy."

In the light of day, Frost, touchy, would disparage summer people, one of whom had pushed his daughter Marjorie off a walk on
her way home. He said he would not stay in Franconia to be a
"spectacle" to them. The natives, though, were no better; they regarded him as a "curiosity." Confiding in Cox, Frost said he had
"dismissed" his contract with his British publisher, Mrs. Alfred
Nutt, who refused him royalties; he had "a gentleman's agreement
with [Alfred] Harcourt of Henry Holt & Co." And he was pleased
that the baseball player Christy Mathewson had just ordered a
copy of *North of Boston*. But though Frost scoffed at academics,
he bragged that Professors Bliss Perry, of Harvard, and Cornelius
Weygandt, of the University of Pennsylvania, were "among his
most unreserved admirers."

During their vacation Cox and Bloch swam, chased Jersey cows,
went blueberrying on Sugar Hill, and discovered a deer lair in an
uncut hay field. One day, while Cox sat in the field on a large rock,
reading a book Frost had lent him (Balfour's *Theism and Humanism*), the poet came by and began to read aloud from Amy
Lowell's *Sword Blades and Poppy Seeds*. Frost labeled her "a
fraud"; Cox agreed. At other times Frost pontificated on: Mase-

field (he was likable, both as a person and as a poet), Vachel Lindsay ("quite a person"), and Shelley ("too thin in imagination, too thick in thought"). Unable to read much of Carlyle, Frost praised Coventry Patmore, Thomas Hood, William Barnes (the Dorset poet and friend of Hardy), Longfellow, and, of course, Emerson. Emerson was a greater poet than Whitman, whose one attempt ["O Captain! My Captain!"?] at traditional verse Frost said was not successful. Poe was "not truly great, [his] chief feeling [was] that derived from throwing stones at [a] tomb." Although Frost was a friend of Wilfrid Gibson's, he didn't like Gibson's poetry. Sara Teasdale was "given to love affairs," and Joyce Kilmer was "a Catholic who claims to control American poetry through the *Times Book Review* and *The Bookman*." There were "few, hardly any good American critics. Most of what they write is limp, derived stuff. Such a one was Stedman." [1] (Two years later, Frost was to urge Cox to become a "critic—first-class *American*.") The poet interspersed his impressionistic criticism with readings from F. S. Flint, the imagist; the popular Joaquin Miller (he was "not much"); [2] the Victorians in *The Oxford Book of English Verse*; and his own poetry and drama—"The Ax-Helve," "Snow," "A Way Out."

Talking again about his sound-of-sense theory, Frost pointed out that there may be differences of temperament which affect tones, but all good sentences must have some tone. And the sound image need not be any more obscure than images of sight. The sentences of mere statement are the least interesting and naturally have least tone; they are varied by changes in arrangement.

During the week Cox and Bloch hiked to see once more the Great Stone Face and the Flume in sunlight. On an evening stroll with Frost, they stopped on a hilltop to watch the moon rise over Mount Lafayette. The silhouetted trees, the stars, and the mountain reminded Cox of the popular illustrator Maxfield Parrish. "Maybe he's not altogether bad," Cox said. Frost replied that it wasn't right to justify Parrish: "Much in nature is stagey." Like a good painter, the poet "must not be afraid of the ordinary—must call a broom a broom and not the magic wand of the goddess of the hearth, Hestia. All good writers now say the Moon, not Diana or Luna. Attempts to heighten or dignify the facts do not succeed.

It is a shame to rely upon classical allusions. He [Frost] had been accused of that when at the close of a poem he referred to the *calypso*—a rare orchid he had been looking for."

Frost's hatred of fraud surfaced again in gossip about Robert Louis Stevenson, whose work Frost regarded as "amusement." Stevenson's family, he said, was angry with a book on him by Clayton Hamilton.[3] "No physician thought Stevenson had consumption. Stevenson himself found out how profitable it was to be sick. He saw people in bed when there was nothing the matter with him; and was, in short, a poseur."

When Cox and Bloch left the Frosts, on the morning of August 16, 1916, "the family was at hand for our departure. Mrs. F. was particularly lovely, Lesley stiff. Mr. F. walked a mile with us and said warm words at parting." It was a visit Cox had enjoyed, and he went home carrying Frost's copy of *Theism and Humanism* for his father to read, as well as a photograph of Frost, a parting gift from the poet, Cox's idol.

NOTES

1. Edmund Clarence Stedman (1833–1908): poet, critic, anthologist, businessman. Among the first to trumpet American literature.
2. Joaquin Miller: pen name of Cincinnatus Hiner Miller (1839–1913), a poet who celebrated the vigor of the American West.
3. *On the Trail of Stevenson* (1915).

ALS, 4 pp.

# 38.

Dear Mr. Frost,                    30 July 1916   Schenectady, N.Y.
Alex and I intend to start on another walking trip next Saturday. We intend to take train to Burlington, Vermont, walk part way to Montpelier, and having reached Montpelier by train, to walk into the mountains making Franconia our objective. We are accepting your suggestion that we come to Franconia and get board at some farm house. You and Mrs. Frost are not to entertain us at all. But we hope to be able to see a good deal of you, and that you can take some trips with us.

We are likely to reach Franconia sometime in the middle of the week of August 6.

From Franconia we shall go down to Plymouth and around by Asquam; walking I hope. And if things go according to my desire I shall stop not far from there and be at home.

For my Father is leaving southern Illinois, and it looks now as if he would accept a pastorate in New Hampshire. That accounts for my unexpected waiting here at Schenectady, and for my affording to go on this trip even though I am going to enter Columbia in the fall.

I think "Out Out" is a tremendous poem. Isn't it about the best you have published? Alex likes it. But some of my optimistic acquaintances think the close is uncomfortable. In other words it is too sincere for them, and they fail to sense the tender sympathy. I like the one about the Home Stretch, too, but it is not so stirring.

I was at first rather displeased to find, last night, a poem called "Ruins" written by Theodosia Garrison "in the manner which has been popularized by Robert Frost," as the shallow-seeming commentator in the Literary Digest said.* But I was relieved to find that it lacks the deep sincerity and originality of your poems. And, though the writer has essayed to catch the sounds of speech, the effect is in places strained. And after all it fails to convey the impression of a genuine experience. I hope all are well at your house. We shall be glad to have a line from you before we set out.

Yours sincerely,<br>Sidney Cox

*Theodosia Garrison (1874–1944): American lyric poet, author of *Joy O' Life and Other Poems* (1909) and *Earth Cry and Other Poems* (1910).

ALS, 2 pp.

## 39.

Dear Folks,                    9 August 1916    Franconia, N.H.

We're here, I am anxious to hear from Father. We must, as usual, accept what comes, without discouragement, even if it is disappointing.

Mr. Frost is as fine as ever. He gave us a good welcome.

Our trip so far has been interesting enough to give me a new store of things to talk about. Yesterday was the most delightful— air fine and scenery very satisfying. I care particularly for the pointed firs.

Last night a second experience impressed us with the advisability of avoiding cheap hotels. We had "the best rooms in the house." That was at Laconia. We left there at quarter of ten this morning and had a pleasant leisurely walk. We came up here from Franconia about noon in a rather heavy rain.

Mrs. Frost gave us and a visiting professor from Amherst a good lunch. There was no excitement on the part of any member of the family at our arrival. And we began to feel at home at once. This afternoon Prof. Stark Young, Lesley, and Mrs. Frost went with Mr. Frost to the large Forest Hill House here where he read some of his poems for the benefit of the French war sufferers. More than ninety dollars were taken.

Alex and I got along even more friendly than last on the trip. And though I see imperfections in him, I like him much.

We are rooming at a farm-house about a quarter of a mile from Mr. Frost's house with rooms adjoining from the front one of which we can see Mt. LaFayette. We are made less apprehensive about beds, in spite of last night bugs and bites, by the knowledge that Mr. Harcourt, Mr. Frost's publisher,* and his wife roomed here when they visited the Frost's, and by the pleasant, attractive looks and manner of Mrs. Herbert.† We are to come in at night when we please, and to have breakfast at half past seven or eight.

As before I'm keeping a diary. And so I'll not write long letters. But this time I can tell you about my observations and impressions in a fortnight or so when I see you. I wish it might be in ten days.

Miss Comstock says that you can go to their house and have the room that was mine when you first go to Schenectady, Gertrude, until you find one that you think suitable. I doubt if there will be a scarcity of rooms. But you will be lucky if you find a room with people who will compare either as landladies or as friendly acquaintances with the Miss Comstocks. Miss Carrie Comstock pleased me by saying that they will try to help you to find a good place.

Lovingly,<br>
Sidney

c/o Mr. Robert Frost
1 wk.

---

* Alfred Harcourt (1881–1954): editor at Holt (1904–1918), founded his own firm, Harcourt, Brace and Howe, in 1919.
† Cox and Alex Bloch stayed with the Herberts, half a mile up the road from the Frost Place. Willis E. Herbert had moved there after selling his farm to Frost.

ALS, 4 pp.

## 40.

Dear Mr. Frost,          18 August 1916   New Hampton, N.H.

Alex left this noon. Isn't he a likeable man? We have lived as close, nearly, as bride and groom for two weeks and nothing has come between us. As he said, That is rather remarkable.

Down at the station at Bristol I suddenly remembered that I had forgotten to give him the photograph you gave me. He was so disappointed when we got down to the willow bridge, because he hadn't remembered to ask for the one you promised to him, that I said I'd let him have mine. Sometime you'll send or take him one, won't you?

I guess we were both rather sober at leaving. We talked hardly at all until we ate on a green spot behind raspberry bushes the lunch Mrs. Herbert put up. Soon after that we were surprised to meet a

man walking. He was from the Franconia Notch, and was bound
for it. He carried a heavy stick, and he said he was glad to meet us
because it was a lonely road. But I guess he wasn't afraid. Alex
thought he was a professor. At any rate he was agreeable.

We were both glad that we went to the Lost River. I never saw
such wonderful quarrying and scooping work done by water. It's
strange I've never happened to hear much of the place.*

We reached North Woodstock a little before six. After we had
looked up trains we went dusty and spotted with mud to the
Mountain View Hotel. When they told us they didn't think there
was a room Alex was suspicious that they didn't want us. But
when they showed us the bath-room to wash in, told us to stay to
supper, anyway, and recommended Deer Park for the night we believed the excuse. The landlady indicated that she was interested in
our walking. And when we told her we came from Franconia she
asked us what hotel we'd stayed at. When we said we'd been visiting Mr. Robert Frost she said, "O, I read all about him in the papers." We did stay at the Deer Park and sat on the porch—after
dark, and had a game of pool before we went to bed. In the morning we had breakfast there. And we saw hardly any signs that our
rough appearance was noticed.

Yesterday we made twenty-four miles on foot, were carried
about a mile in an auto and rode from Woodstock to Campton—
about ten miles—on the train.

Though this hamlet is high they say "You know we are down in
the valley." There are but few houses, most of them painted white.
The church is substantial looking outside, and exceptionally neat
and comfortable inside. And the parsonage seems large and comfortable, too. It has conveniences that we have done without—fur-
nace, bath and electric lights. There seems to be a good public library here. And a sort of semi-intellectual tone is given to the place
by the Literary Institution. I understand that it has about 100
pupils. There is a very decent small campus with six or seven
buildings on or near it. I came near leaving out of this rambling
description that there are shaded and prettily winding though
sandy roads entering the place in several directions; that beautiful
hills surround it, and that there are many fine elms along the sides

of the streets. Tomorrow I'm going to test the statement that from all the near-by hills one can see the Franconia Range.

It is five miles to Bristol, but that is the terminal of the train up from Concord. It is only seven miles to Ashland, and people go over there often. If sometime when I'm here you can stop off to see us that will be the place for me to meet you. Newfound Lake is two miles from Bristol, and so a little more than seven miles from here at its nearest point. We did come through Bridgewater—not through much of a settlement.

The pleasant wife of the doctor at whose house we are staying says she read in "The Christian Work" or some such paper that you are the foremost living poet in America. (It bolsters me to hear of such an authority after the fact for what I have said in the uncertainty of ignorance.) The pretty girl who was for a few days visiting the Sophomore son heard you at Plymouth and boarded with you and your family. Do you remember Miss Hardy (or Harding)?

I am very glad I can hope to see you in New York. And I hope that I can hear from you once in a while. Our whole trip was interesting and fine. And our week in Franconia with you was one of my happiest and best weeks. I think I could say the same for Alex.

When I get my trunk I'll look for my stamps for Carol. I'd like to have my Father casually pick up Theism and Humanism. But, anyway, I'll send it back before long.

Yours,
Sidney Cox

* The Lost River: glacial caverns near the Great Stone Face, just north of Woodstock, New Hampshire.

## PART FOUR

# Frost at Amherst, Cox at Missoula
## 1916–1925

*Lets be as stupid as is necessary to be good.*

ROBERT FROST *to* SIDNEY COX
*8 September 1921*

B Y THE FALL of 1916, Robert Frost was on his way to be-coming America's most famous poet. Edgar Lee Masters and Carl Sandburg were two contenders about whom Frost worried. Masters's *Songs and Satires* of 1916, however, was a critical fail-ure, so that Frost could pronounce this rival "dead." Sandburg was not so easy to dismiss. For the rest of his life Frost had to com-pete and be confused with the white-haired Illinois poet whom he saw as a phony—"He is," Frost said, "probably the most artificial and studied ruffian the world has had." [1] In June of 1916 Frost had been Phi Beta Kappa Poet at Harvard. That November he was elected to membership in the National Institute of Arts and Let-ters. His third book, *Mountain Interval*, was published on Decem-ber 1. Less than a year later, "Snow" won *Poetry* magazine's prize of 100 dollars, the "first real prize in a long life," Frost wired the editor, Harriet Monroe.

Financial gain followed critical and popular acclaim. Frost now had some income from royalties; and he was teaching at Amherst College in January of 1917 at a full-professor's salary. By making "sacrifices on all but that highest plane of the spirit," Frost stub-bornly and sometimes painfully proved that his genius could pro-vide for him and his family, although they were never secure until he was over sixty.

*Mountain Interval* was praised by both readers and critics. Padraic Colum in *The New Republic* and Monroe in *Poetry* gave this book (Elinor Frost's favorite) sympathetic and perceptive re-views. When Sidney Cox, in November 1916, jocularly addressed Frost as "Oven Bird," the poet mildly rebuked him. For Cox had hit a nerve. Cox was probably the first to see that the Oven Bird was a symbol of the poet himself, who "knows in singing not to sing," and frames the significant question of "what to make of a diminished thing"—post-lapsarian life. But Frost was not recep-tive; he pooh-poohed Cox's interpretation.

That fall Cox had enrolled as a doctoral candidate in English at Columbia University. He studied under two of Columbia's best-known teachers: the kind, scholarly, imaginative chairman of the

English department, Ashley Thorndike; and the wide-ranging, witty, creative John Erskine, author of *The Private Life of Helen of Troy*. Reading Elizabethan literature with both, Cox tried repeatedly to interest them in Frost's poetry, and was ecstatic when they finally agreed with him that it was good.

In August of 1917 Cox's first article on Frost, an essay-review entitled "The Sincerity of Robert Frost," was published in *The New Republic* (which paid him thirty dollars for it). Cox stressed Frost's "fundamental and embracing quality, sincerity—sincerity in perception, sincerity in thought, sincerity in feeling and sincerity in expression." With insight, Cox noted Frost's realization of his sound-of-sense theory: "Read aloud it ["Birches"] shows, sentence by sentence, a startling reproduction of the sounds of speech." Moreover, Cox added, "Not only the language but the souls of Yankee men and women appear as they are upon Mr. Frost's pages." Cox effused, "Mr. Frost is always tender; he always cares."[2] Unknowingly, Cox helped shape the mask Frost wore in public: the kindly, whimsical, witty, and sincere country philosopher-poet.

A Russian-born economics-turned-English graduate student, Eugene Kaydon, became Cox's good friend. Together, with Frank Hill and a Mr. Schluter, they studied, read literature aloud, argued, and wrote. Talking with Thorndike about a possible dissertation topic—Cox wanted to write one with cosmic dimensions on freedom—Cox felt he would finally achieve the coveted Ph.D. But the entrance of the United States into the Great War intervened. At first the war seemed wrong to Cox, but three things caused him to enlist: President Wilson's "*great* mind"; Professor Thorndike's serious, sad comments supporting the war; and "a talk with Mr. Frost," who then, as later, felt war brought out the best of man's qualities—courage.

Earlier, at a friend's wedding, Cox had met an intelligent, mercurial, and witty young woman, Alice Macy Ray. A New Englander, related to the Macys of Nantucket—where she had grown up—Alice Ray had been graduated from Simmons College and worked as a secretary for the Texas Company in Boston. Extremely creative, she studied sculpting and enjoyed acting. Years later

she was to write that Cox came to Boston, convinced her she was
in love with him, and married her. But at the actual time of courtship she wrote that she was impressed with Cox's learning and
deferential toward his scholarship. As their romance progressed,
she visited Cox in Morningside Heights, where they found a private place to talk and kiss in the dimly lit side chapels of the Ca-
thedral of Saint John the Divine.

Cox left his graduate studies—temporarily, he thought—in the
spring of 1917 to enlist. Sent to an Officers Training Camp in
Plattsburgh, New York, he wrote Alice of maneuvers, tests of skill,
and his self-doubt and fear of failure. But he successfully completed his training and was commissioned a second lieutenant in
the summer of 1917.

Before going overseas, Cox, almost twenty-eight, married Alice
Ray, twenty-five, on August 15, 1917, in Waverley, Massachusetts.
The couple took a brief wedding trip in New England, stopping at
Franconia to see Frost. Unable to be at the wedding because of
Elinor's illness, the poet, upon meeting Alice, liked her. But he re-
minded Cox that the young man owed him "something . . . not
much, but a little. Not enough to make your wife jealous of me."
Earlier, Cox had spoken prophetically when he told Alice, "Proba-
bly you'll never make such a hero of him as I have, but I'm pretty
sure you'll get to like him."

Ordered to England in 1918, Cox served at various aerodromes
with the American Expeditionary Forces. After the Armistice,
he returned to New Hampton, New Hampshire, where his parents lived, and began to search for a teaching position. He would
have to relinquish his pursuit of the doctorate—temporarily he
thought—in order to earn a living. Columbia thought highly of its
doctoral student, and he taught there for a semester. The summer
of 1919 he taught at Hunter College, in New York City. In the fall
of 1919, Cox was appointed chairman of the English department
at Academy High School in Erie, Pennsylvania. But, his heart set
on becoming a college English professor, he began to look west for
a job, where salaries were higher and faculty appointments more
readily available than in the East.

In the fall of 1920, Cox proudly took up a new position, assistant professor of English at the State University of Montana at Missoula. He and Alice had started their family. Their first child, Arthur, had been born in May 1920; their second, Barbara, in 1921. Cox continued his writing, publishing articles in *Sewanee Review*, *Modern Language Notes*, and *Candid Opinion*. His first book, an anthology for college students, co-edited with a colleague, Edmund Freeman, was published in 1926, under the title *Prose Preferences* (New York: Harper).

Cox threw himself into his teaching, sharpening his techniques of arguing and debating—and encouraging his students to think, to analyze, to judge. He wanted to make his students aware of literature's power to enlarge their minds, to influence their decisions. One of those Missoula students was A. B. Guthrie, who years later became famous for his novels *The Big Sky* (1947) and *The Way West* (1949). At first, Guthrie has said, he "did not like Cox," because "he challenged my unexamined values." The student had to grow older before he realized how the teacher had enriched his life.[3]

Once settled at Missoula, Cox wanted to bring Frost to Montana on a barding, and several letters discuss the details of a possible appearance there. Through H. G. Merriam, the chairman of Missoula's English department, Cox hoped to make a lucrative arrangement for the poet, but, despite repeated attempts, the necessary funds could not be budgeted.

In the summer of 1923 the Coxes began hunting for a larger home; Cox wanted a bigger place both to shelter his expanding family and to entertain the Frosts if they came to Montana. Alice Cox was pregnant again, and on September 20, 1923, Robert Cox, probably named for Frost, was born. The new baby, soon nicknamed Robbie, was healthy and grew rapidly. Then in November 1925 all three children were sick with chicken pox, the baby suffering the most, and by Thanksgiving Robbie was dead. Cox wrote that the "longing for Robbie . . . is like a terrible hopeless hunger." He told Frost of their loss, and the poet, probably thinking of the death of his son Elliott, responded immediately. Frost's letter of December 5, 1925, shows how deeply he was stirred, how much he wanted to comfort his friend, and how bit-

terly experienced he was in trying to come to terms with an insolv-
able mystery: the death of a small child.

The same year Robbie had been born, 1923, Cox had the additional happy news of an "utterly unexpected" invitation to teach
creative writing the following July at the Bread Loaf School of English, near Ripton, Vermont, the summer graduate school of Middlebury College for English teachers and students interested in
writing and dramatic production. The offer had come through the
influence of Frost, who had told the director, Wilfred Davison,
that Cox was the man he would like to see carry on the work
there.

The entire Cox family spent the summer of 1924 at Bread Loaf,
living in a cottage from whose broad piazza at sunset they could
see the peaks of the Adirondacks. Happy with the work of his students, Cox also enjoyed his hours of leisure. He played tennis, pic-
nicked on one of Lake Champlain's little islands, tramped in the
woods with Alice, who acted in the school's plays and returned to
her sculpting. Popular with the students—though perhaps not so
popular with some of the faculty and the young director, Davison,
who seemed jealous of Cox's success—Cox had, on the whole, a
pleasant summer. The highlight was a visit from the Frosts, who
came over to Bread Loaf from their farm in South Shaftsbury, Vermont, where they were now living.

Cox showed Frost a book he was working on: a collection of his
own essays. Frost liked the writing, but urged Cox to be less overt,
less preachy—to look into himself more. And he asked Cox to
leave out the article on Frost. The poet was also interested in another visitor at Bread Loaf, Henry Seidel Canby, who had been appointed editor of a new magazine, scheduled to be on the news-
stands in August, *The Saturday Review of Literature*; Frost told
Cox that if he had anything important to say, he should try to
write for that magazine. The climax of Frost's visit was a hike the
three men took along the Green Mountain Trail to Silent Cliff,
where they had a fine view of the surroundings and looked down
on a luxuriant pine forest.

If Frost could be a demanding master to Cox—and a somewhat
exploitative one, using Cox as an intermediary for his lecture en-

gagements—he was also generous. He read the draft of Cox's manuscript, offered encouragement as well as sharp criticism, and kept an eye out for opportunities for the younger man in the Eastern academic world. Canby, too, tried to help Cox: the editor sounded out the president of Vassar College, Henry Noble Mac-Cracken, on a position there for Cox, who wanted to return East, because Alice did. But the possibility of an appointment at Vassar came to nothing; Frost believed that Wilfred Davison, prickly in his relations with Cox, had disparaged Cox to MacCracken. But despite the friction, Cox was asked to teach again the next year at Bread Loaf. That summer he also went over to Hanover, New Hampshire, to visit Dartmouth and to meet the college's administration.

Returning to Missoula in the fall of 1925, Cox was promoted to associate professor, was appointed acting chairman of the English department, and was named faculty moderator of the university's literary magazine, *The Frontier.*

As adviser, Cox allowed the magazine's student editor, John Frohlicher, to publish a sketch, called "Tone," in which recurred the phrase "son of a bitch." The magazine also ran a prose piece that was a description of a sleazy rooming house and its female inhabitant. Probably neither piece would have attracted much attention had not the university—to publicize the campus in its recruitment of students—distributed copies of *The Frontier* to high schools throughout Montana. Then, suddenly, across the state, newspaper headlines blazed with statements like "Use of Vile Language in University Publication Proves to Be Sensational."[4] Principals wrote scathing letters of protest to the college. An editorial in the influential *Anaconda Standard* (in which the powerful copper-mining corporation may have had an interest) demanded that Cox be disciplined, accusing him of filling "the minds of his charges with nauseating, slimy, suggestive filth."[5] Cox was threatened anonymously with a tar-and-feathering and with a cross burning on his front lawn. Alice Cox was frightened; but the teacher calmly took his stand.

Missoula's president, C. H. Clapp, in a public letter to the principal of the Sweet Grass County High School, defended Cox: "He is sympathetic, unselfish to a fault, and of the highest moral character. He would rather cut off his right hand than do anything he considered immoral or vile. . . . I wish I could convey to Mr. Cox's critics some idea of his essential honesty and clean-mindedness and at the same time his abhorrence of censorship."[6]

The chancellor of the state university, M. A. Brannon, after conferring with Cox and President Clapp, presented the entire controversy to the state board of education, in Helena. There the governor urged that Cox be reprimanded. The board reviewed the case and voted, "with plenty of rambling ferocity and uprighteousness," to delegate to Brannon and Clapp responsibility for disciplinary action.[7] The two officials decided that Cox should make a public apology and guarantee that the incident would not be repeated. Offering his apology, Cox was autobiographical: "I hate anything that is vulgar . . . I was reared under very careful surroundings. My father was a member of the ministry, and I grew up with a particularly guarded tongue. I believe that I could have been called a prude, and I know that at the present time I have been called a Puritan." Even though the sketch "Tone" was a good piece of writing, Cox said he had been "indiscreet" to allow its publication. In closing he said he was sorry to "cause offense to some good people."[8]

A. B. Guthrie, commenting on the incident fifty-two years later, claimed: "My information is that the fine-haired sons of bitches with the Anaconda Company and their sons-of-bitching followers didn't like to see 'son of a bitch' in print."[9] Like one of his favorite writers, D. H. Lawrence, Cox, a pure-minded man, had been branded a purveyor of filth.

The incident was unpleasant, discomfiting, but, as Frost implies, Cox in some way enjoyed the "fracas." Just as the furor was dying down, the student newspaper, the *Montana Kaimin*, on April 30, 1926, headlined Cox again: he was resigning from Missoula to become assistant professor of English at Dartmouth. Probably prompted by Cox, the paper carefully pointed out that the Missoula associate professor was not taking a demotion, as Dartmouth did not have that academic rank. Cox would be an assistant professor on a three-year contract—at the end of which he was assured a full professorship. His teaching would include considerable work in composition, an area in which Dartmouth students needed improvement.[10]

It was not the *Frontier* incident that caused Cox to leave Montana. He had begun applying to Dartmouth two years earlier, in 1924, when he sent an initially unsuccessful inquiry to President Ernest Martin Hopkins. Since then Frost, once again, had helped Cox, by heartily recommending him to Hopkins. After Cox was hired, the poet, in avuncular fashion, advised him on how to behave at one of his "favorite colleges"—the school from which Frost as a confused freshman had run away in 1892.

Meanwhile, Frost throughout the twenties was consolidating his position as America's greatest and best-loved poet. In spite of the influence of T. S. Eliot's tradition-shattering *The Waste Land*, Frost continued to go his own rhyming way. He had never liked Eliot, privately expressing his distaste for the man who had revolutionized poetry and who was championed by the avant-garde.

In October 1920 Frost had sold his farm in Franconia to a trusting Raymond Holden, who had moved to Franconia only to be near Frost. Wanting to be closer to New York, Frost moved south to South Shaftsbury, Vermont. There his son Carol, eighteen years old (who was later to die by his own hand), proved himself a farmer, though not a poet, which he wanted to be, like his father. In the fall of 1921 Frost became one of the country's first poets in residence, at the University of Michigan at Ann Arbor. His *Selected Poems* was published in March 1923, and in November of that banner year an entirely new volume, *New Hampshire*. The Frost family spent 1924 at Amherst and 1925 at Michigan. At fifty-two, Elinor Frost, fatigued by the constant traveling, suffered another miscarriage before the Frosts moved once again, this time back to Amherst, where they were to stay until 1938.

In 1924 Frost reaped literature's rewards: Middlebury and Yale conferred on him honorary Doctor of Letters degrees, and he won his first Pulitzer Prize, for *New Hampshire* (which includes "Stopping by Woods on a Snowy Evening," possibly his greatest lyric). In 1925 he was celebrated in New York at a "Fiftieth Birthday Dinner" (he was actually fifty-one), at which he read his comic

Irish play, *The Cow's in the Corn*, to guests from the literary establishment, including Sara Teasdale, Elinor Wylie, Willa Cather, Wilbur Cross, Carl and Mark Van Doren, and Louis Untermeyer.

Frost was now a national figure enjoying the recognition he so longed for, and Sidney Cox was now moving into his most productive years as a teacher.

### NOTES

1. Robert Frost to Lincoln MacVeagh, May 1922, *Selected Letters of Robert Frost*, ed. Lawrance Thompson (New York: Holt, Rinehart and Winston, 1964), p. 277.
2. 25 August 1917, pp. 109–11.
3. A. B. Guthrie to William R. Evans, 28 June 1978.
4. Helena *Independent*, 5 April 1926, p. 1.
5. 4 April 1926, p. 4.
6. Helena *Independent*, 5 April 1926, p. 2.
7. Sidney Cox to his mother, Elizabeth Cox, 6 April 1926.
8. *Montana Kaimin*, 6 April 1926, pp. 1–3.
9. Guthrie to Evans, 10 August 1978.
10. p. 1.

ALS, 4 pp.

# 41.

Dear Oven Bird,              16 November 1916   New York City
    I am happier tonight than I have been for many days.

After a rather dull session of the Victorian Seminar with Professor Thorndike, I went for a walk with a Russian fellow-student who, I think, is going to be a friend of mine. Before starting I went into the University Book Store to see if my "Mountain Interval" had come. It had. And we read a few poems as we walked up Riverside Drive until Kaydon was diverted to Shakespeare's sonnet, "Let me not to [the] marriage of true minds admit impediments."

We had dinner and then came to my room to read a few poems. He did not want to stop; so we kept on and read them all. The way I know he appreciates and likes you is by the way he reads.

In fact the first thing that made me like him more than others was the way he read "The Road Not Taken" from an old Atlantic of mine. Or rather, it was "The Sound of the Trees," more especially.

He read that again to-night because he likes it so much. We read several of them once each and then again. He disliked the way I read "A Patch of Old Snow," and he read it well. It seemed to him much like Browning's "Memorabilia." So we read that; and I saw why. We didn't try to think he had discovered a "source" or an "influence," by any means.

The first time he read "An Encounter" in the magazine he did not understand it. I told him what I thought I had seen in it when I pondered over it afterwards. And tonight he read it well. And liked it much.

I defy my admired professor—for I do still admire him—not to find a "convincing" new contribution of yours this time. For instance I think he'll find a tremendous thought that's not too subtle for him in "Hyla Brook."

Mr. Kaydon is scholarly. He only switched from Economics to English after two years of graduate study and three years of teaching because he thought universities were making that study too much a matter of preparation for business. But he is imaginative and sensitive, too. And Professor Thorndike has praised some translations of his of Russian poetry.

Frequently after a poem he said "A splendid piece of observation," or something else really appreciative. But that wasn't all. He thought you succeeded where Masefield fails, in such a poem as "The Hill Wife." He thinks Masefield doesn't suggest anything—doesn't leave enough for the imagination. After we had read "Brown's Descent," he said he thought you were doing, for one thing, what Cowper was trying to do at the close of the eighteenth century. Not what Wordsworth did because Wordsworth didn't see the things you see.

Kaydon recommended that I write about "Mountain Interval" and send it to the North American Review or one of the more dignified periodicals. But I'm not competent for anything of the kind.

I was disappointed at the repetition of a line and the omission of the one that should have stood where it stands in "Snow" (p. 88 1.6). And I missed "The Axe Helve." Perhaps you've decided to have the *play* acted before it's published.

The added stanza in "Bond and Free"—which you gave me in manuscript at Plymouth—is good. [I hope to find it true, and join the "some" who say it.] Of the poems I have not heard or seen before I was stirred most by "The Oven Bird." But I can't tell how much of that thrill was pride at my discovery. The connection (with Shakespeare) established in our minds by the title "Out, Out——" is, for me, at least, sustained by the poem. *Great*, too, I dare to say, are "The Hill Wife," "The Bonfire," "The Sound of the Trees" and "Snow." But I meant not to say anything of the sort. When are you coming this way? Prof. Erskine helped us to know what Theocritus was like, this A.M., by allusion to you.

Yours,

Sidney Cox

Good wishes to you all!

p.s. As I read this over I see that it gives no expression to the exultation and delight which filled me when we had finished reading.

I doubt if you intended any reference to your poetic aims when you described the oven bird. Perhaps no such significance suggested itself to you even after it was written. Your voice as a poet is not loud, certainly. But I trust you won't be offended at my flaunting what seemed to me a discovery before you are able fairly to see who I am.

I'd tear this letter and wait and write another if I was sure its defects are not mine. I could read it aloud and comment on it so as to spoil it utterly. But you won't. Perhaps you can read what I felt and thought but failed to write.

S. H. C.

ALS, 4 pp.

## 42.

[Franconia]

Dear Cox                                    [c. 7] December 1916

It gives me real pleasure to hear of your pleasure and your friend's pleasure in the book. Why mar it by raising the specter of your poor past professor, to argue with? It can do me no good to be reminded of him. It's uncomfortable to be at a feast with a fellow who suddenly pushes back his chair and gets up to gesticulate with his napkin at somebody nobody else can see.

I know you do it from conscientiousness—not to hide from me anything that may be bothering you. You needn't be so scrupulous with me. I shall forgive you if you keep some unimportant doubts from me.

You do awfully well with the book. I could ask no more generous reviewer than you would be. But you mustn't be misled by anything that may have been laid down to you in school into exaggerating the importance of a little sententious tag to a not over important poem. The large things in the book—well I won't name them—you know better than to think the Oven Bird is of them. Probably the best thing in the book is The Old Man's Winter Night. That seems to be the consensus of opinion among the professors I get letters from—if we are going to leave it to professors.

I like different people to like different things. I shouldn't mind your exalting the Oven Bird so much if your reasons were better. Let's not strain, let's not worry. Have a good time most of the time.

I shall be off professoring a little on my own pretty soon and if I have a chance I shall try to find you in New York. The trouble with New York is it thinks people ought to be glad to read to it for nothing. Thats why I keep away from it.

Always yours

Robert Frost

ALS, 2 pp.

## 43.

Dear Sidney Cox:                          3 March 1917   Amherst

Dont you want to come out here and talk over some weekend. I've meant to look you up in New York but I been on nothing but the fly and the jump every time I've been through New York this winter. I'd write you a letter but that I've soured on letter writing for good and all.

Keep a stiff upper lip and maybe the Germans won't hurt you.

Where shall we lock Block?—I mean if we start interning. Things begin to look pretty internal for the stray Hun.

Laugh and the world laughs with you.

I'm now a third-rate authority on The Four PP, Gammer Gurton and such.*

Allers yourn

Robert Frost

* *The Four P's*: an interlude by John Heywood. It is a debate among a Palmer, a Pardoner, and a 'Pothecary, with a Pedlar as judge, to see who can tell the biggest lie. First performed c. 1520. *Gammer Gurton's Needle*: a domestic comedy, probably by William Stevenson, first performed c. 1566.

ALS, 3 pp.

## 44.

Dear Sidney:                          12 August 1917   Franconia

I am going to be very sorry not to be at your war-wedding and you are going to be sorry not to have me there. But I can only be with you in thought. I promise to be wholly that on the forenoon of August 16th. I cant be more. My own marriage keeps me from your marriage so to speak. That is to say things that follow in the train of marriage keep me—babies and the fear of babies. Since some time before you were with us we havent known just what we were in for. We don't know now. It seemed like a last putting forth. At times we have been afraid it was something more serious if no more solemn. At any rate I dont think I ought to be away from Elinor as she is.

But you must come to us and receive our blessing as soon as you can. It wont be safe to go without it too long. You are [to] stay a day or two with us—not to be entertained—you will take us as you find us and take pot luck with us—but to say our hearts out to each other on the eve of what is to come.

Always yours
Robert Frost

ALS, 2 pp.

# 45.

Dear Sidney:          [c. 17] September 1917    Franconia, N.H.
Here it is, then, in all its sympathy, understanding and devotion. Do you remember the misunderstanding we began in that night when we watched the normal school dance from among the empty chairs along the wall? I didn't suspect then that we were to live to owe each other so much. You do owe me something, too, I think. Not much, but a little. Not enough to make your wife jealous of me, because it is nothing in comparison with what you owe her for being what she is. It made us happy to see you so happy on your way with her. Keep her my friend as I shall remain

Always friend of both of you
Robert Frost.

ALS, 3 pp.

## 46.

Sidney Cox:                    27 December 1918   Amherst, Mass.
    Proud memory be canned!
    The way to do is to make a point of seeing me good and plain
once in so often so as not to depend for friendship on the letters I
dont write any more. What's the matter with your bringing Alice
up for a day and a night with us toward the end of next week? I'd
say sooner, but I've been very sick with influenza and must give
myself time to get back to my talk before I begin to meet people
again.
    We're only three or four hours from Boston and there are no
changes if you come on a morning train that starts from the *North*
(not South) Station. You would have to look up the exact time.
    Great to have a look at you and hear you on your plans and
prospects. I can hardly keep from advising you what *I* think you
ought to do next. I'll hold myself in though till I see you. (I want
you to be a critic—first-class *American*.)
    Well say you'll come and meanwhile our love to you both.
Thanks be that the war has spared you to me.

Always yours
Robert Frost


ALS, 8 pp.

## 47.

Dear Sidney:                    5 January 1920   Amherst
    The further from New York the better for a whole lot of rea-
sons. Out there there ought to be something new for you to get the
hang of for yourself. In New York there is next to nothing that
somebody else hasn't already got the hang of for you. New York's
as completely formulated as Abraham Lincoln. The last Englishman to arrive knows as much about it as the most pains-tak-
ing Greenwich Villager is ever likely to know. Our minds are so

crowded with what we have been told to look for there that they have no room for accidental discoveries. And thats the way with whole tracts of knowledge. We can only turn away from them to Montana.

And even at three cents a mile I dont suppose Montana is as far off as California we'll say. And where are you in California when you get there? Almost brought through on the other side again— nearer East culturally than you would be in Montana at any rate.

The worst of it is that the difference between East and West or between this country and Europe seems to want to be blotted out in colleges. Colleges will be colleges wherever found—colorless and cosmopolitan. But I shall trust you to take measures to keep from missing Montana people in your preoccupation with a college faculty probably largely transplanted from Eastern colleges and mostly wishing they were in London or Paris at this moment.

Why do we oppose the introduction into English of idioms not English such as "gives upon"? Does it seem so small minded of us? And yet we are asked to let in all their continental sex notions. I say lets try to get hold of what we have here however accidental and then hold on to it to it to the exclusion of everything foreign the importer has a pocket-interest in importing. There ought to be something springing from Montana soil that needs a friend to keep the trampling foreign off it.

We have a little mountain pony that came to us with the name Beauty which we couldnt stand: so without her finding it out we changed her name by imperceptible stages to Beaut to Butte and Montana Butte, or Butte, Montana. That will give us a fellow feeling with you as long as we keep the pony and you stay in Montana.

What New Year's resolution did you discover worth taking? I resolved not to let anybody put a book to any use it wasnt intended for by its author—if I could help it. Some will ask how they are going to kill three hours a week in an English course and not put an occasional book to an occasional use it wasnt intended for by its author. Embarrassedly twiddling thumbs if necessary. Or if that suggests too much a country courting, let them read aloud a good deal and teach others to read aloud. Shakespeare says good orators, when they are out, spit. There is something will suggest itself when other things fail.

You may have heard that at the time you wrote me about your proposed book I was hung as it were between two publishers and not in a position to do anything for you with either. Harcourt my friend had quarreled with my friend Henry Holt and started a new firm of publishers, Harcourt Brace and Howe. It looks now as if I would belong to Henry Holt because he refuses to surrender me to Alfred Harcourt on demand and representation. I'm like the lady who didn't care much either way as long as it was settled one way or the other. I'm not sure about the value of your anthology for schools. Everybody is doing it. I told a friend in Houghton and Mifflin without getting any particular encouragement. You'll have other ideas for books I can help you with. Let me know when you do. Only keep athinking. You've got things where they can't happen too fast for you now.

The unhappiness that attached to me in your dream wasnt so far wrong. I don't believe I am very happy about this college. And yet it is a better college than plenty of colleges. It tries hard to deny its nature. I mustnt ask it to dissolve into a mere school of experience to please me.

I promised to send you a poem or two. These can wait and take the place of a letter some day when I am less in the mood for a letter than I am today.

So at it now for genuineness. A minimum of class work and all kinds of work for mere exercise. Remember that some of us have got by without ever having written a thing for exercise. Dorothy Canfield was telling me the other day that she had. She's a Doc of Phil of Columbia too.* Make it real and you'll beat the Dutch.

Best wishes to you and Alice from us all.

Affectionately Robert Frost

* Dorothy Canfield Fisher (1879–1958): novelist, essayist, and short-story writer; Frost's neighbor in Vermont.

[Included with this letter are typescripts of six poems: "Fire and Ice," "The Onset," "Plowmen," "Silver Lizards," "A Star in a Stone-Boat," and "Two Look at Two." All are in *The Poetry of Robert Frost*, where "Silver Lizards" appears, with minor changes, as "A Hillside Thaw." Line five of "Fire and Ice" in the typescript reads, "But if I had to perish twice," instead of the final version's, "But if it had to perish twice." The first line of the typescript "Plowmen" reads, "I hear men say they plow the snow," rather than "A plow, they say, to plow the snow," in the final version.]

ALS, 4 pp.

## 48.

Dear Sidney:                              17 July 1920    Franconia

I trust you know I think of you away off out there at least a thousand times to every once I write you.

You tell me about yourself when you write and I'll tell you about myself now.

I've kicked myself out of Amherst and settled down to revising old poems when I am not making new ones. I published a set of four in the July Harpers which you may or may not have seen. I'm sure you liked them in either case because they were mine. I shall enclose with this a few more. Try them on the baby and if they do no harm it will prove that my work ought to have been included in a recent anthology of verse for children that I hear it was left out of. Never mind. The main thing is that you like your job in Montana or you would have written to me to complain of it. Teaching is all right and I dont mean to speak of it with condescension. I shall have another go at it before the last employe is fired. I believe in teaching but I dont believe in going to school. Every day I feel bound to save my consistency by advising my pupils to leave school. Then if they insist on coming to school it is not my fault: I can teach them with a clear conscience.

We seem on the point of leaving Franconia. The hawser is cast off in fact, though we lie still against the wharf. They say when you run away from a place it is yourself you are generally running away from and that goes with you and is the first thing you meet in the next place you turn up. In this case it is frosts we are running away from and Frosts can hardly help going with us since Frosts we are ourselves. If you ever see any talk of me in print you may notice that it is my frostiness that is more and more played up. I am cold, snow-dusted and all that. I can see that I am in a way or I would write to my best friends oftener. Don't say amen to that too fervently if you don't want to hurt my feelings and your own prospects.

My best to the whole family of you.

Always yours
Robert Frost

ALS, 3 pp.

## 49.

Dear Sidney:                1 March 1921    South Shaftsbury

Tell those young poets they did well: I liked their poems and especially the poem about the fish. You know how to take them to put them on their feet. Praise them in the absolute or not at all.

Did you see how your old friend Misgiving had turned up unaltered by time in The Yale Review for January? Mr Cross thinks it shows a marked improvement on what I was doing in 1915.*

Would you be interested in taking in hand an old rhetoric by William Vaughn Moody and bringing it up to date? Mrs Moody was asking. I doubt if you would. But don't hesitate to contradict me if you see money or advantage in the job.†

I dont write letters lest my pen become hateful to me. I take it out in wishing I could see you. What do you say to seeing if you could find me a few engagements at $125 a piece out there next year? I only speak since you suggested the idea. I get all I need for a living from eastern clubs and colleges. Don't have me on your conscience for one moment. It just crossed my mind I might be tempted to bring Elinor out to see you both and the baby.

Our best to you both—and the baby.

Affectionately
Robert Frost

* Wilbur Cross (1862–1948): taught English at Yale, 1894–1930; editor of *The Yale Review*, 1911–1940; governor of Connecticut, 1931–1939.

† Harriet Converse Moody (1857–1932): widow of poet William Vaughn Moody (1869–1910), opened her luxurious Chicago home to visiting poets. The book may be the extremely successful *A History of English Literature*, which Vaughn Moody wrote with Robert M. Lovett in 1902.

ALS, 1 p.

## 50.

                                            South Shaftsbury
Dear Sidney                         [c. 8 June 1921]
   I have a good-looking book I should send you if I knew you
were still there.

                                            Ever thine
                                            R.F.

You havent written for so long.

ALS, 4 pp.

## 51.

Dear Sidney:                 8 September 1921   Franconia
   And I want very much to talk with *you*. I dont see why the engagement with Michigan University should keep me tied up at
Ann Arbor all the long year. But I suppose I ought not to be gone
more than a week or ten days at a time and that not more than two
or three times. You *must* have me out there for one of these. Let
me tell you how I should like you to arrange it. Perhaps you could
crowd enough into a week so that I could come clear off with
$500 above expenses. You might have to run a day or two over the
week. My demand lately has been $100 for one "lecture" or sev-
enty-five apiece for two or more in the same place. All would depend on how far apart your places were and how much time had
to be wasted in travel. I'm vague about your distances. Whatever
else you plan for you must be sure to leave me a good day or two
outright to loaf around with you. That's more important than the
$500 and expenses. Suppose you only get me $300 and expenses. I
shan't weep. Better keep the rates up though. Don't you think so?
   Remember you promised I was going to see two babies instead
of just one.
   If I had time or Lesley I could make you a copy of Paul's Wife.
But Lesley is in South Shaftsbury and I'm hurrying to get back

there to get ready for Michigan. You'll have to wait till it appears in The Century in November. And then there's Maple!* The next Yale Review will have Maple. I havent written much this summer. Having to come off up here has broken me up.

I want to hear about your literary plans. Have they had any check that you should sign yourself stupidly. Or is it just that you are resolved to be stupid for fear of being tempted to be as smart as a column writer in this columnar age? I am with you there. Lets be as stupid as is necessary to be good.

Our best to you both.

Affectionately
R.F.

---

* Frost's poem about a girl named Maple, in *New Hampshire*.

ALS, 4 pp.

## 52.

My dear Sidney,—          15 September [1921] South Shaftsbury

After spending 3½ weeks with Robert in Franconia, I came home last Monday morning, and Robert at the same time started on a walking trip through northern New Hampshire & Vermont to Lake Willoughby. I will forward your letter to him there, and I hope he will pause there long enough to answer it, before starting back to Franconia by a different route. If not, he will be home here again Friday or Saturday of next week. I should think he might set a time for the western trip now as well as later.

I wish I could go out with Robert to Missoula and see you and Alice again, but travelling is so expensive now that perhaps I ought not to think of it. I am glad you feel settled and happy there, and like the work. It seems hardly possible that Alice is soon to have her second baby. How time does fly! I hope she will get up well and strong. I remember how hard it was for me to take care of two little ones.

We have had a very nice summer on our new farm which is very home-like and charming, though it hasn't the grandeur of Franconia scenery. We still have Butte, and she is considerably bigger than she was, and as fat as butter this summer. The children don't ride her much now, but they are so fond of her that they don't like to sell her.

The children and I send our love to you both, and wish you could look in on us here. Carroll* is just going to buy a new camera, and we will send you some snap shots taken around the farm.

Most sincerely yours,
Elinor Frost

* Carol Frost informally changed the spelling of his name to Carroll to distinguish it from what he said was the feminine spelling. In letters mentioning their son the Frosts used either spelling.

ALS, 4 pp.

## 53.

21 September 1921
Dear Sidney:                                    South Shaftsbury

I'm just back from a long walk too, but one through tamer wilderness than yours. I did the three notches, the Willoughby Lake, the Franconia and the Dixville. One of my toes went wrong but I came through all right on the other nine.

I dont believe I understand very well what's wanted of me out there. I should think I might undertake to give one lecture and one class room talk for $125, if that is your idea. One hundred of it would be my regular fee for a public lecture, twenty five for expenses. That would account for all the money and I would throw the class room talk in for good measure. Or are you asking me to think of it in some other way. You say nothing about expenses. Perhaps it would be better for simplicity to offer me up in one lecture and one class room talk for the $125 flat and never mind expenses.

I should like very much to go in for an all-round-the-place series of talks, recitals, songs, dances and sitting-up exercises for my money after the manner of Vachel [Lindsay]. But you don't want to take it all out of me in one winter. Save a little of me from these people if you can for a specimen.

If I seem a little greedier than I used to the English invader is to blame. I shall be asking the $125 less for the money as I keep saying than for the honor of getting at least half as much as you will pay second rate Englishmen.*

Not to wobble and look weak and silly suppose we put it that way with finality $125 flat for a lecture and a talk, $150 flat for two lectures, $175 flat for two lectures and a talk. I'm largely in your hands. Save me and my pride all you can but make me do my duty.

Aint we business-like? Oh and about the time. I should say any time after the first of January. January or February should be a good month.                                    Affectionately Robert Frost

* Possibly Siegfried Sassoon and Theodore Maynard, both of whom gave poetry readings in the United States about this time.

ALS, 4 pp.

## 54.

Dear Sidney:                         12 October 1921   Ann Arbor

That looks like such a little money for such a lot of wear and tear knocking round in the cars that I have half a mind to call it all off but perhaps two engagements right close together. You dont want to see your grandfather's grey head brought down in sorrow to the grave for fifty dollars a lecture. The distances out there are more than we figured on, either of us. I haven't any right to ask any of you to bear the expense of them and I can't afford to bear it myself. It is better for me to operate near home. Then I can ask for my expenses and have my hundred dollars a lecture clear. I think I havent had less than a hundred for anything for more than a year. No doubt asking that keeps me out of some barn-storming, but it is designed to. The price seems to be just prohibitive enough to be protective. It saves some of me for poetry.

But I want awfully to see you, and having gone so far I'm not going to draw out entirely. I offer to make the trip to Missoula for my expenses. I should give one lecture and meet a class or two. In addition I should like one more lecture close by for a flat $100. I

don't absolutely insist on the second engagement, but I should like
[it] as a sweetener.

If I had the long jump I had when a young cricket! My strength
is retiring from the surface. You will understand.

Always yours
Robert Frost


ALS, 4 pp.

## 55.

[Ann Arbor
Dear Sidney                                    c. 22 December 1921]

Isnt it terrible the way I dont write to you. You'll begin to think
I am mad at having got myself into the engagement with you at
Missoula. I'm not. It's too bad there isn't some easier way to see
you, but as long as there isn't, I'm going to make the best of it.
Don't fail to appreciate what I'm doing though. I'm lazy and I'm
past forty. By rights you ought to be made to come to me. You're
young and on a regular salary and the father of fewer children as
yet than I am. But we won't debate the matter. I'm coming as per
my telegram.

I'm particularly anxious to see you for a talk about what you
are up to in the arts. Your being held in check so long gives me
some hopes of you. You'll keep getting deeper and deeper all the
time unless you find an outlet in foolish complaint. People like
James Chapin run off in talk of their deserts.* Probably there's
nothing the matter with what you write. Never mind. If you cant
improve it you can always intensify its quality. No doubt as it is
it would do very well as it is. Wait patiently till it becomes
irresistable.

I've been a busy man since I came hither. I hardly know myself
for the same old lazybones you saw last in Franconia (wasn't
it?)—no it was in New York at James Chapins, the aforesaid.

It occurs to me Mrs Moody may not have meant a book on rhetoric though that was what she said. If it was a book on American
literature, would you be interested in bringing that up to date?
Probably not. It would be more fun to write the whole book fresh
if you were going to have anything to do with it.†

Our love to you all to the last least baby. Merry Christmas. Happy New Year.

Affectionately Robert Frost

* James Chapin (1887–1975): landscape and portrait painter; Frost's friend.
† See second footnote to Letter 49.

ALS, 2 pp.

## 56.

[Ann Arbor

Dear Sidney                                      c. 7 February 1922]

I wonder if I hadn't better pay for the Flinders Petrie. I haven't lost the books: they are safe in my library in Vermont; but of course I can't reach that far to lay my hands on them now.*

Tell Don Stevens I shall be speaking at Chicago University on February 23rd in the evening and shall hope to shake hands with him on your account and his own.

Glad to hear you are all well.

Best wishes. Always yours<br>Robert Frost

* Sir William Matthew Flinders Petrie (1853–1942): English Egyptologist and editor of a history of Egypt in six volumes, of which he wrote the first three.

ALS, 3 pp.

## 57.

[Ann Arbor

Dear Sidney:                                     c. 2 May 1922]

It seems as if I had been going it nearer the edge of my strength than I had ever been before. The trip to Montana proved to be altogether out of the question. I had the finger I wired you about and now I have been having a wry neck. That's better I suppose than a wry mouth. Well, June is coming I say with something of the same grimness I used to use in the old days at Derry and Plymouth.

Some day I'll sit down and write you a real letter again from the heart. The mood will come. As I feel now I could no more write at any length than I could go back on old friends.

It'll be more to both of us than many letters to meet and talk again. You must look in on us (you and Alice of course) for a night and a day or so in the summer. Then we'll talk fast and friendly.

Ever yours    Robert Frost


ALS, 3 pp.

## 58.

[South Shaftsbury
Dear Sidney                                    9 October 1922]

That was a nice letter you wrote—so full of invitations. It would be fine for Lesley to visit you sometime. I'll send her out. But about me. I've just had a resounding telegram from President Burton to summon me back to Ann Arbor.* And I go. Such are the terms of my engagement with him this year that I dont believe I am free to get in with anyone else for money. Any time I take away from Ann Arbor I am rather expected to use for producing belletr. Would it be looking too far ahead talk of arranging with you for October or November of 1923? My suggestion would be that you and Mr Merriam might give me five hundred dollars and my board and lodging and my wife's board and lodging and find me in the neighborhood not more than five lectures at enough apiece to pay our traveling expenses. Is that as clear as if a lawyer had drawn it up? It would be fun to sit round with your friends out there in the shadow of the Rockies and more fun in October than in November, but probably November would be better for a lot of reasons. We'd talk of a better world than this.

Did my vanishing seem abrupt? I was thrown into a whirl by seeing so many of my understudies at once Walter Hendricks of Amherst and Chicago, Wade Van Dore of Tolstoi and Gandhi and Raymond Holden of the New Republic and half a million dollars.† Once you were as young as these and as much impressed by me. Alice saved your soul.

Faithfully yours
Robert Frost

Thank Merriam for his interest

* Marion LeRoy Burton (1874–1925): president of University of Michigan, 1920–
1925. Sent Frost a telegram on October 6, 1922, offering him a 5000-dollar Fellowship in
Creative Arts.
† Walter Hendricks (1892–1979): visited Frost in Franconia while a student at Amherst;
later founded and was first president of Marlboro College, in Vermont. Wade Van Dore (b.
1899): poet and friend of Frost's, calls himself Frost's "Hired Man." Raymond Peckham
Holden (1894–1972): poet, author of sixteen books and a "Profile" of Frost in *The New
Yorker*, June 6, 1931.

ALS, 3 pp.

## 59.

[South Shaftsbury
Dear Sidney:                                     c. 30 April 1923]

I'm just returning to an interest in life after my fifth fluenza in
one winter. What's come over me? Some one suggests that it may
be I write too much poetry about snow and ice. I am pretty much
inclined to harp on those strings.

It's so long since I said what I would do with you next fall that I
shall have to ask you to refresh my memory of it. I don't see why I
shouldn't give a reading or two to the outside world. Had I said
anything to lead you to suppose that I wouldn't? But tell me exactly what the plan was, as to dates duration and money.

I've been fairly absent from Ann Arbor this year and not half the
sensation in the Michigan papers I was last year. I don't know
what I think of the berth now that I'm about to rub my eyes and
climb out of it. The sleeping in it was only so-so.

Your old friend spoke to the author's taste when he said what he
said about Stopping by Woods. The more I think of it the surer I
am of that there poem.

A woman stopped at our door here in South Shaftsbury last
week who went to school to you and me in Plymouth. I cant say
her name as it then was for the life of me. But remembered her
well. Her father was a house painter in Plymouth and a great fox
hunter on Sundays.

An article in the Bookman accuses me, Im told, of having few
intimate friends. All the better for the few. Dont you say so. As one
of the few you are in a position to judge. Over how much territory

would I have to spread myself to escape the charge of being a cold Yankee? *

Ever yours

Robert Frost

* The anonymous article, "The Literary Spotlight: Robert Frost," May 1923, also found Frost's humor "clumsy."

ALS, 2 pp.

## 60.

I'm at South Shaftsbury Vt

Dear Sidney:                          [18 June 1923]

I begin to think you are having trouble about finding all the money you wanted for me. Don't concern yourself too deeply. Remember what I always used to tell you about taking life as the leaves grow on the tree. I dont have to tell you that perhaps now that your wife Alice looks after you so understandingly and well.

If you can't have me out one way why not propose another cheaper if not quite as good. Of course Im perfectly willing to be farmed out in the town to read a time or two. Maybe two weeks would be all you could afford of me—and enough of me. Let's not be afraid of each other. The worst we can do is give each other offense.

The one thing I am unalterable about in the stipulations is that I shant be exposed to anything as deadly as the spotted-fever-tick.

Ever thine

RF.

Does this help you?

ALS, 6 pp.

## 61.

Dear Sidney                 31 December 1924   South Shaftsbury

I'm not going to take much ink to tell you what I have to tell you. Something went wrong between you and Davison after I left that looks to me as if it had spoiled your chance for the moment of coming East.* I am inclined to think it was your success with your classes and with *some* of your fellow teachers. Your hit with Canby, Farrar and Miss Holbrook excited a jealousy you took no pains to disarm by devoting some of the time every day to self-deprecation.† There alone is where you have to take your share of the blame: you didn't sing puisne for life insurance. You could have kept Davison self-satisfied as easy as $\pi_1$ or $3.141592$. You absolutely had him the last I knew. But you considered him too slight a person to waste the wisdom of the serpent on and the consequence is he seems rather to have enjoyed being in a position not to help you get anywhere. Why would you be so independent?

He tells me he expressed himself to the Vassar people as not particularly impressed, but they mustnt take his word for it: let them apply to Canby and Frost. But after such a beginning they just naturally didnt apply to Canby and Frost, at least not to Frost. They turned to Miss Branch and she put the finishing touch on you. It is too bad to have our fate hang by such threads, but such is fate or luck or whatever you call it. You are enough of a tactician to see that it would do no good for me to interpose in the very teeth of the Vassar ladies unwillingness to be advised by me. Least said, soonest forgotten. We dont want the check to amount to an incident. This chance lost, *our* cue is to get as ready as we can for the next.

I didnt ask Davison particulary what he and Miss Branch found the matter with you. I don't care what they found the matter with you. You dont—because you know as well as I what prompted their criticism. They couldnt name their real objection to you. So they murmured something about the sincerity and radicalism you valued yourself on: you werent half as radical as you thought you were and as for sincerity why make a catch word of it? You cant contend with such talk. You wouldn't want me to. You see you have pressed against them too hard; you have made them feel you too much. A good rule is, Go easy with your self-declarations and challenges, if you dont want common ordinariness to retaliate with a nasty little Pshaw or shucks! Youve got too big a thing ahead for any flourishes in the announcement.

I wish I could see you for a little talk. If Davison asks you back next year, I am half inclined to advise your coming: that is if you could come with colors flying. Of course I wouldnt have you do anything to humiliate yourself. Nor would I have you come if you thought the cards were stacked against you. You know best whether you think the minds are too small for you to have any chance with. Stay away from any certain defeat of course.

Don't you let this business bother you. Teach, write. I dont say where you are going to break into prominence first, and it doesnt matter where. But it will be in one or the other soon I'm sure. I wish it could be in the writing. Keep growing and eliminating there. Put all you've got into one more great think. You're bound to make it—indeed in my opinion you've already made it. But you wont mind giving them good measure. Pile it on till they acknowledge the avalanche.

This isnt a Christmassive or New Yearly missive, but after all you arent suffering where you are. There'd be no special mockery in my wishing you a Happy New Year. You can be happy a little longer where you are if you want to be. So be.

I'm your friend<br>R.F.

Wouldn't it count with your people out there if you came East a second time?

---

*Wilfred Edward Davison (1887–1929): Dean, Bread Loaf School of English, 1921–1929.

†Henry Seidel Canby (1878–1961): founding editor of *The Saturday Review of Literature*, author, editor of more than 100 books. John Chipman Farrar (b. 1896): editor of *The Bookman*, director of Bread Loaf Writers' Conference, 1926–1928.

ALS, 6 pp.

## 62.

Dear Sidney                    5 July 1925    South Shaftsbury

If you see any of the aftereffects of physical labor in this letter you may know that it is from hand mowing—my brow is still wet with what Longfellow called honest, and this being Sunday I am just after having broken the Sabbath quite traverse like a puisne tiller. Great to be home farming.

For you to say when you will come down and see us. When
Davison was signing up his faculty our voyage to Europe looked
far more probably than it does now though between you and me I
can't say it was ever more than probable enough for an excuse to
go to a ball game or stay away from a lecture. In other words we
have *subsequently* decided not to go to Europe enough so's you'd
notice it. Peace is more my style than Europe. Orestes like I pray
for it or like Dante in the not-too-well-known-and-in-danger-of-
being-forgotten poem on him by T. W. Parsons the American
dentist.*

But we'll save me and my needs to talk over when you come and
you and your needs too. I confess Davison threw a slight scare into
me and right after seeing him I might have been inclined to think
that what you needed was—well cautioning. I now know better. I
thought maybe you had been inordinately erring on the right
side—as in farming for instance. I hold that all farming is erring
on the right side. So don't be offended. But as I say I now doubt if
you erred at all. On every hand right, left, before and behindhand
reports are that you taught 'em dizzy. Sally Cleghorn was the
latest. I heard her say unasked that a fellow named Cox with his
breezy western energy was worth the price of admission to the
rodeo. I saw my chance to shock her by telling her you were from
Bates. It shocked her like a bit of or bite off conservative dogma.
Her eyes went round and round like the Hermit's boy who then
doth crazy go. She couldn't get used to that. Which just shows
you.†

While I am about it I may as well enquire if you ever found one
crumb of the erotic in the four Gospels. You know Plato virtually
says himself two thousand years before Freud that the love of the
invisible, philosophy is a sublimation of τὰ ἐρότικα, sex love the
mans love not only of fair girls but also of fair boys. The metaphor
with him is always drawn from sex. Is it ever a single moment with
Christ? Great play has been made with the ladies, not all of them
sinless, he had around him. Is it anywhere hinted that his business
with the most sinful of them was other than to bid them sin no
more? Is the erotic note ever struck?—with or without charm?
The great test would be the analogies of argument. They're never,
are they, sensual or even sensuous. It's reached a point with me

where I've got to have it out with myself whether I can think of Christ as but another manifestation of Dionysus, wine in his beard and the love leer in his eye. Is he even a little Pagan? Isn't he pretty nearly all Puritan for better or worse?

Always yours<br>Robert Frost

The real reason for our decision not to go to Europe was Elinor's health. I doubt sometimes if she ought to risk the sea-sickness. Maybe she'd stand it in a big swift boat.

---

* Thomas William Parsons (1819–1892): dentist, poet, translator of Dante's *Inferno* (1865); wrote the poem "On a Bust of Dante" (1841).
† Sarah Norcliffe Cleghorn (1876–1959): pacifist, socialist, antivivisectionist, author.

ALS, 2 pp.

## 63.

[Ann Arbor<br>c. 5 December 1925]

Dear Sidney:

I just think it is too terrible. There are absolutely no consoling thoughts about it—not of this world anyway. It is the worst form of balked desire. Let it die down if you want to. Talk will help it die down of course. Some people encourage talk for that reason. But dont let it die down if you dont want to. We have a right to keep any memory we please even to soul sickness. Repression is not forbidden in the Bible. I should use repression if it did me any good—I mean gave me any satisfaction. To Hell with the new ways of being good and the new reasons for being good. They are simply unresolved equations that look what they aren't.

Im sorry sorry.

Affectionately yours<br>Robert Frost

ALS, 4 pp.

## 64.

Pittsfield

Dear Sidney:                               [c. 1 January 1926]

You are probably well out of it at Bread Loaf I'm glad Davison let it go at parting as friends. You and he might have confessed to antipathy before all was said and done. But you havent (have you?), and I'm relieved. I guess I'm not very good about judging who should be joined together. I'm sure I never would have submitted you to him for criticism if I had given it a moments thought. I'm too proud of your kind of teaching.

You're a better teacher than I ever was or will be (now). But I'd like to put it to you while you are still young and developing your procedure if you dont think a lot of things could be found to do in class besides debate and disagree. Clash is all very well for coming lawyers politicians and theologians. But I should think there must be a whole realm or plane above that—all sight and insight, perception, intuition, rapture. Narrative is a fearfully safe place to spend your time. Having ideas that are neither pro nor con is the happy thing. Get up there high enough and the differences that make controversy become only the two legs of a body the weight of which is on one in one period on the other in the next. Democracy monarchy; puritanism paganism; form content; conservatism radicalism; systole diastole; rustic urbane; literary colloquial; work play. I should think too much of myself to let any teacher fool me into taking sides on any one of those oppositions. May be I'm wrong. But I was always wrong then. Its not just old age with me. Im not like Maeldune weary of strife from having seen too much of it. (See Tenn)* I have wanted to find ways to transcend the strife-method. I have found some. Mind you I'd fight a healthy amount. This is no pacifism. It is not so much anti-conflict as it is something beyond conflict—such as poetry and religion that is not just theological dialectic. I'll bet I could tell of spiritual realizations that for the moment at least would overawe the contentious. That's the sort of thing I mean. Every poem is one. I know I have to guard against insisting on this too much. Blades must be tempered under the hammer. We are a political nation run on a two-party system: which means that we must conflict whether we disagree or not. School must be some sort of preparation for the life before us. Some of our courses must be in *row*ing. Dont let me oversay my position.

They say time itself is circular and the universe a self winding clock. Well well just when it reaches the back country that the universe is a mechanism and what reason have we to suppose we are anything but mechanisms ourselves the latest science says it is all off about the universe it isnt a mechanism at all what ever we fools may be. It will take fifty years for that to penetrate to the Clarence Darrowians and Daytonians. The styles start in Paris and go in waves, ten years from crest to crest, to the ends of the earth. Let us put in some of our time merely sawing wood like William II.

Be good

Ever yours

Robert Frost

No I mustnt think of teaching this year. Perhaps another year if you stay on in Montana that long.

* In Tennyson's "The Voyage of Maeldune," the Irish hero Maeldune, after a long search for his father's murderer, returns home, where he finds the murderer but is too weary to fight him.

ALS, 8 pp.

## 65.

[Ann Arbor
c. April 1926]

Sidney Sidney,

I'd laugh at you if you said the word. But at least you want the predicament you are in taken seriously. I suppose I can laugh at what you say about my warning of last summer. I've forgotten the warning. Would it if observed have kept you out of this mess with editors, chancellors and viziers? Then you ought to have observed it to the letter.

You'd call this shining in a way I suppose. And I can tell you how you can shine more if you think it would help you any to become a national figure. By calling in Mencken and Mark Van

Doren in the case. You could do it through me or on your own. I'd
stir them up. Only I should want to be sure you were prepared to
get out of teaching entirely and go onto the stage or into independent journalism. You'd have to make a place for yourself in those
even. There wouldn't necessarily be one waiting for you in either
of them.

This may decide you in favor of getting out of teaching into
something where you wouldn't be forever having to mind your
step. If its got so you find things daily that teaching keeps you
from saying and doing it is a slavery: you ought to leave it. You
can see the relief Stark Young and Stuart Sherman feel in having
escaped from professorship.* Some people belong in New York
and it's no use their hiding it from themselves.

The boy (G.D. Eaton) who was personifying frankness to the
Michigan campus when I was here two years ago went your Frontier stuff several better. He stirred up such a stink and managed his
public rumpus so skillfully that Mencken took his part and helped
him on graduation to a columniatist job on The N.Y. Telegraph
where I saw him holding forth a week or so ago on Jesus Christ's
Old Man. I dont know how much he has had to play up to
Mencken. But something has gone against his conscience in their
relation I take it; because he has lately turned on Mencken and
bitten the breast at which he fed. Perhaps he wanted a change of
diet from milk to blood. He has become almost the strongest ex-
presser in N.Y. His owners however instead of showing pride in
him have just decided to economise by discontinuing his department. He has performed very heroically. He is now writing heroically right and left for people to say they cant get along without
his column. I've seen his circular letters in the pockets of some of
the boys here. In low politics this would be called working up a
false clientele. Its a hard world and doesnt get any easier.

I tell you all this to cheer you up the way my emergency nurse
from Camp Devens cheered me when I had pneumonic flu with
tales of the deaths she had been in at there. She took my hands and
showed me how I could tell myself when I was going to die by the
blackness that would come to my finger nails.

I'm not blaming you for not wanting to have to get along with
the kind of man who wrote the Anaconda editorial. But you'll

have to get along with somebody of course you know even at
Hanover. There may be some ideal office where the employees fall
forward in orgasmic exhaustion from saying simply everything
only to rise, resume, and fall forward again all day long, but I
wouldnt know where to find it. There are bounds set in all company. I'm sorry—almost. I make it seem sad anyway by putting it
so baldly.

Gee I wish you could get to Dartmouth and settle down. You're
just as capable of being original in what you are bothered by as in
other things. Everybody today goes in for being bothered because
he cant say simply everything to ladies and in print. I choose to be
bothered because if I am reminded of a book in conversation everyone thinks it must be a favorite with me or one I was just reading last night. No one makes any allowance for the power of liken-
ing to call up a remoteness. What will yours be? And let's change
our favorite thing to be bothered by in the people and country
every few months. But let's stick to our wives and children. Remember what Swedenborg used to say about the "sin of varieties."
And by the way I see The Dial is going to mix us religion (Catholic) with its sensuality—an old familiar blend.

Is there anything new? I mean in your situation now. Louis [Un-
termeyer] didnt put you up to sanctioning the number did he?[†]

Nobody knows it here but the President. I'm not coming back
next year. Going to have another aberration back to the land.

You should have heard me standing off a club of scientists the
other night on the subject of evolution. I'm not a good debater but
they are so sure of themselves in evolution that they havent taken
the trouble to think out their position. All I had to do was ask
them questions for information. The last one led up to was Did
they think it was ever going to be any easier to be good. I wouldnt
call it an evolution unless there was hope of screwing virtue to the
sticking point so it would cost less effort and vigilance than now to
maintain. Amelioration was as much as they could make me see.
The funny thing was their surprise at my unscientificalness. They
made more awful breaks. Sometime I'll tell you about them. I believe I'll never forget them. They just jumped off the edge. Me, I
didnt have to expose myself, I was just out for information. Tell
me, I'd say.

We've had a long seige of sickness. Marj has been in bed sixteen weeks with several things and three times at the hospital—one for an operation. Elinor is much worn.

But our best to you all.                    Ever yours Robert Frost

I'll throw another word into Lambuth.[‡]

---

[*]Stark Young (1881–1963): left Amherst in 1921 to become a full-time poet, novelist, drama critic, and translator. Stuart Sherman (1881–1927): left the University of Illinois in 1924 to become editor of the *New York Herald-Tribune*'s "Books" section.

[†]Louis Untermeyer (1885–1977): anthologist, poet, close friend of Frost. See *The Letters of Robert Frost to Louis Untermeyer* (New York: Holt, Rinehart and Winston, 1963).

[‡]David Lambuth (1879–1948): colorful English professor at Dartmouth, 1913–1948; chairman of the department, 1921–1925. On Frost's visits to Hanover, the poet frequently stayed with the Lambuths.

ALS, 4 pp.

## 66.

Dear Sidney                    17 May 1926    Ann Arbor

I'm totally glad. Not the least of its beauties is that it comes so exactly in the nick of time to leave your enemies wondering where you disappeared to. It couldnt be more fun.

And I couldnt wish you a better place to bring up in than Dartmouth if I tried. Dartmouth is one of my favorite colleges, though unfortunately I cant say I have its yell at my tongues end for this great occasion. And thats a large hearted lot you are going to find around you—all men and not one of them an old woman—not one of them cursed with fastidiosity.

You'll dive in and do us all credit with your teaching. You are one of the two or three best teachers going up. Lawrence Conrad here is another and Hughes Mearns author of Creative Youth seems to be another.[*]

Be good to Lambuth and Robinson them and their wives and to Brooks Henderson, him and his epic, and to young Morse (whose uncle was an old friend of mine) and especially to Donald Bartlett when he gets back from Europe next year or year after next. Like prim Harold Goddard Rugg in the library too for my sake. And old Lord who taught me Greek in 1892 and remains one of my pleasantest memories! The dean was a classmate of mine so be careful how you make him jealous. The head librarian Goodrich is one of the good minds. I wish you were going to see something of my friend Dallas but he has gone to be bishop of the diocese at Concord, N.H. There's a story about him I must tell you some day. I mustnt tax you with too many people to swallow whole for no reason but my command.[†]

I like to have you like what I wrote about Amy Lowell. I wonder if Louis [Untermeyer] is right about it being better taken in discon- nection from her. He may be. I leave it to you to decide. The two main ideas in it came to me quite apart from her. Still I thought maybe they applied. I never was a great reader of her work.

My best to you both.

Always yours in all   Robert Frost (vague about
puritanism)

---

*Lawrence Conrad (b. 1898): of the University of Michigan, author of *Teaching Cre- ative Writing* (1937); Hughes Mearns (1875–1965): of New York University, author of *Creative Youth: How a School Environment Set Free the Creative Spirit* (1925).

†The Dartmouth people Frost refers to are: David Lambuth (see footnote to Letter 65); Kenneth L. Robinson (b. 1892), professor of English; Brooks Henderson (1887–1939), as- sistant professor of English; Stearns Morse (1893–1976), instructor of English; Donald Bartlett (b. 1902), who became instructor of biography in 1927; Harold Goddard Rugg (1883–1957), assistant librarian and instructor of modern art; George Dana Lord (1863– 1945), professor of classical archaeology and associate in Greek; Craven Laycock (1866– 1940), dean of the college; Nathaniel L. Goodrich (1880–1957), librarian of the college; John Dallas (1880–1961), Protestant Episcopal bishop of New Hampshire.

## PART FIVE

# The Further Ranges of Friendship
## 1926–1951

*Thrusting in where I did not want you.*
ROBERT FROST *to* SIDNEY COX
*c. 19 April 1932*

B ETWEEN 1926 and 1952 Frost's popular reputation flourished; but those years were also marred by personal grief. Six volumes of poetry appeared: *West-Running Brook* (1928), *A Further Range* (1936), *A Witness Tree* (1942), *Steeple Bush* (1947), and the two blank-verse plays, *A Masque of Reason* (1945) and *A Masque of Mercy* (1947). These new books, as well as the various collections of his previously published poetry—the *Complete Poems* was printed in 1949—evoked diverse critical comment. In one camp were reviewers like Mark Van Doren, who said of Frost: "He is really read; he is read widely; and he is loved." In the other camp were influential critics, such as Newton Arvin, Horace Gregory, Rolfe Humphries, and R. P. Blackmur, who attacked *A Further Range* for its political conservatism; later, Malcolm Cowley and Yvor Winters laid siege to Frost's entire oeuvre. Frost knew, however, he could count on broad public support, as well as favorable criticism from such friends as Louis Untermeyer, Bernard De Voto, and Sidney Cox. During those years he won three Pulitzer Prizes, eighteen honorary degrees, and was hailed America's unofficial poet laureate. The United States Senate, in 1950, passed a resolution felicitating him on his seventy-fifth birthday.

But in those years Frost saw death at close hand. In 1929 his sister and sibling rival, Jeanie, died in a state mental hospital. Suffering from obsessive delusions, she had been committed to the hospital by Frost, who felt that, unlike her, he had rescued himself from the cliff's edge. In 1934 Frost's daughter Marjorie, always frail—she had a long bout with "nervous prostration," like Cox's sister, Gertrude—died of complications following childbirth. (During the many years of her illness Marjorie had incurred large medical bills, a source of worry to Frost and his wife, Elinor; in response Cox, who was struggling along on an assistant professor's salary, generously offered to share with them the royalties from a book he hoped to publish on the poet.) Then in 1938 Elinor Frost, who had been operated on for cancer in 1937, died of a heart attack, in Florida. Aware of the suffering he had caused her, Frost sought her forgiveness as she lay on her deathbed. But Elinor, perhaps like the woman in "Home Burial," kept her grief to herself and did not ask to see him. After the initial heart attack, she suffered seven additional ones—and perhaps she was not sufficiently conscious to think of him. Frost, remembering his insistent sexual demands that resulted in so many pregnancies, the financial insecurity that caused so many uprootings, and his lack of sympathy toward her illnesses, was tortured by guilt. All these memories stabbed him, and he felt responsible for her death. Stricken by a severe cold, he was not permitted by his doctor to attend the cremation rites for Elinor in Jacksonville, Florida. At a memorial service held for her at Amherst College, Cox was an honorary pallbearer. In 1940 Carol Frost, after an all-night session with his father—who thought he had assuaged his son's depression—killed himself with a deer-hunting rifle; he had been devoted to his mother.

In June 1938 Frost severed his ties with Amherst, the college he had been associated with on and off for eighteen years. He enjoyed the classroom; there, exuberant and expansive, he dared verbal and philosophical risks. But correcting the poems and papers of amateurs he found irksome and even, as "A Minor Bird" shows, annoying. He had felt the same way so many years before in Plymouth, at the Normal School. Moreover, at Amherst Frost, always hypersensitive, became increasingly aware of his colleagues' resentment. He was being paid, they felt, for doing practically nothing. They resented, too, being subjected to what they considered the superficial chatter—termed "guest lectures"—of Frost's friend Louis Untermeyer. Submitting his resignation to President Stanley King, Frost grudgingly acknowledged that Amherst had given him more than money; it had given him leisure to create, as well as prestige. But if Frost's long tenure at Amherst was not altogether satisfactory to the college, it did help to establish the academic position, familiar today, of writer in residence. And in 1949 Amherst gave Frost the life appointment of Simpson Lecturer in Literature, and later named its library for him.

But in 1938 Frost was in a state of confused agony. Guilt-ridden by the death of his wife, stung by the bitter accusations of his eldest daughter, Lesley, who claimed that it was his selfishness that had ruined her mother's life and had caused so much injury to his children, Frost was wracked by turbulent emotions. He had always been moderate in his drinking habits; now he turned to liquor. He felt, he said, "wild, wild."

Help came unexpectedly through Kathleen Morrison, the wife of a junior faculty member at Harvard, Theodore Morrison. In 1936, when Frost gave his poetry readings at Harvard, she had entertained him in her home, holding a small reception after each lecture. Extending her sympathy at Elinor Frost's memorial service, Mrs. Morrison offered Frost her hospitality "whenever he felt the need of housing or company" in Boston. Frost took her lightly given though sincere invitation literally.[1] As she says, he threw himself on her mercy; and, with great dedication, she helped him reorganize his affairs. Acting as his secretary-manager, Mrs. Morrison brought him back to a fulfilling life.

A quietly forceful woman, who recognized that the poet had to shore up his energies, Mrs. Morrison kept Frost free from entangling engagements and demanding friends. Though Cox complained to his family that Mrs. Morrison prevented him from access to the poet, her strength gave Frost the strong emotional ties he needed during his crisis. He was able to resume his bardings. In 1939, making an extensive lecture tour, he read his poems in Iowa, Wyoming, Utah, Kansas, Indiana, and Michigan. His "second college," Harvard, honored him: in 1938 he was elected to the Board of Overseers; in 1939 he was named Ralph Waldo Emerson Fellow in Poetry.

That summer he bought the Homer Noble Farm in Ripton, Vermont, near the Bread Loaf School, where Theodore Morrison was now director of the Writers' Conference. Frost proposed to the Morrisons that they lease the main house from him and he would live farther up on the property. They agreed, and after cleaning out a kitchen full of chickens, the Morrisons settled down in the white New England farmhouse that would become their summer home. Frost took as his retreat the rustic three-room cabin a few hundred yards up the hill from the house. Here he could write and brood in privacy. If he looked out, he could see a stone wall, an apple orchard, and the sweep of the Green Mountains. If he needed conversation or listeners, he could walk down the hill to chat with the Morrisons or mingle with the students, faculty, and writers summering at Bread Loaf.

In 1943, Frost, fifty-one years after he had run away from
Dartmouth, returned in triumph to his alma mater as the George
Ticknor Fellow in the Humanities. But, initially, the triumph had
a drawback. Torn between Sidney Cox, whom Frost now complained of as being "possessive," and David and Myrtle Lambuth,
who "pulled him around"—the Lambuths were social leaders,
who saw Frost as their star—Frost smarted under conflicting social demands. His daughter Irma Cone, who lived in Hanover and
was suffering from mental distress, was also demanding. John
Sloan Dickey, the new president of Dartmouth, observed the
prickly situation—and intervened. Playing the role of host, he so
diplomatically arranged Frost's schedule that the poet was rescued
from his friends and admirers.[2]

One Dartmouth friend to both Frost and Cox who did not want
to own the poet was Stearns Morse. Fifteen years younger than
Frost, four years younger than Cox, he was probably Cox's closest
friend at Hanover. Frost had known Morse's great-uncle, a country lawyer and farmer in Bath, New Hampshire, fifteen miles from
Franconia, where Frost had farmed helter-skelter fashion in 1915–
16. Morse, brought into the English department by Lambuth in
1923, met the poet in 1924. The two men saw each other frequently during Frost's sojourn in Hanover. A lively teacher and
sometime farmer, Morse had an ebullient humor, a sense of style,
and a keen understanding of human nature. As dean of freshmen
from 1946 to 1956, he often introduced Frost to student audiences. In one preamble, he played with the case of Frost "as the
freshman dropout, lighting out for the woods or for home . . . but
finally returning, still the freshman, prankish and wayward, yet
now the college's more wise than wayward son."[3]

Morse felt that Cox's "reiterated adulation" of Frost put off
many of the faculty; but Morse recognized Cox's strong contribution to Dartmouth life as "a great teacher." And he judged Cox as
"a romantic whose romanticism and idealism had been modified
by Frost's realism."[4]

Cox was at Dartmouth for more than a quarter century. Those
years have no dramatic climax, no significant turning point; their
pattern follows the design established at the outset of his teaching
career. He had a rich family life—he watched his three children

grow, mature, and marry: Arthur Macy Cox, Barbara Alden Cox Vallarino, and Wendell Hayes Cox. He had his wife, Alice, whose delight in fun, earthy wit, and practical realism complemented his own seriousness and idealism. A creative woman, Alice Cox sewed costumes and acted in the Dartmouth Players' productions, sculpted, painted, gardened, and refinished the antiques she found in her forays into the New England countryside.

To earn a living, Cox taught in season and out. Dartmouth semesters were succeeded by summer stints at the Cummington School of the Arts, in the Berkshires. During the Depression Cox, far less conservative in politics than Frost, lashed out against the capitalists. While he served at home as a volunteer fire warden, Cox watched his students go to World War II and saw the Dartmouth campus transformed by undergraduates training to be naval officers. When he was fifty-six, in 1946, Cox suffered a coronary thrombosis and spent six weeks in Dick's House, Dartmouth's infirmary. Crowning his years of hard work was a sabbatical in 1951, when he and Alice enjoyed a literary pilgrimage to England and Ireland.

Besides Stearns Morse, Cox formed close friendships with Donald Bartlett, professor of biography; Henry Williams, who taught English and drama; and Harry Schultz, who taught English and with whom Cox would go on long walks. He knew well Adelbert Ames, founder of the Dartmouth Eye Clinic, and Emil Rueb, a refugee from Nazi Germany who was proprietor of the local camera store. Cox the teacher saw his relationships with many students ripen into enduring friendships; probably the closest was with William Bronk, the poet from Hudson Falls, New York.

Cox devoted his rare free time to writing. He published a covertly erotic poem, "Color," in *The Bookman*, August 1927; numerous book reviews, some in the *Sewanee Review;* and a number of scholarly articles, many of them on Frost. Co-editing *Prose Preferences,* a widely used college anthology, in 1926 and the Second Series of *Prose Preferences* in 1934, Cox, like Frost, realized the importance of anthologies in shaping public taste, in paving the way for new writers. His *The Teaching of English: Avowals and Ventures* appeared in 1928 and *Robert Frost: Original "Ordinary Man"* in 1929. He tried fiction: two unpublished novels, *Spi-*

*ral,* a turn-of-the-century love story, and *Too Deep for Wading,* an academic novel; an unfinished third novel, *Crude Material;* and several short stories. Cox aspired to be a creative writer, but, as he confided to Frost, although he could encourage others to write poetry and fiction, he himself failed at it. Cox's *Winking at the Sphinx,* a book-length philosophical discourse—praised by Frost—was never published in its entirety. Cox's best-known books are *Indirections for Those Who Want to Write* (1947) and the posthumously published *A Swinger of Birches: A Portrait of Robert Frost* (1957). *Indirections* had five printings and a paperback edition came out in 1962. Favorably reviewed, it is still regarded by writers as a sensitive and inspiring, if not always practical, guide on how to write.

Cox spoke on creative writing to teachers at workshops and institutes. He was an adviser on applicants to Yaddo, the writing colony, serving on boards with such distinguished figures as Malcolm Cowley, Lewis Mumford, and John Livingston Lowes. He swelled with pride at the creative achievements, in all the arts, of his students—the poets Reuel Denney, Samuel French Morse, William Bronk, and Philip Booth; the novelists A. B. Guthrie and Budd Schulberg; the film maker Joseph Losey; the artist Gobin Stair; the scholar John V. Kelleher. Meanwhile, he always had a batch of themes to correct.

His life, then, was one familiar to many college-faculty members—but it attained distinction by two elements: his kind of teaching, and its effect on students, and his continuing friendship with Frost. The friendship was strained by Cox's recurring desire to write the poet's biography and Frost's fear, even dread, of his doing so. But if Cox recognized and admired the risks Frost took as poet, Frost recognized and admired Cox's integrity—the risks he took as teacher.

Called by someone "a country club for barbarians," Dartmouth in 1926, when Cox arrived there, was a self-contained, conservative institution, its English department emphasizing the literature of the past, studying it from the standpoint of sources, parallels, and influences. Literature taught as an interpretation of life, a confrontation demanding an engagement from the student, was rare, if not nonexistent. But President Ernest Martin Hopkins wanted a stimulating faculty, scholars who were not bound to departmental lines, who could shake up students. In his initial interview with Cox, Hopkins challenged the teacher "to be his own man in a department where there was enough stuffiness probably to make Cox feel something like a lone voice in the wilderness."[5] Enthusiastic and optimistic, Cox, though uneasy after the Montana incident, took pride in his courage. A few colleagues thought of the new teacher as a fresh breeze from the West. Others, full of rancor that the president had high-handedly bypassed the voices in the English department that opposed Cox's appointment, regarded Cox as the outsider Robert Frost had foisted upon them. And Cox did not hold the Ph.D.

Cox went his own way, the provocateur insisting that good writing was an honest, maybe painful, exploration of self. Using the Socratic method, he forced students to challenge the accepted conventions, the half-truths coruscating from their papers. He did not deliberately cultivate disciples, but word spread among the undergraduates about Cox's exciting classes, the radical involvement demanded of both the teacher and the taught. John V. Kelleher, now professor of Irish studies at Harvard, believes that Cox's success created a "certain jealousy of the man who could attract lively students on the part of those who had little personal following." The students found the English faculty a "rather full and stuffy lot, and . . . Sidney certainly did little to discourage that opinion. He knew that he was a strong teacher and that most of the others were not; and he felt that he was being unfairly discriminated against by the department big shots on the grounds of insufficient scholarship and that this was in fact merely the attack of mediocrity against personality."[6] Another former student, the poet Philip Booth, feels that "in a bland English Department, Sidney self-styled himself as a thorny man and a dangerous teacher."[7]

In Cox's early years at Dartmouth, his frequent citing of his hero did not endear the newcomer to his colleagues. The first thing Cox said to Gerald Warner Brace when Brace came to teach at the college, in 1930, was "tell me about Frost"—Brace had graduated, in 1922, from Amherst, where he had known the poet, though only slightly.[8] Frost in one letter scolds Cox for his public adulation; and President Emeritus John Sloan Dickey remembers that

Frost "was sometimes given in private talks to being critical of what he regarded as the 'possessive' manifestations" of the friendship.⁹

Cox, hired as an assistant professor (Dartmouth did not then have the rank of associate professor), had been informally promised a full professorship at the end of three years; but this promotion did not come. In fact, he was not appointed full professor until 1939, some ten years after he had expected it. But though the failure rankled, it did not embitter him. Cox came to Dartmouth just before the onslaught of the Great Depression. If Alice Cox grew vegetables, wore hand-me-downs, sewed clothes for the children, papered and painted their home, and took in student lodgers on the third floor of their house at 26 East Wheelock Street, so the college, probably abetted by Cox's departmental rivals, was chary of promotions. Cox, who felt that the rewards went to the fawners, the hidebound traditionalists, and dry-as-dust pedants, took obsessive comfort in his status. He had been true to his own vision of teaching; he had not violated his integrity to gain a promotion; but he acquired a "stickleback sensitivity" on the matter. Years later, in 1939, when Cox was belatedly awarded full professorship, Donald Bartlett reports that after he congratulated Cox, he was "met with a most perfunctory 'Thanks,' and then a distressing speech about how he had not lowered his colors to get it. . . . I felt like saying, 'Skip it, Sidney, any fool knows you haven't.'"¹⁰

In spring 1947, when as an undergraduate Philip Booth signed up for a writing class, he found himself in a room with the other writing students, meeting the two teachers, Cox and Tom Braden, who subsequently became a nationally syndicated newspaper columnist. Cox informed the students, in his Maine accent, that they were to be divided into two sections: "If you want to make money, stay here with Mr. Braden. Those of you who want to learn to write, come in the other room with me."¹¹

That angularity, that brusque honesty, was Cox's signature. His concern was wisdom, not intelligence, not conventional education. When he was hired by Dartmouth, he hoped to teach literature as well as writing; but the upper-division literature courses were owned by established department members. And so Cox had to accept the composition and advanced writing courses, but he did so with his usual intensity and zest for experimentation.

Cox's manifesto, which grew out of his experiences, is *The Teaching of English*, in which he admits he cannot tell anyone *how* to teach—but he can relate what he does in his classes. In this book, which influenced English teachers throughout the country, Cox stresses that he offers students friendship. The teacher must be personal. The student should feel free to tell the teacher everything and not feel guilty or embarrassed afterwards. Cox is often frustrated. Some students flout the offer of friendship: "A larger number do not care enough to make the indispensable return. But many come to take it as much as they are able, at the time. And a few keep coming" after they have completed the course.[12] The teacher, Cox says, must have inexhaustible energy and a willingness to be open that may invite rejection or ridicule.

But if Cox can reveal only partially his way of teaching, his former students offer vivid perceptions. Reuel Denney says that when students walked into the classroom they saw a man with a large and "gangly body, oversized head, big ears, large pale blue eyes that seemed a bit runny, but had remarkable vitality . . . and a most mobile mouth—a long pensive upper lip with a pendulous lower lip that was never at rest—the movements of his mouth were like a whole puppet show of questionings, grins and smiles."[13]

Each class Cox took the "big risk," William Bronk remembers, the risk of making a "discovery." Cox would open the class by reading a selection from a famous author, or a piece from *The New York Times*, or a student's submission. The reading would lead to questioning, by the teacher of the students, by the students of one another, by the students of the teacher. On days when a "discovery" was made, "there was general joy and you walked out floating." On other days, when the class was a flop, you walked out squirming in embarrassment for the teacher. How could he be so naked? How could he open himself up to the possibility of appearing ridiculous?[14]

With friendship, Cox offered gruff undercutting to the brash and the instant dogmatists. John V. Kelleher remembers giving him a "clever" paper that would have earned an A in any other class: Cox "read it out and began to agonize over it slowly," while Kelleher "sat there in misery, knowing only that I was never going to try that stunt again—not in this class anyway."[15] Sometimes Cox could destroy a student's confidence all too unwittingly by harsh class comment, but he could also encourage a wavering student with high praise. His criticism "could be terribly demanding without being meant to be personal."[16] Speaking of his students, Cox told Stearns Morse, "I like to get at their vitals—and give them a twist."[17]

Cox was the first person to suggest to the future film maker Joseph Losey, who as a student had intended to be a doctor, that he direct his energies toward a creative art. Losey considers Cox an influence, because he "ruthlessly drove you and coaxed you, led and shamed you into more and more self-analysis and examination of everything around: people, attitudes, the books you read, your use of words."[18] But whatever method Cox used, he made students want to create. Budd Schulberg says that whenever he teaches a writing course now, he asks himself, What did "Sidney do that made us feel we had to rush back to our rooms and *write?*"[19]

Branching out from the classroom, Cox started his tradition of the "Sunday Nights" by inviting some carefully chosen students to his home for readings, followed by brownies and coffee. In the white Colonial house, the teacher "sat in a battered old armchair . . . sunk way down on his spine, with his right leg cocked over his left knee at an angle that showed how loose-limbed he was."[20] Cox would read from a contemporary writer or a student's manuscript to ten or so students and visiting alumni. Occasionally a guest such as Frost or Lewis Mumford—who in the thirties and forties as a visiting professor spent a week every month in various departments—would drop in. After the reading, the group would go deep into argument over the piece's merits. As it grew later, one by one the students would drift into the kitchen, where Alice Cox held court, until Cox was left talking to a lone auditor. Far from being jealous over the laughter coming out of the kitchen, Cox took pleasure in his wife's social success. Budd Schulberg says those "gatherings . . . were the highlights of our college literary life."[21]

Cox's honesty made him dislike small talk so much that at times he seemed shy; embarrassingly long periods of silence were not disguised by chitchat. His own honesty made him take each student's paper as honest; and, as Kelleher writes, "being taken as honest by a wholly honest man . . . is a very chastening experience."[22] Cox had time for the student "who seemed to him serious and intent on working out his ideas, at least if the ideas were 'making ideas,'" Samuel French Morse remembers. "He was willing to listen to what was in process, or unfinished—knowing how much a writer needs an audience." As the faculty adviser for *The Dart,* the college literary magazine, Cox "was likely to be stringent, and at the same time an excellent propagandist for a story or poem he admired."[23] Gobin Stair, the artist, emphasizes that Cox forced him "to work out what I thought of integrity. . . . It is not always easy, this searching, sometimes even brusque, attempt to be true to one's self and one's situation."[24]

Cox's honesty, his seriousness, often made him appear humorless. Because he lacked a light touch, a few colleagues and some cocksure students found him an easy target for mockery. But though Lewis Mumford sometimes thought Cox "abrasively earnest," he "learned to love even Sidney's solemn quirks!" He summed up the teacher as "incorruptible."[25] John Sloan Dickey says that "the overwhelming impression I had of Cox as a teacher was the pervasive depth of his sincerity."[26] Because of that sincerity, that incorruptibility, Frost could write to Cox: "You are one of the few who can sustain years of teaching literature as thought about life."

Literature and the teaching of it were important concerns of the two friends, but they were not the paramount concern in the letters between 1926 and 1951. The paramount concern, sometimes dormant, sometimes overt, was this: Cox's desire to write a book on the poet and Frost's thwarting, encouraging, and then discouraging of that desire. Alice Cox, who ironically referred to Frost as God (as in "You got a letter from God today"), believed that her husband's worshipful attitude toward Frost prevented

Cox from striking out on his own. And in his own mind, Cox was so overshadowed by the great poet that for a vast portion of his adult life he was never able to become fully his own man. Frost enjoyed Alice Cox's wry, frequently iconoclastic wit; he liked her hospitality and the atmosphere in the Cox home; and he was grateful that she was friendly and kind to his difficult daughter, Irma Cone, when the latter lived in Hanover. But Alice Cox would suggest to her husband that he visit Frost by himself, because, she said, both men had a better time when she wasn't there. It rankled her that Cox shared his ideas and information with other Frost biographers, instead of saving for himself his original material and insights.

Frost was well aware by 1926 that he was ripe for a biography—he had been awarded six honorary degrees and one Pulitzer Prize by then. But he was caught off guard when John Farrar, an editor for George H. Doran, asked him to name a biographer for a series the publisher was preparing on contemporary writers. Hating, as Frost put it, to be undressed in public, he mulled over the prospect. After an embarrassing entanglement with a would-be biographer, the English critic Edward Davison, Frost finally invited Gorham Munson, who had praised him as the "purest classical poet in America," to write the biography. Cox had been under the impression that quite early Frost had given him permission to be a Boswell. When Munson, at Frost's suggestion, asked Cox for help, Cox gave Munson a lively account of the poet, which Munson incorporated into his book, *Robert Frost: A Study in Sensibility and Good Sense* (1927); however, on Alice Cox's advice, Cox reserved part of the material he was originally going to mail to Munson.

Feeling somewhat betrayed by his hero who had allowed Munson to write a biography, Cox covered his disappointment with long rationalizations. But the knowledge that there were competitors in the race to be Frost's biographer made Cox work harder. Spurred by Munson's book, Cox, who had been making notes and preparing copy for a book on Frost for several years, began to shape a manuscript. Calling his study "Walks and Talks with Robert Frost," he interspersed his commentary with extracts from Frost's letters. In the summer of 1928, the Frosts invited Cox to South Shaftsbury to discuss the manuscript. Dissatisfied with passages, the Frosts were making deletions. The book, Frost felt, didn't put Cox and him "in the right personal relation." He objected to Cox's saying that initially the poet had sought him out; that he never went to see the poet unless summoned. Daunted, Cox put away that manuscript—Frost kept a carbon copy of it—and concentrated on an extended essay on the poet's characteristics and ideas. In 1929 he sent his rambling, ruminative exploration of the poet's mind to Frost's publisher, Henry Holt and Company, who printed, in a handsome edition, the slim volume *Robert Frost: Original "Ordinary Man."*

Cox may have been disappointed over Frost's rejection of his earlier, longer work, but he did not despair. Periodically he would take the manuscript from a drawer, revise it, add to it, edit it; and the reworkings caused him to analyze and brood on the course of his friendship with Frost. Insistently, he would broach the matter in his letters and conversations with the poet. Trying in 1932 to gain permission to write an extended biographical study, Cox again suffered defeat. Frost did not want Cox "thrusting in where I did not want you." And he insulted Cox: "I have written to keep the over curious out of the secret places of my mind both in my verse and in my letters to such as you."

The intensely private Frost may have felt he had been too revealing in conversation to permit Cox to be his biographer; he may have felt that Cox's literary style was more suited to philosophical analysis than to the shaping of a life. And he may have thought that Cox's enthusiasm and exuberance, his near-idolatry, would make them both appear ridiculous. He wanted to keep Cox's friendship; he did not want him to write the biography. Frost's rejection strained the friendship. A year and a half later, in October 1933, Frost complains of Cox's neglect: "I don't know how you are, but I'm so constituted that I don't seem to mind being neglected by people I am sure feel all right toward me."

Other scholars became interested in writing the Frost biography, and during the next decade or so Cox grew aware of the plans, first, of Robert Newdick and then of Lawrance Thompson, Cox's contenders in a race that Frost encouraged and discouraged by turns. Prodded by Frost, Newdick, in 1935 a junior professor at Ohio State University, communicated his plans for a biography to Cox and gracefully requested information. Cox who was obedient, even subservient to Frost's wishes, shared not only his recollections but also his 1912–1915 file of Frost letters; he probably did not realize that Frost had showed Newdick his carbon copy of Cox's one-hundred-page journal, "Walks and Talks with Robert Frost."[27] Newdick died suddenly in July 1939, and his research was not published until 1976 by State University of New York Press, Albany. Eight years after Newdick's death, Cox asked Frost for permission to use some of the materials gathered by Newdick, but apparently Frost was not agreeable to the idea.

Paradoxically, while encouraging Newdick Frost also weakly encouraged Cox: in May 1938 the poet, in an unsigned letter, told Cox, "I have always hoped you might sometime publicly remember me in writing." Cox seized this hint to show Frost a revised manuscript, but again he suffered rejection. In 1942 Cox felt a jealous twinge when he saw an announcement for Lawrance Thompson's study, *Fire and Ice: The Art and Thought of Robert Frost* (New York: Henry Holt and Company); and, in a letter, he half argued with, half begged the poet: "There is a place too for my effort; and if I last I shall make it, in some form. Now I am asking you: shall the form be biography-portrait, or shall it be just portrait?" In 1947, urged on by Frost, Thompson asked to interview Cox regarding Frost's "'pilgrim's progress' in the realm of spiritual matters." Generous to a fault—a trait that may have been stained with masochism—Cox complied. Behind each request was Frost, who showed Cox's material to other biographers, who played on Cox's loyalty, his blind devotion, who scolded him, insulted him, manipulated him.

The final word, ostensibly, in this extended cat-and-mouse game was in a strange letter of August 1948, which may not have been mailed. Frost speaks of Cox's effort as "your dread book" but tells his friend to go ahead and publish it; he adds a statement designed to make Cox feel guilty: "I am at your mercy."

But Cox did not see the publication of his work. On January 2, 1952, he was hospitalized with pneumonia, which was complicated by a heart condition. He died the next day, his hope apparently obliterated by sudden death at age sixty-two.

## NOTES

1. Kathleen Morrison, *Robert Frost: A Pictorial Chronicle* (New York: Holt, Rinehart and Winston, 1974), p. 10.
2. Interview: Stearns Morse, 10 June 1976.
3. Stearns Morse, "Lament for a Maker: Reminiscences of Robert Frost," *The Southern Review*, 9 (January 1973): 66. On pp. 60–62 Morse discusses the Frost-Cox relationship.
4. Ibid., p. 62.
5. Donald Bartlett to William R. Evans, 11 February 1978.
6. Kelleher to Evans, 27 July 1978.
7. Booth to Evans, 21 October 1977.
8. Brace to Evans, 16 June 1978.
9. Dickey to Evans, 27 February 1979.
10. Bartlett to Evans, 11 February 1978.
11. Booth to Evans, 21 October 1977.
12. (New York: Harper & Brothers, 1928), p. 5.
13. Denney to Evans, 7 February 1978.
14. Interview: 24 August 1977.
15. Kelleher to Evans, 27 July 1978.
16. Booth to Evans, 21 October 1977.
17. Interview: 10 June 1976.
18. Losey to Evans, 16 January 1978.
19. Schulberg to Evans, 27 March 1979.
20. Kelleher to Evans, 27 July 1978.
21. Schulberg to Evans, 27 March 1979.
22. Kelleher to Evans, 27 July 1978.
23. Morse to Evans, 30 March 1978.
24. Stair to Evans, 4 August 1978.
25. Mumford to Evans, 25 July 1979.
26. Dickey to Evans, 27 February 1979.
27. William A. Sutton, ed., *Newdick's Season of Frost: An Interrupted Biography of Robert Frost* (Albany: State University of New York Press, 1976), p. 190.

ALS, 6 pp.

# 67.

South Shaftsbury

Dear Sidney                                    [22 December 1926]

I can think of nothing but how glad I am you are at Hanover safely unhanged. You were too many hours ahead of your time out there on Rocky Mountain Time and there was always danger of its giving you an exaggerated sense of your own importance and so getting you into trouble with the Kew Clucks. Be at peace now and like your opportunities as much as in you lies to like anything human. I wouldnt give a hoot in derision for the difference between the boys in one college and the boys in another. There are the same kinds in all of them, your kind and the other fellow's kind. It will take time of course for your own to gravitate to you. Time is an element, is of the essence of everything.

Don't count on me to do anything for Dartmouth or any other college—unless it is through my poems. Read those to the boy under you, but dont rub them into him. I understand that my last visit to Hanover was a little worse than wasted. It is as I would have it. *I need all* the excuse I can muster for desisting from the colleges. They are none of mine. I didnt invent them and I should be a fool to think in my heart I could really make them over. I'm recessive in teaching. I suppose it flattered me to be called back to meddle in a system as teacher that I spurned as pupil. And that's why I yielded to the temptation. I'm vain like some other people. But I dont stay vain over the same folly all the time. I used to want to think I might become a tennis player by the time I was sixty. I draw in. I'm willing to leave tennis playing to those who start young and give their lives to it—tennis playing to tennis players and teaching to teachers. I'm a farmer.

On with the excitement as Byron said. You do what you see to do and Dartmouth will come all right for you without my interposition. Aren't we funny fanciers? You think invoking me would save the pieces. Be disenchanted. I've got too much Amherst Wesleyan Bowdoin and Michigan on my conscience as it is. Another year I must be free from all but Amherst and one other. I'm in hopes of a few more poems before Gabriel blows his trumpet. You see I already have quite a start in poetry.

At Williamstown, speaking of starts, the other day I heard a workman on the college grounds lament the death of a student worth five millions. "Why weep on an uncertainty," I said. "Wasnt there a good chance of the boy's coming into something better in Heaven than five millions?" The workman (evidently French Canadian and so probably Catholic) gave me a curious look to see if he could make out in what sense I said that. "He'd be a pretty lucky boy to get two such starts in succession," was his answer.

"Then for this reason and for a season
Let us be merry before we go." (Curran)*
Merry Christmas to you all.            Ever yours   Robert Frost

Mrs Irma Cone's address is Rozel Kansas

* John Philpot Curran (1750–1817): Irish orator, judge, and poet.

[Frost included three poems in this letter: "The Rose Family" and "A Minor Bird," handwritten and initialed, and "What Fifty Said," typewritten and signed; all appear for the most part unchanged in *West-Running Brook*. With the first two is a handwritten note: "Plenty of others in New Rep. lately."]

ALS, 5 pp.

## 68.

[Amherst
Dear Sidney:                              c. 7 February 1927]
You *would* exaggerate me into the most conspicuous prose writer in your collection, you doting friend and so disqualify me for doing anything to boost the book.* I don't care if you don't. A little undeserved praise now and then will only make it up to me in advance or arrears for the undeserved blame I am always getting— or suppose I am always getting—I never look in the reviews to see. You have more to lose by your act than I have. I am stopped from using or recommending for use any anthology in which I am made to shine. But as I dont use any anthologies at all or think of them to mention in my travels perhaps you are not so much out there as you might at first seem to be. I did carry your beautiful book so

beautifully printed to my class in philosophy the other day for the dialogue between Hermotimus and Lucian—one of my most favoritest pieces in the known universe. Isnt that a lovely boy in there?[†] Nearly the whole book proved good reading or rereading. And I must say the biocritical forewords are hard to resist. I'm a Fool is probably [Sherwood] Anderson's best though to my nerves it scrapes false in a spot or two. Wilbur Daniel Steele's story has lighthouse in it.[‡] My only wonder is that you didnt find anything of [Stuart] Sherman's to bring in. But I can see how you would refuse to be held answerable for inclusiveness. I'm not particularly in favor of covering in my poetry that I know of.

We are still under the cloud of Marjorie's long illness. Our day in the house revolves round her. She reads a little plays the piano a little and plays cards a little: but she has to be kept from doing even such things too much. Sometimes we get fearfully disheartened. More than glimpses of people seem to exhaust her. She cant be left too much by herself. It seems to me it must be something like your sister's case. The doctors now call it nervous prostration. The nervous prostrates I have seen however were set serious. Marj has her ironies and her grins.

Lesley is on one of the winter tours round the world with a branch of her book store. She's past Samoa by now. The last letter from her was from Honolulu (sp.)[§] With Irma married into Kansas and Carol away off in Vermont we feel a pretty scattered family.

I get a little poem out of it now and then. I might include you one or two in this.

Be seeing you soon.

Best to you all.

Always yours<br>Robert Frost

* In the headnote to Frost's "The Poetry of Amy Lowell," in the anthology *Prose Preferences*, Cox and his co-editor, Edmund Freeman (a colleague at Missoula), wrote: "Robert Frost is one of the best living poets; he is also, when he cares to use it, a master of virile, concentrated prose. He is one good foundation for pride in being an American."

[†]In Lucian's *Hermotimus* an affable skeptic, Lycinus, mildly ridicules the earnest student of stoicism, Hermotimus.

[‡]The story by Wilbur Daniel Steele is "The Woman at Seven Brothers."

[§]Lesley Frost, with her sister Marjorie, had established the Open Book Shop in 1924 in

Pittsfield, Massachusetts, and during the summers they operated the Bookshop-on-Wheels in the nearby towns filled with summer visitors. She also had the Round-the-World Bookshop on the S.S. *Franconia.*

ALS, 4 pp.

## 69.

Dear Robert                                    19 February [1927]
   You have made me very happy on an unhappy day. Such a wonderful feeling of all-rightness comes in your letter. I didn't think I was as close to you as I come by your coming to me in it.
   An unhappy day because Gertrude, my sister, wants to go home, and we don't think she's much better and are afraid she will get worse if she goes. Alice is corroded by the irritation, at Gertrude, she has to repress. And Gertrude thinks our attitude, and that of the very good doctor we have, keep her from sleeping and interfere with recovery. All her faith still reposes in the dubious doctors of the Chicago sanitarium she went to twice. And as long as she refuses to yield to the guidance of some expert who can see her often she will probably remain neurotic. Alice thinks I'm weakly piteous towards Gertrude; Gertrude often thinks I'm rather cruel. She evidently feels that way about my getting Father to say over the telephone that he wished she would stay with us another week.
   I hate to have Marjory ill. She's always seemed one of the few specially lovable people. Your writing poems, in the present state of things, that are more reassuring and courageous and convincingly religious than ever is one of the things that make cynicism and despair impossible for me. "The Soldier" is one of the best poems. I don't believe there's anything so good in so many ways for me in Shakespear. It makes me think of what you said to me about Lycidas; the sound alone, if I could not hear the words, would make me worth more to myself and would give me a moment so perfect I could almost call it absolutely perfect. I like each of the others you sent in a way special to each. "The Minor Bird" is a very lyrical lyric. I shall back it against Shelley or anybody's favorite lyric poet.

I'm nonsensically glad that I had hunted all the poems out of the "New Republic" lately. Stearns Morse told me of one—the one about the Pacific. And I thought it very new for you, not at all expectable, and good, way, way down and in. Later Kenneth Robinson told me of the others. I had a good half hour or so with them. How is it you never fail to make your "doting" friends feel they have not thought more highly than they ought to think?

It sets me up that you like the little notes in Freeman's and my "Preferences". I should have had something of Sherman if, at the time we got the things together, I had read his last essays. I have said what I think a good and true word about him, in an article that I don't seem to be able to get published.

The next literary question for me is whether the book I've finished, all but some revising, on "The Art of Teaching English", can get published. It's got much of the best of me in it, and Mac-Gregor the Harpers man who did such a nice job on "Prose Preferences" told me that he and Canby wanted me to go ahead with it. But the people who recommend such books may not enough of them want my personal essays so that printing would be expedient.*

You know that I am more than a little glad you are coming, after all. I want you and Mrs Frost to spend part of the time under our roof. Won't you? Can't you?

Yours<br>Sidney

*Cox's *The Teaching of English: Avowals and Ventures* was published in 1928 by Harper and Brothers.

ALS, 4 pp.

## 70.

Dear Robert Frost                    19 June 1927    Hanover

I've been waiting for news of some little success to put into my letter. But I'm not going to let myself be permanently prevented from writing to you. I hope that nothing is going to prevent us, either, from riding north in search of a pond sometime between now and the twentieth of July. Maybe we can decide upon a time, now. Can we? You know I go to the U. of Virginia for their second summer term.

My Sherman article has been sent back again, and a short story has been twice rejected, and Harpers think my "Not Really a Class" would go more profitably if a publisher that makes "professional books" on education and text books for high school put it out, though they assure me and reassure me that if I want them to go ahead with it, under the conditions, they will be very glad to do so. I have asked Harcourt, Brace and Company if they are interested.

As far as the teaching goes I have been successful enough. I have made a few good friends, and one or two have said, and others have implied, that I have shown them something. The funny thing is that I seem to be able to help some others to things I can't achieve myself. Recently two mature people who have been taking my lambastings and Bravos and hints, for some time, by correspondence have placed a number of things in good magazines.

Anyway the people who, misled by the Frontier rumpus of last spring, expected me to be rampagious and snorting have been saying they find me a horse of another color. Not a Roan Stallion but a milk white palfrey; I hope that's not it.

The Lambuth's and the Morses were over here to supper last night. Mrs. Lambuth carried it off very well. She told a lively story about the resourceful Freshman who has pleased her surprisingly; and she remarked that at first she had told him they never kept anybody in their house who was not a gentleman in a sense which he had never known. She is that kind of lady, surely.

The MacKaye's took us over to see Percy the other day; and we had a good time. I liked him much better than I do his poetry. He sent his love to you when I told him I hoped to see you soon. (It was Mrs. MacKaye that told him I knew you.) I believe now that minor poets and too artistic-y people are sort of inevitabilities. He praised your wonderful talk, and showed that he thinks your interest is likely to be won only by something "very real." I'll tell you what it is he hopes you may be interested in when we can talk.*

A little while after you left I wrote out something for Gorham Munson. Alice and John Beecher and his wife made me reserve part that they thought very specially mine.[†] They said it was the best thing I had ever written. But Munson seemed grateful for the remainder.

Yours   Sidney Cox

*Percy MacKaye (1875–1956): American poet and dramatist, author of *The Scarecrow*.
[†]John Newman Beecher (b. 1904): an English instructor at Dartmouth in 1927. Cox is referring to the biographical material on Frost he gave Munson for his study.


TLS, 2 pp.

## 71.

Dear Robert Frost          13 November 1927   Hanover

If I were with you now I don't feel as if I should be quite as tongue-tied as I felt the last three times. At any rate I should have this much to say. I hope you will read what Lewis Mumford said about you in the enclosed review of Munson's book. I was so delighted with his indispensable corrections of Munson that I wrote at once to thank him. I called his attention to Munson's ridiculous perversion of your "what is uncommon to expression" as I had already, in a letter that Alice thought too "glad" in its general tone, called Munson's. I had also told Munson of the two main limitations I felt, the very two on which Mumford comments so deftly.*

Tonight I have finished reading Mumford's "The Golden Day". I like it more than any new book except "Death Comes for the Archbishop" that I have read for a long time. It seems to me that if I had kept the promises you thought I was giving years ago I should by now have learned enough and shared my thought enough to have produced a book with some resemblances to that. All I can say is that if I ever do produce anything that gets in whatever is seminal in all my brooding and thinking it will at least not be glib.

I am at something new that interests me enormously, though it is very modest, and gets most of its value apart from me. Even for it my energy after a little teaching is seldom adequate, and at best, it falls distressingly short of its imaginable possibilities.

I had good fun discussing with Upton Sinclair, at the after-meeting; and Stearns Morse called me up the next day to tell me he liked what I said, and that two who went home with him thought— [I] made good one or two points. Stearns said he thought "we almost converted him," a joke of course, but a good joke because it had truth in it.

Some more about my writing; I keep thinking of things of mine that I was disappointed at not getting published that I am glad now were kept from print. Maybe if Harpers delays long enough with my "Avowals and Ventures" I'll be ashamed of that before too late. I am not conscious of beginning to, though. If not I shall have to thank Alice for making me ashamed of some false notes in time.

You are extremely important to me.                Yours   Sidney

*Lewis Mumford's review of Gorham B. Munson's *Robert Frost: A Study in Sensibility and Good Sense* appeared on the front page of *The New York Herald-Tribune* November 6, 1927.

[In this letter Cox is punning on the name of the newly appointed president of Amherst College, Arthur Stanley Pease. Frost had strong disagreements with Pease regarding the terms of Frost's appointment to the college.]

ALS, 4 pp.

## 72.

Dear Robert                              23 April 1928   Hanover

Stacy May let me know yesterday that the little peas you put into the big pod turn out wormy.* I am very vengeful when I allow myself to wish that he might have a "realizing sense" of how picayune he looks. The king of the Lilliputians ordering the threads and tacks for Gulliver. I'll spell his name with a small letter.

Of course you're indignant more than hurt. I hope the presidentkin knows he's too late to prove anything by the putting down of his august foot. An uncertificated man has already done great teaching at two colleges without regular classes, marks or the taking of attendance, and been at the top of the list of regular professionals. That fact thumbs its nose at him.

One more man doffs his manhood to be a president. I'm still wondering a little about President Hopkins [of Dartmouth]. If he compromises too much I shall doubt whether it is possible to keep a soul you call your own and be on the college ridgepole. One tends to slip astride and rupture his integrity. I wonder if president peas has looked up a truss.

I wish I could hear about it all from you. I suppose he was pacifying someone. It's awful to have to sit under Xantippe's potfulls. But, however it may feel to you right now, it means much to me that you have expressed your will and thought, subject, unmistakably, to the conditions and evil possibilities that make most people call such genuineness impractical. If you had always been immune from presidential flurries, cynics would have said that you were faithful to your distrusts because official hands were tied.

People have been hopefully asking me if you were to spend some days here again this year. And a student told Professor Lambuth recently that the desideratum for our much-advertized new English House would be Robert Frost to find there, sometimes, and talk to.

I see much of Stearns this year, and I'm sure he is a real, fine friend to you.

Can I see you some day between the middle of May and the end of June? We expect to hunt a cheap place to live for the middle of the summer, somewhere on the shore of Nova Scotia. The old house is almost on its new foundations, and we shall come back to it in September. I wish you might be the first from out of town to cross the stone doorstep.

I liked "The Bear" better than ever when I saw it in the *Nation*, the other day. Is a new book nearly ready?

All goes well with us, and I hope you aren't feeling too much the opposite. My sister is getting along in a Hartford (State) library, and she says her head is comfortable. May her marvelous improvement be a trustworthy augury for Marjorie.

Yours affectionately    Sidney

---

* Stacy May (1896–1980): economist, an assistant professor of citizenship at Dartmouth in 1928.

† Arthur Stanley Pease (b. 1881): president of Amherst in 1928.

TLS, 2 pp.

73.

Dear Mrs Frost                    25 May 1928   Hanover
Next week I expect to turn over to a stenographer the manuscript of a book I want to call "Walks and Talks with Robert
Frost," and, with my manuscript, extracts from Mr. Frost's letters
to me, especially those from England in which he wrote a good
deal about his thoughts on poetry. I have been careful to mark for
transcription nothing that I thought Mr. Frost might prefer to
keep unpublished for the present; and Alice and Stearns Morse
have confirmed my selections.
    When the manuscript is completed I want to bring it to you so
that if you want to you can pass judgment on the acceptability to
Robert and you of any or all of it. You know Robert told me in
1922 that he did not object to my Bozwellizing him if what I
talked about was his ideas. I think Mr. Munson's fairly good
but inadequate book makes the publication of mine—which, of
course, I don't think is adequate either—rather appropriate. I expect you will like it.
    I am saying all this to you instead of to Robert because I don't
want to embarrass him by putting him into the position of having
authorized it. I shall leave you to decide whether he shall know of
it or not before it is in print.
    The editor of Harpers Magazine has expressed a desire to consider printing part or all of it in the magazine, and I hope Harpers
will publish it as a book. I propose to divide the book royalties
with Marjorie Frost. That is only fair as a great part of the value of
the book as well as a great part of its attractiveness to buyers will
be in the selections from her father's letters.
    Please tell me some news about all of the Frosts. From what
President Hopkins told me on his return from Michigan about the
calming of the situation at Amherst, I infer that my earlier letter to
Robert about the way I had heard President Pease was treating
him was almost as ridiculously out of time as somebody's singing
the last measure of the Doxology after the organ has stopped.

Here are some snap-shots we took at Carol's on our way east nearly two years ago. We lost our camera with that film in it for a while, and only had the film developed a few weeks ago.

I very much hope all goes cheerfully with you now. I read in two book review magazines recently about Lesley's taking a position with Doubleday-Doran, and still keeping on with her two book shops.

Alice has had good times this year acting in several plays, drawing, getting the rest of the furniture for our new-old house, and devising ways to make that house a good home. The carpentry work on the house has got well started. I hope you and Robert will come to see us in it during the first year we are there.

Arthur and Barbie have had a good year in school and out. And I have had some great times teaching. Knowing Stearns has been one of the best things in the year. And writing my book and reading and rereading the letters has been another.

Without any intrigue on my part, Robert Frost's "Selected Poems" are going to be used next year, not only in my Sophomore writing class as they have been these two years, but also in all the special sections, and I think the general sections, too, of the entering class.

Yours affectionately<br>Sidney Cox

ALS, 6 pp.

## 74.

My dear Sidney—            31 May [1928] South Shaftsbury

Thank you very much for your letter. I am very much interested in the book you have written, and should greatly like to see the manuscript when it is copied. I am sure I shall like it. Could you not bring it down, and we could all talk it over and see if we want it published now—or if you ought to keep it until after Robert's death. I do not know if *letters* are ever published during anyone's lifetime. Do you know about that? Probably you have chosen parts which are almost impersonal—and that would be all right. As you say, it is a favorable time to publish it, in one sense, though naturally one shrinks from too much personal revelation.

Any time after next week will be convenient for us, except two or three days around the 20th of June. Could you not drive down as you did last summer? But don't be in such a hurry! It is most generous of you to offer to share pecuniary results with Marjorie. If you feel that you would like to do it, I am sure it would be very thrilling for her. She is much better. She spent 8 weeks in bed at Johns Hopkins in Baltimore, and 2 weeks at Atlantic City on the way home, and gained in all 24½ lbs. She is going on with the treatment—the rest—the quiet, and the heavy feeding, and I am hoping that in a few months, she will be quite a vigorous girl.

Irma and her 8 months baby are with us now. She was unhappy in her married life on account of the persecution of a perfectly fiendish mother-in-law. Just now she and her husband are separated, though they correspond. If he is willing, later, to leave his father's ranch, they may have a home elsewhere, but it does not look now as if he meant ever to leave. I should feel more sad about it, if I did not see that her love has greatly diminished through observing how great an influence an awful woman like that one in Kansas could have on her husband. She wishes to take a year's work in the Normal Art School, and fit herself to teach drawing in the public schools.

Carol and his wife and little boy are well.

I am so glad that Alice and the children are well and happy. Sometime you must bring them all down for a visit.

With love and best wishes for you all. Sincerely   Elinor Frost

When you have planned ahead will you let me know when you would like to come?

ALS, 2 pp.

## 75.

Dear Robert                           16 June [1928] Hanover
   Can't you and Mrs. Frost make us a little visit between July 1
and 6? A year is up since I saw you last, and I have things I should
like to tell you. A lot of people who would want to make a fuss
over you in ordinary times will be out of town then. And our
house will still have the freshness I should like it to have when you
first visit it; and green ought to predominate over brown in the
lawn by then. But if those dates are too soon and too close together I'll want you after the last (twenty-fifth) of August if Alice is
feeling fit.
   I'm going to teach a writing course, and a course in some modern novelists at the Albany teachers' college, from July 8 to August
17. That's why I'm limiting the invitation the way I am. A Montana student friend is going to be here from June 24 to 29.
   One of the best evenings of this spring was when I read from
Robert Frost, at their suggestion, when a little woman's poetry
group entertained their husbands. Mr. MacKaye—you remember—found a good deal he had failed to find before, he said. And
Stearns Morse was amazingly emphatic in his praise. Three deep-
dyed New Englanders, yes four, were pleased with my catching of
the talk. Stearns said it was "inimitable"; and he knows.
   But if that puffed me up, I've had things to deflate me.
   I do want to see you, and to have you in our own house.
                                   Affectionately   Sidney

               Grounds of Faith

         The shine of the sun
         On a shovel over a shoulder,
         October red
         Round a crumpled tin can,
         Two grandiose tones
         From plumbing,
         Ought to have told her

Not to renounce
The emergence
Of modified splendor in man.

        With unflagging affection   Sidney

TLS, 1 p.

## 76.

Dear Robert          11 July 1928   New Hampton, N.H.

Here is another chapter to make any necessary elisions from. I have decided I want to call the book "'Time to Talk' with Robert Frost." I don't know yet whether to trust people to recognize the source of the first three words or to remind them with the quotation marks.

The other day I had a letter from Mrs. Lambuth in Harrisonburg, Virginia, asking for all kinds of materials, and two anecdotes from me, two from Alice, and three from Stacy May—to whom I was to pass on the letter—to be used in helping a group of her friends to "love" your work. I sent her a copy of the chapter I just finished.

Did you know that Bravig Imbs, once at Dartmouth and the Lambuth's, has just won praises for a novel called "The Professor's Wife"? *

I can't place the enthusiast Woodman who writes that he is sending me two copies of his "Contemporaries", composed, I take it, of work done by his students. He wants me to review it, and to see if it isn't as good as "Creative Youth". He says he is sending you two copies, too. Calls himself a New Hampshire boy, and writes as if he and I knew each other of old.

Let's not let my book be a thorn in your flesh.

                         Yours
                         Sidney

* Bravig Imbs (b. 1904): Dartmouth '27, published a satirical roman à clef, *The Professor's Wife*, in 1928. As a student, Imbs had worked as a butler for the Lambuths.

ALS, 2 pp.

# 77.

Dear Robert                    7 October 1928    Hanover
I suppose one reason why I liked your two letters was that I have for quite a while been reluctantly giving in to the suspicion that the things you say in them were true. We'll hope that instead of being a leopard who cannot change his spots I'm a creature enough like a toad to be able to shed a skin that he's outgrown, and then eat it to reassimilate whatever's in it suitable for life.

It is something that I am not discredited at Dartmouth enough to prevent my being one of the recipients of a $300 increase in salary. I have been assigned new honors students in spite of the vociferous request of my former two. But one of the new ones particularly wanted me, and they both seem to fall in with my way of working it.

I've cockles in my heart if not as guarded a sanctuary as is estimable, and you warmed them.

Yours    Sidney

[Helen Thomas, in World Without End (1926), speaks frankly of the love of her husband, the poet Edward Thomas, for Eleanor Farjeon. Although Frost deals with sex in a number of his poems, he was usually reticent about it. His friendship with Edward Thomas was extremely valuable to Thomas, and Frost felt a closeness to the writer who was like him in many ways.]

ALS, 4 pp.

# 78.

London Eng. now: but I'll be home in S. Shaftsbury early in November. Want to see you.

Sidney, Sidney                    11 October 1927 [1928]
It won't do. You'll say I've been long enough coming to that brief conclusion. I practically had to wait till I had grown into another person so I could see the problem presented with the eyes of an outsider. Looking in on it from another country and from another time with all the disinterestedness possible I find I'm against

the book—at least in my lifetime: when I'm off the scene you can decide for yourself. My greatest objection to the book is that it doesn't put you and me in the right personal relation. I think you would realize that if you took time. Your repeated insistence on the fact that you never came to see me except when summoned has the very opposite effect from what you intend. Instead of making us out equals in friendship as I should have thought we were, it puts you in the position of a convenience used and sent for whenever I had anything for you to set down for posterity. I dont like the picture it makes of either of us. It isnt a true picture either. I cant remember exactly when you asked my permission to keep a record of the best of our talks. But Im sure it was late in our lives. I invited you to visit me and I wrote to you many times before you could have been so self conscious about it all. I might have to search myself for my reason in singling you out for a conversation a year. I can tell you offhand I never chose you as a Boswell. Maybe I liked your awkwardness, naivete and spirituality. We wont strain for an answer.

Meeting Helen Thomas fresh from her experiment in reminiscences of someone else has probably helped me to my decision. You probably read her "As It Was" between her and Edward Thomas—suppressed in Boston. Its a good piece of work in a way, but it took a good of squirming on her part to justify it. I wondered if she wasnt in danger of making E T look ridiculous in the innocence she credited him with. Mightnt men laugh a manly laugh? E T was distinguished at his college at Oxford for the ribald folk songs he could entertain with—not to say smutty. Worse than As it Was are some other chapters in his life she has been undressing to the public since. In one she has him invite to the house a girl he has met and come home full of admiration of. She gives herself away by calling the girl "this paragon of women." But she finds the minute she sees her (how homely she is) that she can conquer her with magnanimity, or conquer her jealousy of her with magnanimity. All women are sisters that the same man loves, she tries to make herself think. Once in the woods listening to a nightengale in the dark E says to the two of them We are knowing, but the nightengale knows all. Then he kisses his wife and to keep the score even his wife makes him kiss the other woman. She pretends to think that is large and lovely but I happen to know it was a dose she was giving him and rubbing in. These things are hard to do sincerely. And unridiculously. In another chapter she has him carry her off to bed on his last leave of absence before going to the front. It reminds me of Schnitzler's Whatsername.*

No you'll have to forgive me and be as good friends as if nothing had ever happened, but it wont do. You'll have to reason our relationship on to a better footing than it has apparently been on lately. Lets not be too damned literary.

Really faithfully yours<br>Robert Frost

* Frost may be referring to the prostitute Leocadia who seduces a soldier in Arthur Schnitzler's play *Reigen* (*Hands Around* or *La Ronde*).

ALS, 2 pp.

## 79.

Dear Robert                    2 November 1928    Hanover

I liked your letter. And I don't feel that I have anything to forgive. That is because you and Alice convinced me that my book wasn't good enough, and that it did invite misinterpretation, and, even as sympathetically interpreted, showed a weakness in me that might as well be unpublished.

I can trust you, if anybody can be trusted, not to go to the extreme, and say you were wrong in liking me because a person who would be so worshipful must be a sucker. You won't make the easy mistake of suspecting that I *wanted* to be a *mere Boswell*, even though I was foolishly self-conscious. I haven't thought of either of us in the light of a convenience to the other, nor wanted you as capital. You know.

I should think you might see how I could feel you to be my best friend, and still *look up* to you. I won't even admit that looking up is all weakness, or silliness. But I am sorry I am so easily impressed that I capitulate too completely. On the other hand having been so admiring and affectionate toward you has made me confident in many natural tendencies and preferences I was born with, so to speak. And I believe it is partly deep kinship and not just impressionability that has drawn me to you so almost subordinately.

I think you will see no false tone in the essay about you I am just sending off to Dr. Thornton.*

Won't you come and see me first this time? If you can't, I want to come to you.

Affectionately   Sidney

* Richard H. Thornton, Ph.D. (1889?–1977): head of the trade department at Henry Holt and Company in 1928; president of the company, 1932–1938. Editor, *Recognition of Robert Frost: Twenty-fifth Anniversary* (Holt, 1937).

A L S, 4 pp.

# 80.

Dear Robert                         2 December 1928   Hanover

Thank you very much for the beautiful book. I could think of strong words and true ones, but they wouldn't be *good* enough, to say about the poems. I have had two or three very good times reading them aloud; and Father and Mother and Alice all liked them, each according to his kind. No kind of lover of any good kind of poetry can fail, I should think, to find something beautiful in "West-running Brook". Even those who want "beautiful beauty", as you call it, and those who want organ tones, or harps and flutes. And yet every poem has something no one could possibly be looking for, because it never existed before, and it was never clearly desired before. All of them are full of you, the same you that's in "A Boy's Will"; but "West-Running Brook" strikes new lodes as well as new notes, and frets new strings in readers. It does more than carry on.

I made a list of those I like best for the time being. And I'll tell you what they are, when you come up, if it makes any difference to you.

Do come. And if you must wait until your visit to the college, please manage to stay with us—part of the time if you can't all.

This snow will keep our Ford bound to this region until spring. And I want to see you and have meals with you and burn lights late with you before that.

Mr. Thornton pleased me by sending the new "Selected Poems". I'm glad of the additions, and glad they made so nice a book of it.

Did my earlier letter, saying you had not only persuaded but convinced me that my book wouldn't do, reach you? I'll do a better one some time, and in the meantime something else.

I hope Marjorie is much better, and that Mrs. Frost is well. We want her to come to see us, too, if possible.

Did Louis Untermeyer surprise you? He hadn't succeeded in making what-had-been non-existent, apparently. I wonder if he has lost any of his over-smartness. Will Mrs. Jean believe that she has got him now, and relax a little? I'd like to have a sight of Mrs. Virginia's mind.*

I'm listening for some news of a play by you.†

I think it was generous of you to let your friends have the "West-running Brook" poem. Joseph Conrad said, after he'd written several books, he was sure that his writing was done for friends. I use the word in his sense, I think.

Yours affectionately   Sidney Cox

* Untermeyer had been married to Jean Starr; divorced from her, he married Virginia Moore; after two years, he divorced Moore and remarried Starr.
† Either *A Way Out: A One Act Play* or *The Cow's in the Corn: A One-Act Irish Play*. Both were published in 1929.

ALS, 2 pp.

# 81.

[South Shaftsbury

Dear Sidney:           c. 17 December 1928]

I'm home from almost everywhere somewhat dazed. But that ought not to prevent me from telling you you did all right the second time. You did better than I deserve, but we wont let it trouble us. We'll accept unscrupulously the luck of the draw. You dig in with a stiff-lipped scoop.

Dont make me write any more now. Im sick with my third over-
lapping cold since the fog settled down on London. And I dont
know exactly where I am, out with a new book or at home with
the family.

I'll want to see you soon.            Ever yours   Robert Frost

you knew Brickel was going to make a book out of your article. It
made them all look at me with fresh eyes down there.*

* Herschel Brickell (b. 1889): head of the trade department at Henry Holt and Company
after Lincoln MacVeagh resigned, in 1923. The book is *Robert Frost: Original "Ordinary
Man"* (Holt, 1929).

ALS, 8 pp.

## 82.

[Franconia
Dear Sidney:                              c. 19 September 1929]
    I may want to write you two or three letters as I think over all
you came up here with yesterday—and I may not. One thing I will
write about at once that I didnt quite bring myself to talk about
face to face. It reaches me from many directions sometimes with
the kind of smile I don't care for and sometimes with an out-and-
out sneer that I am too much with you in the class room. I am sure
you have used me to your own hurt at Dartmouth. I'd just like to
see what leaving me entirely out of it for a year or two would do—
not severely alone and out of it but just gently and unobtrusively
out of it, so that no one would notice the omission till some day
toward the end of the two years someone uncommonly observing
should wake up and exclaim "Let's see! Whats become of Frost in
this course?" I doubt if our friends, wives, children, or even ourselves are to be looked on as resources in classroom work. Off-
hand you might think it was an advantage in teaching contemporary literature to be personally acquainted with me. On the
contrary it is a great disadvantage in my way of looking at it. I
keeps you from talking about me as modestly as you could talk
about Mrs William Rose Benet [Elinor Wylie] for instance. Everybody knows something has to be kept back for pressure and to

anybody puzzled to know what I should suggest that for a beginning it might as well be his friends, wife, children, and self. That would be the part of *mature* wisdom. Poetry is measured in more senses than one: it is measured feet but more important still it is a measured amount of all we could say an we would. We shall be judged finally by the delicacy of our feeling of where to stop short. The right people know, and we artists should know better than they know. There is no greater fallacy going than that art is expression—an undertaking to tell all to the last scrapings of the brain pan. I neednt qualify as a specialist in botany and astronomy for a license to invoke flowers and stars in my poetry. I needn't have scraped those subjects to the point of exhaustiveness. God forbids that I should have to be an authority on anything even the psyche before I can set up for an artist. A little of anything goes a long way in art. Im never so desperate for material that I have to trench on the confidential for one thing, nor on the private for another nor on the personal, nor in general on the sacred. A little in the fist to manipulate is all I ask. My object is true form—is was and always will be—form true to any chance bit of true life. Almost any bit will do. I dont naturally trust any other object. I fight to be allowed to sit cross-legged on the old flint pile and flake a lump into an artifact. Or if I dont actually fight myself, the soldiers of my tribe do for me to keep the unsympathetic off me and give me elbow room. The best hour I ever had in the class room was good only for the shape it took. I like an encounter to shape up, unify however roughly. There is such a thing as random talk, but it is to be valued as a scouting expedition for coinable gold. I may say this partly to save myself from being misunderstood; I say it partly too to help you what I can toward your next advance in thought if not in office. You'll find yourself most effective in things people find out by accident you might have said but didnt say. Those are the things that make people take a good reestimating look at you. You have to refrain from saying many things to get credit for refraining from a few. There is a discouraging waste there as everywhere else in life. But never mind: there is a sense of strength gained in not caring. You feel so much in in having something to yourself. You have added to the mass of your private in

reserve. You are more alluring to your friends and baffling to your
foes.

Ever yours you know,
Robert Frost.


ALS, 2 pp.

## 82.A.

Dear Sidney                    19 September 1929    Franconia
Take another letter in the same envelope.
You may have been right in having searched yourself and in having helped others search you for certainties. You may be the better
in what comes next for having gone into yourself as you have. But
you will be wrong if you continue in that phase to forty. Your help-
less immersion in the phase proves your reality. But all this to-do
about it must make you too self-conscious for reality. You are in
transition plainly. You could only turn backward on principal
from obstinate policy. Onward is into a phase more objective. This
is all that is critical in your situation. You are perfectly right about
a lot of things. There is no knowledge without thinking. Stick to
that. You have them there. The kind of person who would know
what was good in literature—that is the person we aim to cultivate. How I like to hear you say such things. Fight it out on those
lines. But dont compromise a good cause with personalities.

R.F.


ALS, 1 p.

## 83.

Amherst now for three months
Dear Sidney:                    [c. 19 November 1930]
Thats a good letter—a fine letter—free from non-essentials.
Why dont we use sheer poems oftener for letters? It might be good
for the poems.
I didnt get you up to see me at Woodsville. The uninvited

crowded in on me to the exclusion of the invited. I must see you before long.

The ordeal of addressing the alumni trustees and faculty has just been barely survived by

Yours always
Robert Frost.

TLS, 1 p.

# 84.

Dear Robert                        22 March 1931    Hanover

Louis Untermeyer brought us very bad news about Marjory, and told us you have been having a rather wretched winter. I am very sorry about Marjory. It's all dreadfully too bad.*

I am going to New York for a few days next week: and I'd like to stop off and see you Monday (the thirtieth) if it is a suitable time. I'll take you somewhere for a meal, and after we have talked I will go to a hotel in order to save bother for Mrs. Frost. If the time of my return, Tuesday, April seventh, will be more convenient, I can stop over a train or so then.

You know without my saying it that in proportion as I particularly want this trip to include seeing you I would not want the mere fact that I am going back to press a visit if the time happened to be wrong for you. You say.

Yours    Sidney

[Handwritten note on this letter from Robert Frost]
Mrs Sidney Cox
Dartmouth College
Hanover N.H.

Just got Sidneys letter—Can you get word to him I am at The Holley, Washington Square New York.                        R.F.

---

* Marjorie, Frost's favorite daughter, was ill with tuberculosis in 1929. Sent to Colorado, she married Willard E. Fraser there in 1933. A year later, after giving birth to a daughter, Marjorie died of puerperal fever.

ALS, 2 pp.

## 85.

[South Shaftsbury
Dear Sidney:                              c. 1 October 1931]
    I have a vague recollection of your having asked me in a letter
sometime this summer not to pity you. Dear Sidney you're a joke.
Why didnt you offer to bargain: you wouldnt pity me if I wouldnt
pity you. What could have put pity into your head unless it was
that you were feeling pitiful. Pity you? You dont get me. Damn it I
blame you: I dont pity you. I blame you for letting the basteds in
on you by inviting (not just incurring) their criticism of your
teaching. Thats all; and its not much though its a good deal. So
forget it. Only remember that as a grown-up man whose further
improvement is your own private affair, it becomes you to look
and act and speak henceforth when anybody starts to take you to
task as I do now, it becomes you, I say, to look and act and speak
as if you couldnt permit of personalities. Keep the basteds out.
Forbid them. I know you're one of the best of teachers. You know
it. Never again ask any one to say that at least you do the children
no harm. Bless the children anyway. I wish you could write and
talk with them less in mind—them and their teachers and their
teachers' teachers. Let's think mostly of the non-school world. The
worlds a stage not an academy Shakespeare says.
                                        Ever yours
                                        R.F.

We're just back from seeing Marj at Boulder Colorado and Carol
& Lillian settled at Monrovia California.


ALS, 9 pp.

## 86.

[Amherst
Dear Sidney:                              c. 30 March 1932]
    You got what you wanted a dossier; which I suppose wont seem
complete without a word from me.
    They say what you teach is subsumed in what they teach.

You might say what they teach is subsumed in what you teach.

Then the President ought to say what is better to leave subsumed, what is subsumed in your teaching or what is subsumed in theirs.

Nobody seems to say definitely enough what the thing is that with them is implied with you brought to the surface.

Of course it is Responses.

Nobody seems to say definitely enough what the thing is that you imply and they bring to the surface.

Of course it is records on paper or on the mind. With them everything must be cited or quoted. Every idea must be put in the mouth of an authority. The most they presume to be themselves is authorities on authorities. There is this to be said for their way, that they gain a certain objectivity by putting everything off on someone else ahead or above them. It is the same objectivity I gain by putting everything into the mouths of characters. Only mine are characters while theirs are authorities.

We won't scorn records. But responses are better than records because [they] include records and much besides.

Let's see what responses are. They are the same to things read that they are in conversation to things said. First of all they are witty and spirited. They abound in metaphor and analogy. They throw light on, they enlarge on, they create diversions from, they go off at tangents from, they make unexpected play with, whatever offers. They are insights and associations. They are more additional than subtractive though they may well be both. And they are addressed more to the subject-matter than to the form.

I speak of them as they go in good company.

But there is this about them: they are so much a matter of luck and excitement that I should be as hesitant in announcing a course in them as I should be in announcing one in love and friendship. I should be sure they would happen in my classes and your class much oftener than in most classes. But I should want something like sandwiches and tea and cigarettes to lie low with and pretend I wasnt waiting for anything in particular in the hours when responses refused to be. Inspiration is too delicate a thing to talk much about. So is giving birth to ideas, not to mention babies.

You have been influenced by me a little in past years. I wish you would be guided by me outright and not want to give a course in the artistic mind. What you mean is responses. That's what you and I are good at and that cant be advertised in a college catalogue. Any plain-sounding course we give will be one in responses. And we can't help ourselves. It's too large a subject for any one year. Narrow it down for modesty. A course in Shakespeare's periods and commas. A course in the final couplet in Shakespeares sonnets. Call it anything definite (but of course honest and real) and then ho for a good time. I had one of the best hours I ever had in a class last week over the scene in Richard III where three citizens meet and talk about the death of Edward and the succession of a child to the throne.

All I'm saying is that you dont have to put your kind of teaching forward. On the contrary you can afford to keep it more or less under a bushel basket and it will shine through the weaving. Shrink a little from declaring inspiration. Call your course Merely Coleridge Merely Byron and then let it speak for itself with the years.

I know what I'm leaving out of account. All the responses you ever encourage, all the responses the classes become conscious of having, will make no impression in the department examinations. Your boys can't get credit for quoting as I can from factitious authorities. As Duns Scotus once said in his cups and saucers. Well not everything can be solved. Stick to developing responses and let who will be sodden. You may have to die for your cause. I am resigned.

For gods' sake don't ever let the word Responses loose in a class room. Have them in all their variety but name not their dread name.

And remember that the best of them are beautiful and the second best true. A lot of people aspiring in art waste their lives on truth in the mistaken idea that it is the same thing as beauty. Then they wonder why they have missed being poets or appreciators of poetry. They have missed by the hair or mile that divides beauty from truth.

"Processes" is below the belt. You arent interested in processes but in responses at the level of the work of art under consideration.

And so I might talk on.

Ever yours

RF.  over

Your story about Frazers Golden Bough and Brownings poems is a grand one. I know one on them that doesnt match it. A teacher says, says he, "The only defect of Lowes Road to Zanadu is that it is about two very insignificant poems. If it had been about Gulliver's Travels now, it would have been some thing." "What would it have been?" "The study of a real mind." "You mean an artists mind?" "A great artists mind." That fresh from the Ph.D. Dept of Harvard.

ALS, 2 pp.

# 87.

Dear Robert                    15 April 1932   Hanover

I just had a nice hour with James Thompson [Thomson] and Coventry Patmore. Yesterday with another class it was Andrew Marvell and James Shirley. I usually have poets or pieces of prose as points of reference and departure. You didn't think I'd give a course on the artistic mind without? Your letter was full of good things and a good person. I have liked it twice.

This time I'm writing on business; and it has nothing to do with me. A while ago Miss Mary Walsh, Editor of the Children's Book Department of Houghton Mifflin Company, wrote to ask me if I'd read the proof of a little book on "Writing Poetry", and if I liked it say so.* She said she would also like to have you see it, and say something of it in a letter, if you liked it. Did I think you would be willing, she wanted to know. I wrote her that though I was suspicious of such books as she described, and hardly ever had liked one, I would read it. I said of course I couldn't speak for you, at all; but that, if I liked it when I saw it, I would broach the question to you.

I have read it, and found that Miss Gilchrist knows a great deal more precisely about poetry than most I have read or heard talk about it, and that she writes in such possession of her thought that what the reader has in his bones comes to her asistance. I liked it better than most things I have read on poetry. It is short; and intelligent fifteen-year-olds could read it; and yet I don't think the Children's Book Department is the place for it. People like Auslander, who was up here to disgrace himself and poetry, by vacuity, last week, lack much that it contains.[†]

Many of the verses, which I hope it is the editor and not Miss Gilchrist who is responsible for using to stuff out the book, are pretty trivial and toddling. The book would be worth much more if only the few best were used to show what members of the Cleveland Library Stevenson Room Poetry Group can do. Miss Gilchrist has charge of that room.

I told the editor I would tell you I like the book, and that if I didn't hear from you in about ten days I'd conclude you hadn't time for it, and return the proof to her, though I hoped you'd look at it. I also told her that the several references to, or quotations from things you have said about writing poetry, in Miss Gilchrist's book, might deter you from comment, but that I'd tell you none of the references was in any sense an estimate of you. Shall I send the proof?                    Yours affectionately   Sidney Cox

[*] Marie Gilchrist (b. 1893): wrote *Writing Poetry: Suggestions for Young Writers*, published by Houghton Mifflin (1932).
[†] Joseph Auslander (1897–1965): collaborated with Frank Ernest Hill on a history of poetry for young people, *The Winged Horse*, published by Doubleday Doran (1928).

ALS, 5 pp.

# 88.

                                                Amherst
Honestly Sidney                                 [c. 19 April 1932]
    You are getting out of hand. I'm afraid you aren't going to let yourself be unduly influenced by me any more.
    I grow surer I don't want to search the poet's mind too seriously.

I might enjoy threatening to for the fun of it just as I might to frisk his person. I have written to keep the over curious out of the secret places of my mind both in my verse and in my letters to such as you. A subject has to be held clear outside of me with struts and as it were set up for an object. A subject must be an object. There's no use in laboring this further years. My objection to your larger book about me was that it came thrusting in where I did not want you. The idea is the thing with me. It would seem soft for instance to look in my life for the sentiments in the Death of the Hired Man. There's nothing to it believe me. I should fool you if you took me so. I'll tell you my notion of the contract you thought you had with me. The objective idea is all I ever cared about. Most of my ideas occur in verse. But I have always had some turning up in talk that I feared I might never use because I was too lazy to write prose. I think they have been mostly educational ideas connected with my teaching, actually lessons. That's where I hoped you would come in. I thought if it didnt take you too much from your own affairs you might be willing to gather them for us both. But I never reckoned with the personalities. I keep to a minimum of such stuff in any poets life and works. Art and wisdom with the body heat out of it. You speak of Shirley. He is two or three great poems—one very great. He projected, he got, them out of his system and I will not carry them back into his system either at the place they came out of or at some other place. I state this in the extreme. But relatively I mean what I say. To be too subjective with what an artist has managed to make objective is to come on him presumptuously and render ungraceful what he in pain of his life had faith he had made graceful.

Leave us look at the Gilchrist book. I am curious to see where it touches me.                                              Ever yours   RF.


ALS, 3 pp.

## 89.

[Amherst
Dear Sidney:                                          c. April 1932]

Pay no attention to me unless to figure from what I say the kind you are and want to be still more. I can see, though dimly, that you like the blows you have had at Dartmouth and are somewhat disappointed that I dont like them too. It's not that my element is not injustice as much as yours is; only my nature demands it further up the stream among the rocks and at the spring, yours seems satisfied to bathe further down where the stream is muddied with school or city politics. I'm trout and you're pickerel. Nothing invidious intended. I dont care to be personally observed in a soiled medium. Personally personally—there it is again. Even you dont know and never will know where I get the sense of injustice most in life to keep me living. A lot of injustice will never have the satisfaction of knowing I know it exists. Some of it I make fun of, when it is called comedy. For instance when I am sometimes unjustly praised I accept it as making up for the other times when I have been unjustly blamed. Such is comedy. The only other way to take injustice is the way of tragedy. There I maintain my mystery for no one to pluck the heart out of.—But as I say pay no attention to me.

I forget what I was to do with Miss Gilchrists book. I wasnt asked for a testimonial was I? That's another thing I keep out of from a distrust of myself in the realm of politics. I can tell you I have no objection to the way I am brought into the book. It does all right by me. I mean it comes as near what I have said as I could expect and will ask. The book is mildly good and I should think harmless.—I've been giving it another look before mailing, and I think the book is in a fine spirit. I wish it well. What more do you want me to say?

Ever yours
Robert Frost

ALS, 2 pp.

## 90.

Amherst
Dear Sidney:                              [c. 15 June 1932]
It's too bad, but I shall be in California by that time. We leave South Shaftsbury on June 22nd and shant be back east till November 1st. I should have liked visiting your College, seeing your crowd and seeing you. We haven't had anything but letters for

some time and I'm afraid mine to you have been tyranically preaching. Dont worry about my worrying about you. You know what to do when anyone comes on you too overwhelming as I said to them in my poem at Columbia the other day.*

Ever yours

Robert Frost

* Frost, as Phi Beta Kappa poet, read his political pastoral, "Build Soil," at Columbia University, May 24, 1932.

ALS, 5 pp.

## 91.

Dear Sidney:                    24 October 1933    South Shaftsbury

Things that did themselves have crowded out the things that needed us to do them. I'm dazed to think how long ago I promised to have you here or up to Franconia. I dont know how you are, but I'm so constituted that I dont seem to mind being neglected by people I am sure feel all right toward me. What do you say to coming down Saturday this week and going back Sunday?—unless you have a football game to keep you.—Be careful what you say against football or any other college athletics. I think that as they are taken so poetry should be taken and not otherwise. So I look on them as a model for our kind and a reproach to the other kind of teachers. But I will excuse you from football this week since it will be me you are deserting it for. Come if you can and will. Come as a friend and equal and dont trouble your head or silly old diary with trying to decide which wants to see the other more. I didnt mean exactly what you thought I did when years ago I was so incautious as to suggest that you might like to turn to account some of the theories of school, life, and art I let fall in talk but was too lazy ever probably to use in writing myself. You took it that I was asking to be Boswellized. That has hurt our relationship a shade if you will forgive my saying so. I meant something the most unpersonal. I shouldnt mind a word of credit for an idea of course. A fellow named Gordon Chalmers recently got his doctors degree for a Thesis on Thomas Browne and Metaphor at Harvard that really owed a lot more to me than he was generous enough to declare.* You'd never treat me that way. In my judgement you wouldnt be treating me much better if you went to the other extreme and brought my name and ways in every other word. Some time you might solve for me the problem of how I was going to tell the world the principles upon which I had composed. I shrink from prefaces as you know. Once in a while it comes over me to wish some friend would do my explaining for me. It shouldnt take much and it might better be based on my talk in general than on particular rambling talks with me. Im just now more or less in trouble with well intentioned people who want to publish stenographic reports of my so called lectures in New York at the New School. The objection is the same. I dont want the picturesque setting and charms or uncharms of me. I want the ideas rounded out and rounded up into something more formal than I care to take the responsibility for myself. Enough of this. You'll gather from it more or less why I was against the larger book you sent me for approval. Either the ideas for the ideas' sake and without the dirt and dross of me or no book at all ever while I live or after I die. Try to please me. Gee lets enjoy life. Come for the fun of it when you come.

Ever yours   Robert Frost

* Gordon Keith Chalmers (1904–1956): became president of Rockford College, in Illinois, in 1934, and Frost participated in the inaugural ceremonies. (Lesley Frost had obtained a teaching position at Rockford in 1931.) Later Chalmers was appointed president of Kenyon College in Gambier, Ohio.

ALS, 7 pp.

## 92.

[South Shaftsbury

Dear Sidney:                                    c. 9 July 1934]

   I'm proud of you for a book like that.* Let's see them beat it. It's all front-line stuff and shows how far forward you fight. The little booms are good writing. Where did you find Cooley? He's a real find. I have always admired that book of his, though I doubt if I would ever have had the courage to propose him thus boldly. But

then I am not an anthologist-critic and not trained up to the responsibilities of one. I marvel at Louis Untermeyer in his advocacy
of such as Merrill Moore. What nerve! I should be much surer in
public about Cooley. In private I should be absolutely sure. Two or
three of your names are new to me, I'm grateful to say, and many
of the pieces. It is all honestly fresh material—so different from
some anthologies we know of that merely make themselves out of
prior anthologies. The George Moore has always been a favorite
memory of mine. I happen at this moment to be reading Paul
Elmer More's Socrates in the Shelburne Papers. He's one I've too
long postponed. As far as I've got, I admire your representations
entirely. If I had a word of fault to find it might be for Evelyn
Scott's ineffably old-south feminine snobbish dirt on Grant.[†] Gee
what a painfully great man she makes of Lee. How does she know
that Grant looked hard at Lee and Lee averted his eyes? All you
have to do is read Grants Memoirs to prove he was a very modest
man to whom the situation of the surrender at Appomattox must
have been as embarrassing as to any northern gentleman. I will not
venture to speak for the southern gentleman. That's just the way
the likes of Evelyn Scott would have tried to work herself up to
speak of you or me Sidney. I think it amounts to a betrayal of our
class for you to encourage her. Take Grant's coat she makes so
much of. It wasn't the ill fitting finery she makes out. It was a common private's coat with two chevrons of three stars each merely
pinned on it to show his rank for business purposes—a carelessly
assumed uniform I suppose to go to meet the truly great in. I
doubt if it was chosen to humiliate anybody. Everything of evidence Grant did to Lee showed the noblest consideration of defeat. American History shouldn't be written by women novelists
with English sympathies for the arrogant old slave-holding days.
Your people were probably abolitionists. Mine were not: so I
would have more excuse than you for letting the south have its
way about what kind of people on both sides fought the war and
whether or not it was to free the slaves. Some southerners have
been saying lately (and allowed to get away with it) that the war
was waged by the industrial north to put down agriculture. The
fact is it was the agricultural middle west that licked the agri-

cultural south. The civil war wasnt the smallest incident in the world wide industrial revolution of the last century. Lee and Grant ought to be done together some time for the contrast in generalship more than in clothes and graces. Lee was the tragic figure of a fighter who never saw anything beyond winning battles. His vision wasn't large enough for a whole war or even campaign. His dispositions for battle were beautiful. His two great divisions under Longstreet and Jackson were like pistols in his two hands, so perfectly could he handle them. But ask yourself where he could have thought he was going when he set off on the raids that ended at Antietam and Gettysburg. What was he doing when he let Grant come on victory by victory cleaning up the west till the war was lost before ever he had to encounter him for the final show down? He was the great man of the south. He should have taken it upon himself to think and act on the grand strategy of the whole front from Vicksburg to Richmond. Say he didnt have Jefferson Davis with him. He should have had by force and persuasion. Grant had to teach Lincoln Halleck Stanton and the rest of them. The war was one great turning movement grasped as such, first by the mind of Grant and altogether and step by step his in execution. You may not like generals in general, but you have to concede him rank with the greatest our race has had. The World War brought out nobody to match him. I am touched by Lee, so noble in character, so brilliant and punishing a smiter in the field, but so lost in the larger things of statesmanship and strategy. He was not large enough to see the United States. I suspect he was merely romantic beyond a certain point of mentality. I suspect him of a secret resolve never to set foot outside of his native state but to have it out in Virginia win or lose. Otherwise he might well have gone to deal with Grant before he had assumed such proportions. He must have realized however dimly by the time Grant got to Chatanooga that where Grant was the war was. But he had registered a vow with himself perhaps in consistancy when he gave up all the states for a few of the states that he would really never be devoted to any state but one. He was parochial. He couldnt see largely. I might even represent him in a whole novel, if I wrote history that way, as valuing himself for his loyalty to the First Families of Virginia alone. In which connection, I may add, that my friend J. J. Lankes has been such a success with his woodcuts in Virginia that he has been honored with a chance of being listed in a book of the First Families of Virginia for the sum of five dollars. He was born of German parentage in Gardenville near Buffalo New York and has earned much of his living illustrating tomato cans. I cant see that his Virginian honors have turned his head.

All this merely to amuse you and distract me from our sorrow.[‡] I'll tell you a short story for your third book when you get to it. Oh I do think it the most wonderful short story I ever read. It has everything. It is called A.V. Laider. Max Beerbohn wrote it.

Where are you in the near future?

Ever yours<br>R.F.

* *Prose Preferences, Second Series* (1934) was an entirely new collection, edited by Cox and Edmund Freeman, which included "Life and the Student," by Charles Horton Cooley (1864–1929), a sociologist at the University of Michigan.

†Merrill Moore (1903–1957): poet and psychiatrist; was later consulted by Frost in order to help Carol Frost. The George Moore essay is "Cycling With AE"; the Evelyn Scott essay is "Two Generals."

‡Marjorie Frost had died on May 2, 1934.

ALS, 2 pp.

## 93.

Dear Robert                                    18 July 1934    Albany

I'm pleased that you like *Prose Preferences* again. Evidently my request to my former student who is editing *The New Mexico Quarterly* that he send you a copy of that obscure journal containing the essay I wrote at *his* request was not complied with. Do you mind reading the essay in manuscript? *

The people who aren't afraid to die and who keep firm and sweet to the very end are the most terribly missed I should suppose. Marjory left irrefutable good memories behind. Even for me she is one of the proofs of what a human being can sometimes be, a quiet fortifier of whatever tendency there may be in me to be hard to overwhelm or to embitter. She was one, I think, who protected her sensibility and fineness, and preserved it, not by a shell but by secreting a mineral atom in every forming cell. Her words that Carol told me, "Death isn't sad; it's beautiful" sound with authority. I should like to grow to understand them.

I think I shall be going up to Hanover for the week-end, or part of it, Friday the twenty-eighth. How would it be for me to stop a few hours at South Shaftsbury Sunday afternoon, the thirtieth— Alice too—? Or to go to South Shaftsbury by bus on Friday and let Alice get me there Saturday? Other week-ends I could get in some hours with you, as far as my plans are concerned, are the week-ends starting August 4—Friday, and August 11. After the 15th I'm going to be at Cummington, again. I want to see you some time this summer when you want to see me and are free.

I'm having a great time getting my class to present plays of Shakespeare, rehearsing an act each afternoon, or, now with Hamlet, taking all the parts myself. And my writing class goes animatedly, too.

I've seen and liked three poems of yours since last I saw you.

Affectionately,<br>Sidney

* "New England and Robert Frost," *The New Mexico Quarterly Review* 4 (May 1934): 89–94.

ALS, 4 pp.

## 94.

Dear Sidney,                          10 March [1935]   Key West

It is nearly time for us to start home. I hope you'll have an early spring for us up there. We leave Key West on the 28th and plan to stay in Washington a week or so on our way north. O! I shall be so glad to get home. This is a wonderful climate, and it has done wonders for Robert—and I am very glad of that, but it seems alien to me. Robert is planning to go to Hanover sometime after we get home. Perhaps he hasn't answered your young friend's letter, but I know he intends to go.

There is a young married woman here, who has written quite a good deal, who wants very much to go to Yaddo this summer. She doesn't know Mrs. Ames' full name and address, and I offered to write and ask you for that information, so she could send in her application. Her name is Jenny Ballou. Her husband is the statistician of the F.E.R.A. project here. You know Key West has been taken over by the United States government, and is ruled by a dictator. It is an experiment in state socialism, I think. This girl is a Russian, brought to this country by her parents at the age of two. I don't know just what she has published, but Robert has seen and liked some of her writing in manuscript—a part of a novel. Her husband is a New Englander.

I hope you and Alice and the children have been well this winter. That was a fine picture you sent at Christmas time. Carroll, Lillian and Prescott have been down here in Key West, and have been in splendid health.* Lesley and her little girls have been well and happy out near Chicago, where Lesley is teaching in Rockford College. Little Jacky, Irma's boy, has been sick a good deal through the winter. Well—please give our love to Alice, and also our love to yourself.

Elinor Frost

Will you kindly answer this by a short note at once, Sidney, as I told this girl I would write you some time ago.   E.F.

* Frost's son married Lillian LaBatt in 1923; their son William Prescott Frost was born in 1924.

ALS, 3 pp.

## 95.

Dear Mrs Frost                    15 March 1935   Hanover
    I am writing the same day that your letter came—it was good hearing from you.
    The Executive Secretary of Yaddo is: Mrs. Elizabeth Ames and Yaddo, Saratoga Springs New York is her address. I was appointed adviser again this year but haven't yet been asked to comment on any applicant. If I hear from Mrs. Ames again I will speak well of Mrs. Jenny Ballou. Meanwhile she will write to Mrs. Ames.

I don't see any reform that can make climatic sauce for the gander equally sauce for the goose. I'm sorry you weren't done wonders for by the Florida sunshine and ocean air, too. It begins to look possible that I shall go to Nashville, Tennessee for a year, on leave from Dartmouth, and so give Alice the much needed sauce of a winter that doesn't congeal her marrow and test the marvelous unbeatableness of her nature. The initiative comes from John Crowe Ransom.* I wonder if Robert caused his awareness of me.

I've been waiting all my letters till I know whether Doubleday Doran is going to take my novel or not. They've had it three months, and not a chirp since, after one month, they said it was being read.

Arthur just brought home his H in hockey, and now he's all agog with tennis. Barbie is almost a young lady, and a witty and charming one. Wumpie thrives and is a clog sometimes on his mother's feet.

I thought I was stopping. But I remember Dick Lauterbach asked me to ask you to get Robert to let him know as soon as he can just when he will be ready to speak at Dartmouth, so that he can reserve and announce the date.†

It's just settled that, Albany not having me on their list, I am to teach at Cummington all summer, with my mornings reservable for writing. I've been having many good hours here with classes— and one public lecture—this winter.

Alice sends her love. And so do I to you both.

Sidney Cox

---

*John Crowe Ransom (1888–1974): poet, New Critic, professor, founding editor of *Fugitive* (1922–1925) and *Kenyon Review* (1939–1959).

†Richard Edward Lauterbach (1914–1950): Dartmouth '35, edited the undergraduate humor magazine, *Jack-O-Lantern*.

ALS, 3 pp.

# 96.

Dear Robert                                    19 April 1935   Hanover

Thank you very much for "Three Poems". Ever since I was showed one in the passageway to the Library outside the printing room I've hoped I'd get one. I like the poem about the orchid hunt. And few juvenilia, in the backs of huge volumes, are as good as the other two. I don't feel a clear preference for Kiplings "forget" poem, if it is one of his most famous.

Your Christmas gift poem about "Two Tramps in Mud Time" is about the most deeply and variously satisfying thing I've read new this year. You get more levels of meaning for me than I often find. It is right in all the ways, delightfully. And I specially rejoice in the social implications, the constructive, exhilarating, practical challenge.

You know, I'm lucky. Most of the time my "work" feels to me "play for mortal stakes". That word *play* with its three values is a third strike in the seventh inning, when bases are full, two out, and our side one ahead.

Harold Rugg had a fine two-window exhibit of your books and booklets, letters, manuscripts, in the foyer of the library on your birthday. He didn't have the two or three prose things I have. But he had both English *and American* first editions, and the play poem.

Reading in the *Times* your birthday letter was almost as good as having one straight from you. How well "the mischief" lasts!

I'm going down to South Hadley the fourth of May to help judge their poetry contest. Maybe I could see you the following evening—Sunday.

Herb West, who has written a book about Cunningham Graham [Robert Cunninghame Graham], and other things, and who is a good, virile, thoughtful person and admires you, is eager to meet you when you're up here. Shall I arrange an evening dinner with him and Stearns and Ramon Guthrie, poet and novelist and my friend? * Or shall it be just you and Herb and I? I hope you will stay at least two days. I wish I had room to put you up.

Dick Lauterbach says you joked of suggestions for a topic. It would please me—though I'll be hard to affect in any other way—if your lecture should include some reference to a relation between poetry and the chance for life of share-croppers and half-starved farmers and men without a job.

Whatever your plans and engagements be sure to save some hours and if possible an evening for me.

Yours affectionately<br>Sidney Cox

---

\* Herbert Faulkner West (1898–1974): writer, book collector, Dartmouth assistant professor of comparative literature in 1935. Ramon Guthrie (1896–1973): Dartmouth assistant professor of French in 1935.

[A handwritten, initialed copy of "Happiness Makes Up in Height for What It Lacks in Length" was included with this letter. There are three differences between this version and the final one, which appears in *The Poetry of Robert Frost*: 1) line 16: "The hours went clearly on" becomes "The day swept clearly on" in the final version, 2) line 19: "*may*" is not italicized in the final version, and 3) the last two lines of the poem are reversed in the final version.]

ALS, 3 pp.

## 97.

[Cambridge, Massachusetts?]

Dear Sidney:                                    29 March 1936

It's getting near my next book, book six [*A Further Range*], and I havent sent you the advance poems from it that I promised you. All sorts of things got through the line on me and stopped me in my tracks. You have to remember Im a family man a professor, a farmer, a lecturer a contributor to magazines a publisher, author and a diner-out when I am where they have dinners. I am also as I forgot to say a resorter northward for hayfever and southward for influenza. I think I keep my head pretty well in all this for such an old slow coach, but I dont always keep my promises, especially when it is more to my advantage to keep them than not to keep them. But I dont need to go into my analysis with you who know me better than you used to anyway.

And now if I want to send you a poem in manuscript to make it mean anything it will have to be from my book after the next or from book seven. I always have something back when I go to press so I wont feel too cleaned out or drawn down. I once saw a spider like Robert the Bruce. Only my spider came half way down from the roof of a church and there he had to stop and secrete some more web before he could let himself down the rest of the way to the floor and the lesson he taught was different from the lesson the spider taught Robert the Bruce. Dont attempt anymore than you have secretions for! And some to share.

I have really been on the point several times of sitting down to write you out Departmental and The White-tailed Hornet and Woodwards Gardens and A Record Stride but just then came a letter from my editor demanding manuscript and what was the use of sending you what you would so soon see in print?

But on the other side of this I am going to copy out for you one it will give me some satisfaction to share with you because it is fairly new and I want a friend in on it. It is not to new for that and it is not too old for that. It is in a betwixt-and-between state— where I possibly enjoy a poem most.

I am working hard for me. I am spurting. For once in a way it can do me no harm. There seems always some new situation for the adventurer. My health seems to stand it. Elinor is my chief anxiety. She has to stay out of much that goes on—not out of all.*

Have you any news? You must have seen a lot of water go by.

Ever yours
R.F.

Plus

Happiness Makes Up in Height for What It Lacks in Length.

> Oh stormy stormy world
> The days you were not swirled
> Around with mist and cloud,
> Or wrapped as in a shroud,
> And the sun's brilliant ball
> Was not in part or all
> Obscured from mortal view,
> Were days so very few
> I can but wonder whence

I get the lasting sense
Of so much warmth and light.
If my mistrust is right,
It may be altogether
From one day's perfect weather
When starting clear at dawn,
The hours went clearly on
To finish clear at eve.
I verily believe
My fair impression *may*
Be all from one fair day
No shadow crossed but ours
As through its blazing flowers
For change of solitude
We went from house to wood.

R.F.

\* Elinor Frost had been ill with "a severe attack of grippe" when she first arrived in Cambridge, where Frost was Charles Eliot Norton Professor of Poetry at Harvard in the spring of 1936. In October 1937 she was operated on for cancer.

ALS, 5 pp.

## 98.

[Hanover
31 March 1936]
One day before All Fools
Vacation at Dartmouth

Dear Robert

I seem to have a good deal of adventure, too. In classes, in interchange with former as well as present students, in downs and ups of writing, and at home. But next to none are directly reportable. And I've continued all this year on the verge, apparently, of reportable news about the novel that gets liked and praised and labeled sure of publication and thumbed down. It's because I've been waiting for the up thumb that I haven't written to ask you to send me a *Collected Poems* and the little verse play.

Meanwhile I've done some good chapters on my second novel and had teaching hours when I was amazed at the buds opening red and green and yellow up and down what had been dry sticks.

It surprises me still how much new pleasure there is for me in your poems when I see them in print after I have heard you read them. How can a man of your years be so sly and full of caper if he knows the worst? That, I judge, is a dilemma that sticks sober fellows and window-ripened maids and makes them try not to look at you, like undernourished country kids staring at something commonplace for reassurance when a dazzling horseless carriage happened by the school.

One thing, if the conscientious poetry experts wax solemn over smaller people whose strangeness is not at all profound, intelligent and humorous people who keep poetry in its place and when irritated push it to the wall behind the toy chest along with trimmings from old hats—people like Alice (who hears too much of 'modern art' and of 'reforming the world' and of poetry, and all but brags of her indifference) can't leave your poems alone, can't help remembering lines while working in the garden, can't keep from exclaiming at how nice and funny the poems are, can't conceal her feeling that you know, are really wise.

I'm just saying that one of the ways you have the right to feel you're an exception is that you get on your side the tough-minded, down-to-earth people who leave the earnest artists, the eager social thinkers, the professionally thoughtful severely alone in their devotee-surrounded queerness. Such a lot of modern verse is either the Rosicrucianism camp-following modern physics and psychology or the Crazyrooshianism that would impose an intellectual signet of Marxism on all the unpredictableness and new-possibility of America.

If enough people get enough looks through your eyes and feel fibres in themselves that they hadn't dared to think were there, America won't have to choose between Fascism and Communism. But if the smart (enough to be in Dartmouth and to brag that in ten years they will have their $10,000 a year) keep on using their brains to get and keep the lion's share and find no way to gamble except in other people's security I'd be glad to see enough concerted anger to reduce all of them to one apiece. Most of them don't count 1000 with me. And the few who do, either communists or other honest imaginative persons, only ask to count as one. I'm sick of men owning power plants, mines and the means of growing and making. I'd be glad to have all except the heirs demand that such resources belong to all of us. Then let's see who can make best, grow best. Plenty of incentive there.

Don Bartlett and I did a word dance together over your being called back as a very special honored teacher in your second college [Harvard]. There's nothing left in education but being called to Cambridge or Oxford, and I'd rather you stayed an American teacher. What I'd still like is for educational theorists to be forced to perceive that it doesn't require a magic—called genius—completely denied to bread-and-butter-earning teachers, to have something of the fun and adventure and naturalness and being real in teaching that they have to acknowledge in yours. But as long as we say each real teacher must make his own way they will counter, Yes, geniuses teaching very exceptional students. But most people trying to go their own way, they will keep on saying, just naturally go wrong. And I'll concede to them just before April Fool's Day that if one is part fool, too large a part, his gambling on being real may look less successful than what Ben Pressy, chairman, says our department does: think the right thing the safe thing, the safe thing the conventional thing, and therefore distrust all variation and adventure.* That was apropos an asked-for full description of my writing course.

Yours,<br>Sidney Cox

P.S. We—especially Alice—got all the flood excitement we could out of: listening to Johnstown and Springfield and Hartford on the radio; going down to watch the Connecticut rise against the basement windows in Lewistown—between here and Norwich, you know—going to Wilder to see it suck below its own surface level, rush over and leap back up at, the dam; peeking over a high fence at it menacing the bridge at White River; and going a few days without mail and papers.

And Sunday I saw lumber (back in trees again) using trees, far from the Pompanusuc river bank, as high poles to constitute a sort of fence, and crows nests of flotsam hanging to telegraph poles along the track, and a smart little motor crane dropping huge and smaller hunks of marble with a double-jawed tongs into the edge of the high water to reinforce the B. & M. embankment.

I wrote to a boy out two years who had sent me a letter that marks my kind of success that I lived always on the verge of failure. As I read your extra secretion poem I think how many verges you're on when you write. Sometimes people whose minds have got a squint from looking hard for meanings would pass your poems that show most about how you 'made it', buoyantly and with kept head through all the years, as pleasant, simple little things. I like the gamble on being just right on something many others are fractionally wrong on better than I do the gamble on going where no other sane man has ever gone. To have one day so good it made the world seem light and warm for years proves more to me than being made a chieftain in Tahiti, or rising to become a salon-keeper in Bloomsbury or Paris. To make others believe it possible to have such days in this stormy world with no accessories and yet to be all-but on the side of the defeated instead of hooded from recognition of the fewness of such days, that is selecting chances and running the chances and making good—increasing the sum of good in the world. So free and easy and so measured, always sure the spurt and the slide will make up for the nervy extra lead off from the bag.

Some inquiry sent to alumni got the answer from two students— a neighbor professor told Arthur—that the only thing they got from Dartmouth was Sidney Cox's teaching. As the Bible says of the worldly-minded tithers of mint and cummin or seekers of High seats at feasts and synagogues, even such as I "have their reward". I'd rather be the realest thing in college or one of the realest for a score or so of intelligent and growing boys than a person of importance. But I'm not satisfied.

Yours    Sidney

* William Benfield Pressy (b. 1894): taught English at Dartmouth from 1919 to 1961.

TLS, 2 pp.

## 99.

Dear Robert        12 July 1936    Cummington, Massachusetts

I've just had a superlative evening of a thus-far delightful summer reading poetry to a responsive audience including youngsters in, or just through, high school, in or just through college, teachers in Union Theological and Barnard, our very fine and able master of music, Hugo Kortschak of Yale and the Neighborhood School in New York. I was asked for a sort of panorama, and I started with the Nausicaa book of the *Odyssey* and ended with "Two Tramps in Mud Time". I read, not from the magnificent limited edition you gave me, and for which and for the "Collected Poems" I am exceedingly grateful, but from a first of the trade edition: "Unharvested", "The Master Speed" and "Departmental", and "A Leaf Treader". I included Chaucer, two ballads, Shakespeare, Donne, Milton, Dryden, Pope, Burns, Blake—had to skip nineteenth century except two by Hopkins—which I found more than ever too-too—Lawrence, Cecil Day Lewis—who in the company seemed a little thin and staccato—Marianne More and Reuel Denney, and my two students here who write verse, Lionel Wiggam of *Landscape with Figures* and Samuel French Morse.

Do you remember Sam Morse from our stop at Amherst last spring on the way back from the Mount Holyoke prize contest? He is doing good things, and he is a solid, honest, laughing, knowledgable fellow with a good way of placing accents. He said while rereading from "A Further Range" that while reading it it seemed your best book. He exclaimed, not too excitedly, that you never used a word too many, and another time that "Unharvested" had just what the communists need. It was at his request that I took that first, before I had decided which. He often quotes the little one—it isn't here!—about sitting in the center; and one of his favorites is "At Woodward's Gardens".

I say all this about him because he's from Dartmouth, Senior Fellow this year just past, a thoroughgoing New Englander, and worth watching. He's the same person around here and at Hanover that he is in his verse, unlike Lionel Wiggam who, as I just wrote Alice, lets his ear run away with his bag of poetical memories, and seems around here a sun-tanned kid afraid of serious thinking. We'll watch him and his like, Flaccus, to see if ear and facility fill up with substance and form instead of finish ever comes.* Anyway I saved him from going off from here in a Byronesque, Rupert Brookeish puff of dignity because he had been told he was not cooperating and he thought he had to be individualistic in the stereotyped way.

Hope I shall have hours with you this summer. I peg away at my second novel, sure if I can get what I get into teaching 'running' free and taking shape it will make you sure you never overrated me, but often conscious that I haven't yet done so with the attempt to be casual and close to everyday.

I think I come near enough and progressively nearer—to uniting

"My avocation and my vocation

As my two eyes make one in sight" (possibly accusable of being one-eyed) not to let any of my friends feel too sorry that my compromising colleagues at Dartmouth still refuse to award me the label "full". I'd not let slip one minim of the realness of my teaching to be the most famous full professor in the kentry.

Yours affectionately<br>Sidney Cox

* William Kimball Flaccus (1911–1972): Dartmouth '33, a student of Cox's, became a college professor.


ALS, 4 pp.

100.

[San Antonio
Dear Sidney:                                          1 January 1937]

It was not to be Southern Cal after all. We were divided in preference between California and Florida; so we came as nearly as possible to halfway between. We are over across the Gulf from one and over across the deserts from the other in—San Antonio Texas—at 113 Norwood Court to be exact for you in case you should want to write me a letter about Dartmouth College or

Stearns Morse's party of the vestigial part. I'm sorry not to be where I can see something of you in the wild and unharnessed state. But then I doubt if I should find you very different. You and I are not the kind that can be described as either wild or tame: I always maintain that I would be the same in a society of one as in a society of one hundred and thirty million. My conditioning is all internal. My appetites are checked by each other rather than by anything in my surroundings. Or do I deceive myself? I dont care if I do in this respect. My denial that I am the result of any particular surroundings comes to nothing more than a refusal to think of myself as one who might have been better or worse if I had been thrown with different people in different circumstances. Look out I don't spoof you. About five years ago I resolved to spoil my correspondence with you by throwing it into confusion the way God threw the speech of the builders of the tower of Babel into confusion. My reason is too long to go into tonight (January First, Nineteen Hundred and Thirty-seven. Lucky New Year to you, if you are superstitiously susceptible.) Part of my reason is my dislike of all the printed correspondence I ever saw. You or anyone else could enjoy a better friendship with me if I could be sure you were keeping no records of it in the off-hand letters I write. My public talks owe any felicity they may have to the fact that they are gone on the wind. I wrote down not a word for Harvard last year and it would have thrown me off my phrasing to have known of anyone's taking notes on me in my audience. But I am resigned to what I am in for. You have the hint of what would please me: you will use your judgement as a scholar and a critic in dealing with the case.

You've got a novel to write and I have some prose I should be at if I dont feel to averse to it. So perhaps we are as well apart where we cant take it out in talking. Talking is a hydrant in the yard and writing is a faucet upstairs in the house. Opening the first takes all the pressure off the second. My mouth is sealed for the duration of the stay here. I'm not even going to write letters around to explain to collectors my not having had any Christmas card this year. I'm not going to explain anything personal any more. I'm not going to explain my children, except to tell you that Irma has written us how much she likes Alice. You may not have guessed this. Irma might have difficulty in conveying it to Alice. It would be too bad for you and Alice not to know it. My children are all good but rather offish with the human race. I myself am rather onish. I refuse to explain the discrepancy. I refuse to explain my position on a lot of things we brought up and left unsettled in our talk last fall. Why should I press home my conclusions everywhere. Blessed is he that seeketh not his own advantage. I practice such equalitarianism as I please. I wouldnt let a tiger eat me to relieve its starving kittens.

Ever yours, R.F.

[It is highly likely that Cox, disappointed at not being promoted to full professor at Dartmouth, was searching for a position elsewhere and had asked Frost to write a letter of recommendation for him.]

ALS, 4 pp.

## IOI.

Dear Sidney:                    15 February 1937   San Antonio

I wrote the highest praise of you in answer to this. I stayed on the plane of educational ideas entirely. You are one of the few who can sustain years of teaching literature as thought about life. I said so. I didn't know whether to descend to the level of your determination never to own a dress suit till all your children had got through college. I said many young people owed you much. I might have said if it had come to me in time that you bring readers round to the side of a book from which it was written and make them judge it as if they had written it themselves or might well have written it.

I have scolded you a lot first and last but if you will take one suggestion more from me, let it be this: your long suit will be writing that is ostensibly and in form philosophic. I dont see why you dont go at it. Maybe you want to ripen a few years longer. You are doing the novels as prentice work. In them the cart is before the horse. When you get really going your narrative dramatic will show only in illustration. You won't leave personalities out but you will sublimate them. That's my guess for you. Aw come on leave literature and the literary crowd. Lay down some law. Confute us. Corner us. Make us be good. You have really got further along on that course anyway than on any other. You didnt quite break through. But theres a place waiting for you at the end of one more big go. You might very well shift over into a more congenial department. Literature as learning is pretty nearly universal; philosophy as learning is a good deal less general. There is such a thing a philosophy as thinking about life in our colleges. I've got to speak at the University of Texas before going home; and my subject is going to be The Other Ninety-five Percent of You. I shall mean the ninety-five percent who aren't going to be scholars and where they come in. They get the good of looking on at the development of the scholars. They get some of the crumbs of their discipline. They get impressed with how far short they come of being scholars themselves and should acquire a respect for scholarship that should last them out in the world for the rest of their lives. Thats good for the scholars. It protects the scholar in their position. It is a provision of society I approve of. I want to see the scholars protected. Their security lies in making the largest number possible realize their superiority. (No I mustnt go so far.)

Take me as you like.

Have a good time in my native state.

Oh I forgot to say: I didn't assume that a call to Elmira College would be anything you could even consider. I dont know anything about it of course.

Ever yours
Robert F.

947 West Agareta Ave
San Antonio Texas
February 15 1937

ALS, 2 pp.

## 102.

Dear Sidney:                                    [Amherst
                                        c. 15 April 1937]

I get sick at heart in the search for real reasons among the reasons given by these officials. But we musnt mind the premises of

social life too much. Theres a book just out in England, The Muse in Chains, Pedagogy and English Literature by Stephen Potter we both ought to see for corroboration of what we have both always known.* Others in America will know it too but not till they have heard it from England perhaps. I'm afraid we scared Pres. Pott blue with the form our praise of you took.† You no doubt seemed a monster of enlightenment. The situation looks funnier every time I stop to look into it. I have made all the suggestions I am going to make in your case. The last one stands however. You for the philosophy department by way of some philosophical book. To Hell with novels unless you mean to lighter out on them into the literary ocean like Stark Young.—Oh just one more suggestion and then no more forever. Why not avoid reading The Muse in Chains and write a book of similar deadly aim yourself. Plain sense is all on your side and will prevail in the end whether you do anything about it or not. But you may as well get fame by hastening its day. Drink a glass of Pacific water to my memory.          Ever yours
                                                              Robert

* Stephen Potter (b. 1900): English humorist.
†William Sumner Appleton Pott (b. 1893): president of Elmira College in 1937. Frost probably had written to him a letter of recommendation for Cox who evidently was applying for a teaching position at Elmira.

[In 1936, as a retreat during the hay-fever season, Frost bought two small houses at Concord Corners, Vermont, near the New Hampshire border.]

ALS, 1 p.

## 103.

Concord Corners, Vt.

Dear Sidney:                                    [c. 7 September 1937]

Are you at home and do you want to come up for a day? We could have lunch or dinner or both somewhere together. There's nothing much here on our new hilltop except a view of New Hampshire. I begin to think though that New Hampshire improves on being looked at from Vermont.

                                                              Ever yours
                                                              RF

ALS, 1 p.

## 104.

Dear Sidney                          16 May 1938   Amherst
   Not much in this but the matter in hand. Lets consider it settled
that I will have dinner Wednesday evening with you West and
Bronk. Dont you think perhaps you had better ask my son-in-law
too? The other things we'll leave till we see how I bear up. The
Mitre will expect to have me after the lecture I assume. You might
talk it over with Martin for confirmation.* I like to be with the
boys that hire me. On second thought perhaps you had better not
talk it over with him on my authority lest he should think I was
trying to escape him. I can't stay till Sunday. I am too full of business here emptying the house I am to live in no more and putting
the finishing touches on my relation with Amherst College.

                                        Ever yours
                                        Robert

   *The Mitre, an undergraduate literary society at Dartmouth, was sponsoring a lecture
by Frost, who suggested dinner with Professor Herb West, Cox's student William Bronk,
and John Paine Cone, husband of Irma Frost Cone.

[Cox became a full professor in 1939, but had probably learned of his promotion
earlier. After Elinor Frost died, on March 21, 1938, Frost became distraught.
This letter was mailed, though unsigned.]
ALU, 4 pp.

## 105.

                                        [Boston
Dear Sidney:                            c. 18 May 1938]
   I knew you would want me to be glad but not so glad as to fall
all over myself and knock the telephone receiver off onto the floor
with excitement. You've reached a point of security that ought to
make some difference in your argument: I trust not to take any of
the kick out of it. I had been told your success made you an inev-
itability. Now for the remaining half of your life. Let's see, I make

you out about forty-five. Is that right? One more thing to say and then I have done with indoctrination forever, the agreement to date from the day of your promotion to fullness. I should think you could afford to be a little easier in the spirit without any risk of losing your invaluable effrontery. Positively that's my last. Lets lay off being personal with each other. Let our object be to be objective. Lets tell each other ideas we have. I have always hoped you might sometime publicly remember me in writing, but I got discouraged with the way you started off on my having sought you at least as much as you sought me. What the hell has that kind of inferiority superiority got to do with two people like us? Unless I have got him stopped the poetry editor of Time is presently going to deal with me by some such deplorable scandalousness. Newdick will be too personal. There is only you left to be uniquely mental with me mind to mind. Maybe I ask too much too vaguely. Damn it I dont want to dictate the book. What Henry Holt printed was all right. But you could go still higher into the thought realm for my taste. You know if any one knows I talk on some interesting subjects rather freshly. At Colorado Springs I spoke from the title Who Told <u>You</u> You Could Write. At Boulder it was Plato's Failure to Philosophise the Executive and the Poetic. At Lawrence Mass it was Anthologies as the Highest Form of Criticism. Time I desisted. I lead a life estranged from myself. I had a wretched time in Florida. One friend, my secretary [Kathleen Morrison] has taken me in hand to keep me lecturing and talking as of old. But I am very wild at heart sometimes. Not at all confused. Just wild—wild. Couldnt you read it between the lines in my Preface nay and in the lines?* All the more reason for your being objective with me. Nothing can save me for any more verse but unscrupulous reality.

* Frost may have shown Cox the manuscript of his famous preface, "The Figure a Poem Makes," to *Collected Poems* (1939).

TLS, 3 pp.

## 106.

[Hanover]

Dear Robert                                    1 May 1939

I've been waiting till I could tell you I was no longer an asst proff. Today a letter from Dean Bill makes it an accomplished fact. Dargan told me last January they had "almost unanimously" recommended me.* It means something in a way that I shall not try to explain to any who congratulate me. I'm one professor who has done creative teaching all his twenty-four years, more and more. I'm a proof; it can be done!

I am very grateful for the new Collected Edition of your poems. It's a handsome book. And as one of the four Dartmouth professors most highly recommended in *The Dartmouth* a few days ago I pronounce it the best poetry (in the greatest number of ways of being poetry) that has been printed in English since William Blake. And that is a cautious understatement. Yeats is a good and great poet, but he has a high percentage of sentimentality. There isn't anybody else in my time that can reasonably be mentioned. You suspect I have been reading the newsman's out-of-context quotation from your remark about excellence at Colorado Springs. Most 'nice' people don't acknowledge that great artists care whether or not they *excel*. What tripe! But you know. And I know you know. And you don't need me or any of my most unlike colleagues to tell you so. And yet you may be interested to know the list of poets to be used along with about as many prose writers, novelists and Shaw and Shakespeare, in English 1 and 2 for all the Freshmen in Dartmouth next year: Tennyson, Browning, Arnold, Hardy and Frost. It amazes me to hear men whose taste in several ways is about as far from mine as anyone in the department say that he likes to use your poems in class as much as any book. Flint urged the use of your poems, dwelling on the way they spread from the local and limited gradually to the boundaries of the universe.† Lately I've been hearing your voice over my head so much it's distracted me from my own writing. Literally, I mean; or almost literally: one teacher of Freshman English after another takes his class into the Wren Room and plays records of ten or fifteen of your poems. One of the times I went up from 16 Sanborn and listened. I congratulate you on pitching your voice right for recording. I tried it once, and I wouldn't own the flighty fluting. Next time down, down goes my voice, like Lewis Mumford's on a platform.

He's been around here lately. But the person I liked best—better than I like his poetry—was Auden. He's without side, seriously thoughtful, and more than I dared expect, flexible-minded. He said in different words a good many things I say. By the way, I'm sure you don't know how good a teacher I am. Here's hoping I can yet prove that I'm, if not so good as at teaching, some good at writing. But don't imagine that I'm feeling very bumptious, or that I talk to anyone but you like this.

I was delighted to have Amherst get out that issue of their magazine by your former students, there.[‡]

I hope you'll be round before long. Meanwhile please write. I've been delighted with the new poems, I meant to say—including the one in the Saturday Review article Louis Untermeyer more or less cribbed from you; making up pretty much, I admit, by filling it with you.

I hope you're having adventurous hours and fun.

Affectionately<br>
Sidney

P.S. The new preface is one of the most practically helpful essays on the art of writing anywhere.

---

[*]Earl Gordon Bill (1884–1947): dean of the faculty, 1933–1947. Henry McCune Dargan (1889–1970): professor of English, 1923–1957.

[†]F. Cudworth Flint (1896–1971): taught English at Dartmouth from 1929 to 1963.

[‡]The theme of *Touchstone*, February 1939, was Robert Frost, with articles and letters on the poet by Gerald Brace, Gordon K. Chalmers, Stacy May, Stark Young, and others.

ALS, 4 pp.

## 107.

Dear Robert                    15 January 1940    Hanover
    John says you report yourself as resting on your laurels after
a legal operation. From what I know of laurels their glossiness
wouldn't compensate for their prickly points, and I bet it's uncomfortable. But I'm relieved that you feel well enough to issue your
own bulletins.
    If you've been in any condition to read the papers you probably
know that the second of our idealists and near-poets has signed off
from a world where the opportunities aren't sufficiently golden.
Franklin McDuffee would have loved to "give and hazard" all he
had if only the possible Portia picture to bet his life on had not
been in a lead casket.* But in the actual world the possible out-
comes of ventures were not absolute enough. His conscience was
too sensitive toward grace, decorum, everybody's comfort on one
side, toward the Ideal on the other for his desire to come through
with anything he could respect.
    I'm glad you and Alice and something dogged in myself have
made infinitesimal and almost imperceptible increases in the solid
and the formed seem worth a life-time pegging away.
    I suppose it was the fact that I had that pertinacity that made
Franklin call me in one night when he was near the nadir of dejec-
tion. He said he had to talk to someone, and he thought I was the
most humane person in Hanover except President Hopkins. We
got on well. I suddenly came to like him very much. Partly, no
doubt, because he showed all his weakness to me. But also partly
because he still had more honesty than most of my colleagues. He
could not fool himself that petty efficiencies and decorums made
life worth wrapping in a napkin.
    You know, yesterday afternoon, coming from the funeral to a
meeting of the full professors to vote on a prearranged scheme of
reassignments to carry on his work, I felt that our Wren Room was
more of a tomb than the place where his flower-concealed coffin
had been taken. Whited, too—a whited sepulchre—but not with
falling snow.

We've got it all fixed for the present that Shakespeare is exclusively introduced by Tony Raven, who is as poetic as a typewriter, the Romantic Poets by Francis Child, who would be all right to give talks on his collection of cider mugs and attendant Yankee anecdotes,[†] and the introduction to the arts for Freshmen by a breezy, whipper-snapper-up-of-trifles with a Ph. D. from Yale. English is all safe from passion. And what could be better? Passion is what leads, they fear, to suicide.

The angelic boy-minister (thirty or so) told us at the funeral that Franklin besides being a poet, lover of beauty (He had told me he could get no satisfaction from even a sunset, that he was a cynic, that he never had any fun, or a good time, that he had "a beautiful vocabulary and nothing to say") was a great teacher, a great man, a great spirit, and that he had the Christian faith—which the pale, sweet-voiced preacher elegantly summarized.

I saw all I could of Franklin the few days before he went to California for vacation, and I was hoping I could, by nearness, induce in him a little—even though he was forty-one—of the spiritual energy he said he felt in me. I loved him. If only he hadn't hung all his life to the forget-me-not bordered margin of the slough of despond. If only he could have wanted something limited, enough to go on through!

I don't believe you will feel this a too lugubrious letter. There are so few grown-up people in my world that I can say such things to. And yet my world is such a good one, even when it's full of hell, that I——

One of my most lively students has just been in. He says he can't write about snow in Hanover because when he looks at Balch Hill it doesn't do anything to him. But he's just written a fresh and funny loving poem about the sea. I have some good students, and this one is more.

Get well fast, Robert.
Yours
Sidney

---

*Franklin McDuffee (1898–1940): professor of English when he committed suicide.
†Anton Adolph Raven (1895–1955): professor of English in 1940. Francis Childs (1884–1973): professor of English, a friend of Frost's.

ALS, 2 pp.

## 108.

Dear Robert                    19 February 1940    Hanover
    I've just been reading Edward Thomas to some writers. I liked
both poems and prose so much it sets me writing to you. Your letter to Mrs. Thomas in the new biography I just got for the Sanborn House library is by far the best thing in an otherwise trou-
bling book.*
    How are you? And what are you doing? I don't think I asked
you if you had seen Reuel Denney's "The Connecticut River, and
other poems." It is good, some of it very good.
    If you know a poet within three or four years of thirty, either
way, who would like to teach at Dartmouth and whom you would
like to see teaching at Dartmouth, tell him, please, that we are
looking for such a person. We don't even ask that he be a scholar,
at all, or that he should have done much teaching. From the way
we talk Robert Frost when he came back from England would
have exactly suited our desire.
    Hewette Joyce is the one for the poet to address. He can teach
some Shakespeare if he asks for it, or Romantic Poets, or any poetry course we have or he invents. He should—I slyly suggest—
ask for about $2,400 and an assistant professorship.
    Secretly I am hoping, since I'm sure that there's no one close at
all to that specification, that we cannot find a suitable man of
thirty, and that we shall take Sam Morse.
    I've just had a good time improving "Winking at the Sphinx."
And I've done two short stories that I'd like to have you see in
print.
    Every once in a while records of you reading poems are run
above me; I hear your voice and wish I might go talk. As I also do
at other times.
    Don Bartlett asks me how you are.
                                        Yours affectionately
                                        Sidney Cox

* John Moore's *The Life and Letters of Edward Thomas* (London: W. Heinemann,
1939).

ALS, 4 pp.

## 109.

[New York]

Dear Sidney                              12 March 1940

You tempt me to interfere. But if I knew somebody just right for the position at Dartmouth I should hesitate to name him. My open sponsorship often does more harm than good. It makes the subject too prominent—or at any rate more prominent than it is wise to start off with. Sam Morse is all right for his age and he promises well. But what you have in mind is someone a little further along in achievement and reputation. How about Ruel Denny? His new book seems to have made somewhat of a impression Is it enough for judgement? I havent seen it. Any other names I might bring up I had rather talk about tentatively with you than write about.

I have been very sick largely we now think from some very drastic medicine the doctors tried on me for cystitis. I went crazy with it one night alone and broke chairs ad lib till a friend [Merrill Moore] happened in to save me. I have had a strange two years— not all as bad as it might have been and perhaps should have been. I was in one bed or another pretty much all of December and January—and in one pain or another. Kathleen Morrison took me south pretty much on my back all the way. I got going again in Key West and so on to two or three or even four miles a day of walking. I only furnish you with these data to use on any of my well wishers who may be *living* in hopes of my dying.

When you get Winking at the Sphinx into the shape you want I wish you would try it on the new literary department of Henry Holt with a word to Bill Sloane from me. The frisk of the title runs all through the thinking and yet it is thinking and serious thinking. A profitable number of people ought to find it profitable reading. I feel in duty bound in gratitude bound to find my publishers an Anthony Adverse or a gone with the wind. I really wish them money. But they must learn that some money is enough if it is made on an unusual book of ideas.

I'm sending you for the fun of it a document that will bring back memories of your old bad days in Montana. It contains names we have heard before. Willard Fraser sent it to me. I dont look forward with any special pleasure to the days when our private institutions shall be beaten into public institutions.

You can see from this paper where I have guiltily been.* I got out Sunday.

R.F.

* The letterhead reads: 200 El Bravo Way, Palm Beach, Florida. Frost stayed there when he was in Palm Beach to give a talk at a women's club.

[Cox appended to this letter, from William Sloane (TLS, 1 p.), a TLS, 2 pp. which follows.

## 110.

Henry Holt and Company
257 Fourth Avenue
New York

Dear Professor Cox:                 April 23, 1940

Yesterday when I took a quick look at WINKING AT THE SPHINX I realized that it was not about Robert Frost and I want to apologize for thinking that it was.

I wish that you were not so remote and that I could talk to you about the business of book publishing at closer range. We are fundamentally organized to sell books to book stores, and the trouble is that it is not advisable for a small publishing house like ours to do too many specialized books at once. I do not suppose that it would make any difference in your feeling about the whole thing if I were to tell you that I question seriously whether we could sell as many copies of this book as could a University Press. Such however is the fact.

Nevertheless, I would like to think about the whole proposition for a little while longer and I shall write you as soon as possible after my return from Durham.

Sincerely yours,
William Sloane,
Manager, Trade Department

[Hanover]

Dear Robert                                              24 April 1940

You can see that Mr. Sloane is easing me down. If there is any way to induce him to make an exception of "Winking at the Sphinx", to take extra means to make the book known to people looking for something fresh and free in serious thinking and push it to success, I have concluded I want such a way to be taken. It may be illogical and irrelevant to avail myself of your hold over Holts. But I would do it. I got a letter this morning from a winner of one [of] the Hopwood prizes in poetry at the U. of Michigan—a *Cummingtonite*, two summers ago, who just spent a day with me here; he does not praise me, but he chafes at the contrast between my kind of criticism and teaching—and understanding conversation, and what he gets at Michigan. And the letter confirms my feeling that I have something for more people than I reach, and that all measures for getting my kind of hard yet flexible thinking a chance to meet more minds might be worth taking. I have proved a few things that many people are looking for and generally getting told can't be. Why shouldn't I exhaust the possibilities for getting a hearing? Without deceptive optimism I can—and do—put another experienced shoulder to the wheel of real education, real human relations, real creative action; so why shouldn't I be heard? Why shouldn't a publisher be told that here is something worth taking exceptional pains about? Thus I argue with myself, and consent to asking you to push Mr. Sloane.

A University Press publisher wouldn't recognize my book as University kind. But things that don't fit categories shouldn't just fade out. I guess Holt is my last ditch for *Winking*.

It was good to talk with you. It took a tuck in the web of passed time and made mock of space. You know—I'm glad you're here.

Yours
Sidney

[Frost's only surviving son, Carol, at thirty-eight committed suicide at South Shaftsbury, Vermont, October 9, 1940.]

ALS, 1 p.

# 111.

Dear Robert                    10 October 1940    Hanover
   If I can do anything that will be the slightest help I want to. I don't think you will buckle even with this added.
Let irrelevancies like my affection count all they feebly can.

Yours
Sidney Cox

[Unfortunately, the letter from Cox to which Frost replies here, apparently has been lost.]

ALS, 2 pp.

# 112.

Dear Sidney:                    11 January 1941    Boston
   I dont know what you are talking about in your letter. I dont assume that I need to know. It sounds as if somebody had been telling you what somebody else—what he thought somebody else had been telling me he thought you had been saying about my literature. Never touched me. Never came within a mile of me. I'm resting comfortably and I trust you are. Lets hear no more about it. Explanations only tend to confuse the issues and bring on wars.
   You went to the last war like a good boy. I dont know what you think of this war. I peek at the papers just enough to have about one idea of my own a week about it. For instance, last week I was just beginning to resent the word appeasement in the mouth of a party whose boast has been all along that it has appeased the proletariat and saved the country from a revolution. If I may be permitted to speak for the proletariat we refuse to be appeased. Todays news makes me wonder if perhaps George B. MacClellan wasnt right in his letters to his wife about the countrys need of a dictator and Lincoln wasnt wrong in muddling along demo-

cratically through the crisis of Sixty-one-to-four. Little Mac may have been the most smeared man of his generation. Sandburg hasnt remarked this. He has gone right on with the self-righteous work of smearing the already smeared. Roosevelt is too self-conscious a second-come Lincoln to notice discrepancies however glaring. A time like this doesnt seem *very* much harder to understand than any other time. Living alone I am made aware of how regularly I am supposed to make up my bed fresh every day. Just so my mind.

I think your summer school of philosophy is a good idea. Philosophy it will be in reality. You cant fool one of the people any of the time. Refer 'em to me in droves.

Ever yours
Robert

TLS, 7 pp.

## 113.

Dear Robert                    5 April 1941   Hanover

I wonder if you have a good notion how much and how often I think of you, not only as one of the whole world's handful of best poets and people, but as just you, and somebody special to me, in this particular century and week. Can I say things like that? I suppose when one doesn't say much there is danger of his saying too much when he does speak.

You wondered in your last letter how I take the war. I'm trying to get my young friends and my twenty year old Arthur to see it as a concentration of the everlasting struggle between the growth impulse and the machines we always keep mistakenly trusting to take the place of growth. I know both the growth impulse and the machine are on both sides. But the nazi side has run tanks over the growth impulse more than our side. And if the more honest and imaginative in America find their hearts turned against fascism they can do a bit to make our side mean more than they believed sides could mean in war. I am glad when a forceful and vigorous student looks at all the ways of taking the present and decides to back the defense movement, knowing it is taking a chance. Some of my ablest and best friends, not long since students, can't see anything but impersonal necessity in answering the draft. They are doing their best where they are, and I don't blame them. But I differ.

Did you notice that Reuel Denney was one of several young poets to win a Guggenheim? It means more in his case than in the case of R. P. Blackmur and Delmore Schwartz because he is a better poet. He has suffered a little from the all-but prevailing modern disease of trying to make a mechanism to keep life in control, but in the main he controls life with life.

It's disgusting the way all the prominent minor poets are, both here and in England, formularizing everything and writing and talking as if it were better for them and for those they treat with solemn unction, like Pound and Eliot, to translate thoughts into multiple symbols that smart connoiseurs can decode. They more and more ignore the few, and great, who think from their feelings and find their inner meanings in what they see and otherwise perceive in the literal happening, act and object. They act and write as if they never knew anyone who *talks* nuclei of poems, and when he's going well speaks and tosses into the void of their ears better poems than Dylan Thomas or William Carlos Williams or Auden ever wrote. (Not that I don't see the good in them.) They write articles about the isolation of the poet, and apparently it never crosses their minds that the poets are too damned detached. Detached not only from equally live and sensitive human beings but also from the roots through which whatever they really know has one time risen.

My long search for a real poet has revealed one young one who is much richer and sounder than Reuel Denney. And at the moment, having just glanced at the last *Kenyon* and leafed the introduction to *The Faber Book of Modern Verse*, it irks me to realize that (again) *he* will have to make a long, slow revolution before he will be taken seriously by the cognoscenti. He will win a popular hearing first, unless the publishers turn all their poetry manuscripts over to "modern" poets and fear to publish anything that doesn't bear the fashionable quirks.

This Ted Boorum, twenty-four, ex-guard in football, weighing

195, has the playfulness and freshness of an energetic child, the wisdom to win the confidence of my deaf, eighty-two year old new testament father and the maturity to understand war, science and religion. His poems are about sea-gulls trying to shake off spider crabs, old housemaids dusting birch logs and the evolutionary and growth transition ground of that part of the beach which at high tide is under water (the strand.) He feels and revels in the concretes and doesn't set down in good set terms the meanings. He plays all the time, and in all his play there is philosophy, and self-possessed responsibility, with full regard for death and danger, but no sickly wail. With one male exception and one female he's the most adequate and sure human being I have known. But *Poetry* and *The Atlantic Monthly* turn him down, though ironically enough *The Partizan Review*, which belongs to the barkers up electric light poles which they take for tree of knowledge and of life, and with which he is on only laughing terms, has given him his one acceptance.*

I've just been rereading Keats and Byron. Neither of them can hold a candle, except in "Ode to Autumn" to the first rate few. Nor can Yeats, though I would put him before Byron and all of Keats except that one. Why doesn't someone discover that T. S. Eliot is no more than an extremely competent voice of human giving-up, first in sneers and then in prayers?

One other modern that wins my grateful admiration is Katherine Anne Porter—in short stories. Saroyan, too, with big reservations, and, lest I seem madly exclusive, Sigrid Undset and, despite his grandiose pontificating, his being toward the fairies a bit, Thomas Mann. I like health. And I know the healthy who are sensitive and sympathetic know more than the fairies and the feeble.

Yours affectionately<br>Sidney Cox

Of course I read all your new poems that I can lay hands on. Not of course, I like them all, too. And I'm looking forward to the book of prose, "Talks Walking."†

*Theodore Montgomery Boorum (b. 1917): Dartmouth '40, became a businessman, lives in Antrim, New Hampshire.

†A collection of Frost's prose, *Selected Prose of Robert Frost*, ed. Hyde Cox and Edward Connery Lathem, was not published until 1966 (Holt, Rinehart and Winston), three years after the poet's death.

ALS, 1 p.

## 114.

Dear Sidney                          31 March 1942   Cambridge
   You and Rugg must apportion me.* I can leave it to you two. I
know you wont overdo it. And you'll both have the boys chiefly in
mind. I should want to spend one night with John and Irma, but
they havent a place for me in their new house yet. As it is I must be
satisfied with a meal out there. The Lambuths haven't spoken up. I
don't know what may have come over them from Johns break
with Larsen.† I've never been into that trouble. Too many other
things in the family to think of. You sound pretty much yourself in
your letter. I'm all right too. We'll talk a lot. I'll stay up there till
the last train Sunday.

                                          Ever yours
                                          Robert

Draw John Troxell into something will you?‡ And you wont forget
Donald [Bartlett].

   *Harold Goddard Rugg (1883–1957): assistant librarian and instructor of modern art
at Dartmouth.
   †John Paine Cone, an architect, Frost's son-in-law, was associated with Jens Fredrick
Larson (b. 1891), who, as Dartmouth College architect, designed several buildings for the
campus.
   ‡John Gross Truxal (b. 1924): Dartmouth '45.

TLS, 4 pp.

## 115.

Dear Robert                          19 July 1942   Hanover
   This summer I am spending a great deal of time with you. Concentrated, exciting, delightful. After reading "The Witness Tree"
and some of the poems in it repeatedly I started at the beginning of
the collected poems and am reading each as if I had never read it
before. With both my Dartmouth writing class (for the first time)
and my summer conversations on writing (for the second time) I
am using poems by you to start off the conversations and to illustrate. They have copies; they also read aloud. We have kept away

from disputation, and nobody is having or feeling that he is having anything thrust upòn him.

As I got more and more refreshed and furthered in my reading I took it into my head to reread my walks and talks manuscript. I saw with stripped, stark plainness why you vetoed its publication. And I can't wonder if ever since you read my own parts of that you have all but distrusted your original liking for and trust in me. I don't like my parts. They are mostly humorless and puppyish. And yet you were not wrong. I have what you saw in me in 1911 and other times and that blundering left foot forward all the time gait, too. I still have some of that. But I'm still growing and maturing. And I'm still about your best reader. I'm still going to write a book about your meaning and how it grows: how it grew in you, and how it grows in readers and may grow a little in America.

I see with some, but surprisingly not much, disturbance in this morning's Times the announcement of [Lawrance Thompson's] "Fire and Ice; the Thought and Art of Robert Frost". It will be a good book if it does justice to that inclusiveness. But it won't forestall mine. I shall fight shy of it. I shall take my time. And I will try to write a book, about you and wisdom and imagination, that will, without saying a word on the issue, undermine most of the oversimplifications of the so-called modern mind, and to make it as whole and deep-working and actuating as all sorts and conditions of people always find my teaching. Maybe I'll add two or three more to the years I've been becoming ready: thirty-one on one scale, fifty-three almost on the other.

Ted Boorum had a fine time going down on the train with you, and he felt that the agreeableness was mutual. He has the stuff.

I didn't buy "A Witness Tree" at once because I wanted one from you. But when I did, I didn't say it was your best, nor that it was less; it was you, different and the same. Full of surprise, full of confirmation. Nobody can find the wire to fasten a name-tag on you that doesn't either burst off or get grown around without a scar. That's what bothers the professors and the poets who are outdoing the professors.

I'm to conduct a little conference next October on creative writing (the teaching of writing classes, I shall assume they mean) before the New England section of the newish College English Association. They have discovered a new way to be dull and safe, in revolt against The Modern Language Association. They are the nice and liberal teachers who dare confess to reading contemporaries, but remain contraceptive. I'll have fun, and be cagey enough, too, I hope, not to make them rescind their extravagant notion of me.

I'm having an adventurous summer, in spite of the Jitters. Hope things go well with you.

Affectionately
Sidney

ALS, 1 p.

## 116.

Dear Sidney                    8 August 1942    Ripton

You needn't worry about having written and consigned to the mails (beyond recall) a letter somewhat too intemperate. It was all right as long as it was to me. I know exactly how to take you in most of your manifestations. God bless you, you shall have your copy of my book and from the heart as you have had the rest of the set. I haven't forgotten you for new companions. Nothing is as for the moment you seem to imagine. You should have had the book sooner; but I had used up all the promulgation there was in me publishing and had none left for distributing. I am restored and ready to go to work doing up parcels. I had better be. You cant be the only friend who has been laying it up against me for my seeming neglect.

And you may be wise in not reading Larry Thompson's book about me till you have written your own. You have your own ideas of me that you dont want to get all mixed up with his. I hear Larry has done me well. I have come to make it a rule not to read anything about myself till it is in print, and not necessarily then. I shall read how Larry understands me. He has been close to me in my latter days and come closer still in going out to be the only soldier I can call my own at the front. He is on sea duty and as I think on a merchant vessel gunning for submarines. I seem to want to win the war not for the Russians, nor yet for the British (much as I admire the Russians for sticking at nothing to accomplish nothing and much as I owe the British for my start in life) I want to win it for the U.S.A. in general and for Larry Thompson in particular.

I am expecting you to write a book on and for me some day— and a deep one. You may not have noticed anything, but I have been taking measures steadily to put off the day till you should assume the toga as a man and my equal. You made a bad start with the note of inferiority you struck in your first chapter, long ago. You were afraid people would think you had sought my society rather than I yours. I was ashamed for you. I probably did seek your society. I administer this with benevolent malice. I remember seeking you in Plymouth at least once for the pleasure of teasing the young fellow I had found so easy to tease on our first meeting at that dance at the Normal School. What added to the wicked pleasure was revenge for your having asked Silver or someone if drink was the explanation of my not having got anywhere at my age. After I came to like you, I can't tell how it was, whether you sought me or I you. I naturally live above or below such considerations with my friends. I am almost morbid in my avoidance of the subtler forms of rivalry and strife. Take this matter of biography between us for instance. Why should you be writing mine and not I yours. You are just as much of a character as I am. Why has it never occurred to me before? I know a lot of good stories about you. I am not going to have it said of me that I let people write biographies of me without returning the compliment.

Ever yours   Robert

TLS, 4 pp.

## 117.

Dear Robert                    2 January 1943   Hanover
Happy New Year! You contributed definitely to my having an unusually happy Christmas by the gift of the handsome limited edition of THE WITNESS TREE, and the particular words you

wrote in it with your pen.* The words you earlier wrote with your typewriter gave me new delight at Christmas time, too, as I read some of them aloud to Arthur [Cox], home from his good job at Washington, and my good student and roomer, Ed Eubanks.

Has anyone singled out "The Subverted Flower" to be glad about? I like the ugliness in it, as you remind us again that if we can't make something of mixtures, turn them into sound compositions, always smelling a little of iron and brimstone to close sniffers, then our fineness festers.

I have kept my word about Pearson's book, though I liked a good deal his article in Harpers about submarine suppression.† At times I get irritated at the small notice taken of the book. Evidently I ought to get into a relation with the book and magazine world that will make my name mean something before I come forth with another book about you. Yet I don't much expect to; I'm so incorrigibly and exhaustively a teacher. I sometimes wish I could have the privilege of taking from Mr. Newdick's materials. Not to make it a chronological, conventional biography, but to have more "local habitation" in addition to the poems to occupy, inhabit with my essentials and ultimates, on the subject. You know how I have always tended to boil off the sap of my experiences and be deficient in snow to crystalize it on. And you, certainly, never, never give the smell of coffee without the cupful.

I don't want, either, to make a book of the grounds. All I want to do—if I can find out how—is what I do when I read your poems aloud, show that they ring true with my voice, too, and give shape to what has gathered in me. Shape that encourages me, as I withdraw from the poems, to pull together my own form for my own nature and experience. For the greatest thing good poetry does is enhance just a little the force, the patience and the balancing play always approaching balance with which the reader can become a composer of meaning, too.

A fact or two about you, remembered with delight or amusement, or with a small difficulty in reconciling, often helps me in showing what it is to read your poems with increasing fulness.

Speaking of facts about you, Max Baym insists that he met a nephew of yours last year in Boston. It's hard for me to suppose you have a brother I never heard of or have completely forgotten.‡

I like Max. We saw each other many long hour sessions and walks. But he hasn't escaped the mortmain of schoolmen. He just sent me three reprints, all very boyishly learned and noteful. But none really noteworthy. A short statement of what he made of any one of his characters, Baudelaire, Henry Adams, William James or Shakespeare would be worth more. He is still afraid of the red pencil, still proving that he knows all the people who ever said anything at all resembling what anyone else says; as if soon he might be granted the authority to have a thought of his own. Oh, I all but forgot: he wants to know where to look up Charles's "Master of the Palace School".⁵ He told me I'd have to trace the source. We musn't understand anything until we know all that led up to it. But luckily he breaks down on that rather ambitious principle.

I wish you much health and fun, With affection,

Sidney Cox

*In the signed, limited edition of 735 copies (New York: Henry Holt and Company, 1942), the inscription reads: "To Sidney from Robert as aforetime."

†The book may be *The American Diplomatic Game* (1937), by Drew Pearson. The article, "Our Battle Against the Submarines: As Seen from Inside the Control Room, Eastern Sea Frontier," *Harper's Magazine*, October 1942, pp. 449–58, is by Lawrance Thompson.

‡Max Baym (b. 1895): taught English at the Polytechnic Institute of Brooklyn; wrote *The French Education of Henry Adams*.

⁵Baym may have wanted to trace the source for Alcuin, the master of the Palace School in Charlemagne's court and a major figure in Frost's "The Lesson for Today."

ALS, 4 pp.

# 118.

Dear Robert                          2 July 1943   Hanover

Hearing Elmer Davis speak of Guadalcanal just now reminds me that today a former member of my women's class in writing whose son was my student told me that he wrote from the Pacific that what he wanted sent was your Collected Poems and *Come In*.* I like to feel that this war is being partly fought for what readers find realized in your poems.

Yesterday I read with pleasure Stearns' [Morse's] article "The Wholeness of Robert Frost" in the Virginia Quarterly.

Ray Nash is a good friend of mine and of yours. (He asked

Stearns for the article to have published in England—you may not know.) He likes my *Indirections* and says things that make me more glad that I wrote it. And he honestly read it as if he were a publisher's reader. I respect greatly his frankness in telling me he can't see how a publisher could make money on it, though he has no doubt there are many who would like it and benefit by it, if they could be brought in touch with it.[†]

Right now Del Ames, one of the simplest, most germinal and energetic men I know, is reading that and "Winking at the Sphinx". I had just read some papers of his recording a strangely similar cluster of conclusions, set forth scientifically, that ostensibly start with a study of the nature of sensation. You know he is the founder of the Dartmouth Eye Clinic. He says he is tremendously excited, to find us like two men's hands with one set of fingers fitting between the fingers of the other hand.[‡]

Ray says my book is "too sound". He, Del Ames, says in order to say anything, with so new a sense of mind growth (knowledge) you have to say everything at once. But he seems to hope that his offering and mine can make a way for each other. He says my "Indirections" is as much, he is sure, for painters as for writers. (He was a painter, once.) And he thinks it is equally for musicians, and all who think imaginatively. But he hasn't finished that book. He got fascinated with "Winking".

Dartmouth is changed, and so is Hanover—with about 2,000 navy and marine trainees. But we'll keep something alive here beyond military discipline. (So, for that matter, will God.) I hope, very much indeed, that you are coming to help us. I want to see a lot of you.

Affectionately
Sidney

*Elmer Davis (1890–1958): popular American journalist and radio commentator.

†Ray Nash (b. 1905): printer, artist; taught art at Dartmouth.

‡Adelbert Ames (1880–1955): close friend of Cox's, was professor of research in physiological optics at the Dartmouth Medical School in 1943 and a pioneer in visual perception.

ALS, 3 pp.

## 119.

[Cambridge, Massachusetts
c. 20 May 1944]

Dear Sidney:                                    Ripton Vermont from now on

I have just this day been seeing my oldest friend in this world, John Bartlett of Boulder Colorado; and it made me think of my second oldest you the Hanoverian. It must be my letter in question never got to you or from the nature of it you would have been moved to answer it. Now don't get excited in either the cerebellum or the cerebrum. "By the nature of it" I mean no harm and I say no harm. On the mistaken assumption that you had been bothered by some jest of mine that had reached you on the subject of the two aspects of education I began with a poet I'll bet you cant spot: "Aint Uncle Sidney funny man? / He's childish most as me." * and thence proceeded to worse by making the steps of education seven, the old fashioned sacred number that has been displaced in popular superstition by the New Deals sacred four [Four Freedoms Four Nations (by stretching a point to include poor China) Four Freedoms of the Air (to fly anywhere, to land anywhere to pick up freight and passengers anywhere and to land freight and passengers anywhere) and Four Terms].† But to get back to my seven phases of education. They are: Compression—Before the birthburst. Repression—On the principle that bursting bombs should be seen and not heard. Impression In the grades and high-school Expression In college entirely
Depression By marriage
Refreshion By adult education
Suppression By acclamation.

I have designs on post war education but then I have always had designs on all education. So why should the department of education worry? Letting the system severely alone and simply concentrating is my only chance of bringing a better day. The same people are using Wooley's Handbook and attending I.A. Richards talks on Basic English. Basic Balls, or if I may be pardoned the baseness Why, baseballs or Balls.

I liked your figure about the Fire Tower and Ivory Tower.
                                                Ever yours
                                                R F.

* Apparently a parody by Frost of James Whitcomb Riley's "Uncle Sidney" poems.
†Frost's brackets.

TLS, 3 pp.

120.

Dear Robert                    3 March 1945   Hanover
    I was thinking about you when this jongle began in my head.
And so I am going to send it to you, not asking for a comment on
what kind of jongleur I am, but hoping for a letter about what's in
your mind, not ready yet to come out as a poem. I think "A
Masque of Reason", which I have read to others twice and to myself three or four, is the most amusing serious poem I know, the
most serious amusing poem I know. I would like to have Milton,
Dante, and Thomas Hardy, all the metaphysicals and Pascal gather round in heaven to ponder it. Might let Yeats in, too, and Eliot
up, if he could stand the disappointments of an actual paradise. If
he understood the masque I suppose it would be hell for him. The
writer of the first forty-two chapters would be there by irresistible
psychic magnetism. And he would say, "Well, something *has* happened down there since my day. More at home, even than I was
with religion: that whirlwind of mine sort of got out of hand."
    A not otherwise very distinguished Freshman V12er wrote of
his own accord a little paper on Robert Frost.* One thing in it
gave me much pleasure. It's mainly apropos of *Birches*. "Frost, by
his returning you to earth, brings you a true message. He paints
you a picture, then hangs it in your own front room, doesn't leave
it in some obscure museum." Quite a number of boys in my three
sections, last semester, began to like poetry.
    Please let me know what time in this or next month I would
stand best chance of seeing you, on my little trip to Boston.

## Trundle

Give a whoop for your hoop,
   Let it roll
You have made ends meet
   In your soul.
Press your stick, keep your feet
As it bounds, whirling leap,
   In control.

With a tap lest it droop
   Make it go.
You have joined extremes
   Out of woe,
Won a joy from your dreams
As you found how to coop
   In your O.

Let it bounce, let it whirl,
   Leave it loose.
You have linked goal with start
   Good with use.
Keep abreast, guide with art
As your whole with a twirl
   You produce.

Give a whoop for your hoop
   Let it roll.
You have made of a naught
   A blithe soul.
Not for nothing you thought
Fusing truths in a loop
   That will bowl.

I hope the good spirits of mischief and of known affection will attend your loneliness all this month and on your birthday.

Yours
Sidney

* V I 2ers: undergraduates in a Navy program to train officers during World War II.

ALS, 2 pp.

## 121.

[Miami

Dear Sidney                                        c. 7 March 1945]

You're the same old Sidney I have to enjoin once in so often. You can say all those nice extravagances to me privately but you must hold in a little in public. We'll hope R[h]adamanthus will say I am as good as you claim. But let's have a good time anyway. When you come down I'll read you A Masque of Mercy. Dont imagine I'm not stirred by what your letter says in prose and verse. I like you to like my "works."

So you're turning the Volunters Hose on me.* It is a grateful bath down here in the summer heat. I am not supposed to enjoy baths. If the weather would only stay hot enough I would bathe every day.

I am not too terribly lonely. Kathleen was down helping me for a while and Lillian and Prescott are here all the time. Prescott is a junior in the University of Miami.

Prescott interests me though we have few interests in common. He is now beyond calculus in mathematics and away beyond the general physics that I had. He excels in those subjects and sighs and even groans over the big book of all English Literature he has to get through in the next two semesters. He has his tendency to mathematics from his mother. His health is fairly good considering what he was put out of the army for.†

Let me tell you my plans. I must be at Duke University about the middle of the month. I must be at Henry Holts office for a birthday lunch party with the firm and no one else on the twenty sixth. The ten days intervening havent been thought out. I may have to spend some of them in New York. If I dont but go on to Boston I shall just have to come back and fulfill some obligations later. Come to think of it I have two lectures (so called) to give in New York one on each side of the Twenty-sixth. Tell me about your plans. Let's fit plans together.

Occupations: watering our grove of twelve, building stone wall (nearly forty linear feet) walking two level miles for groceries and eating papayas. Let's see what else. Kathleen and I went down to

Key West to see old friends. It is a cramped little island. We had a talk with John Dewey there. He's eighty-five. We are giving it out that I am practically seventy and I been yours in friendship exactly half the time.

R.F.

Had you stopped to realize it? Thirtyfive is exactly half of seventy. Gee!

---

\*The letterhead of Letter 120 from Cox reads: "Village Precinct of Hanover, New Hampshire, Hanover Volunteer Hose Company."
†A deflated bronchial tube.

TLS, 2 pp.

## 122.

[Hanover]

Dear Robert                                                    18 May 1945

I am nearly through with one delectable leaf from your "Book". I can't say it is to be compared with any of the other books you have given me, or with the Christmas card poem that I still painfully miss from my collection. But I am almost too grateful to be, as it were, hinting. Not being a cigar-smoker you can't know how grateful I am, nor do you, perhaps know how superior these cigars are to those I occasionally buy.

I see by The New York Times that you are at last a doctor of laws, and will not have to be reminded at commencements that the highest honor, as the presidents say, in the gift of the colleges is being withheld for politicians. Now I want to see someone award you the D.D. It would be amusing but no joke.

Just got a holograph of a light poem on the Dickensons and Todds from Melville Cane. I'm going to try to get him to leave out one word, but he has that kind of flair.\* I'm sorry Marianne Moore didn't get the Pulitzer. She's ten times as original, has much more up her sleeve—if only she could learn, "Easy does it." I think more of Dillys Laing than I do of [Karl] Shapiro, though she still goes soft and anxiously timely. But she has overcomings to suggest and a gift of phrase and an ear.†

Just read a fierce and fine commencement address delivered last

June by George Whicher. A male fist in a suede glove for morality in education.[‡]

I've been surprised to find [Glenway Wescott's] "The Apartment in Athens" so firm and beautiful. It ended in grief but left me happy; the things that matter were going *on*. That and Elizabeth Bowen's "The Death of the Heart" and Arthur Koestler's "Darkness at Noon" are the best novels I've read lately. I didn't like Robert Penn Warren's "Night Rider" so well; it has a hurt tone and I suspect he isn't quite big enough to get over something. Except in a few grim and amusing poems he cannot shed the smell of the smoking student lamp.

Alice says God and she are still friends; He spared her apple blossoms when most people around lost theirs. She is doing a wonderful job on our living room. Right now she's painting the ceiling. I, at least, washed the ceiling and she and I took the paper off the wall. But the best thing so far has been restoring the mantle and the window sills. They have a nice design, hitherto covered by many layers—she says ten layers—of paint.

Arthur has divulged his hope. After the war he's going to write. He'd rather be a writer than a senator. He hopes to be home for a pre-Pacific leave next month.

Here's luck with your fowl play. Hope we'll soon have weather for doing things outdoors. If you say so I'll go against radio advice and make a war-time journey to Ripton before I resume teaching. So far the leave has been fun and I haven't honed for student ears.

Yours affectionately
Sidney

---

[*] Melville Cane (1879–1980): poet, lawyer, author of "Robert Frost: An Intermittent Intimacy," in *American Scholar*, 40 (Winter 1970–71): 158–166.

[†] Dillys Bennett Laing (1906–1960): poet, novelist; was married to Dartmouth writer-teacher Alexander Laing (see footnote to Letter 129). Karl Shapiro (b. 1913): poet, critic, editor; won the Pulitzer Prize in 1945 for *V-Letter and Other Poems*.

[‡] George Frisbie Whicher (1889–1954): writer, English professor at Amherst. The address was "Education for Democracy."

ALS, 2 pp.

## 123.

Dear Robert                    14 January 1946   Hanover
   The neat little package "for my collection" gave me a lot of pleasure. The poem will give me pleasure many times. Your Christmas
pop corn is a nice petard to hoist the solemn—like Louis M. Such
kindly malice, yours is, when it's all "collected". Your innocuous
looking explosives will help the few, so determined, to keep the
bright new *ratios* from lasting till all variety and venture are in secure and sanitary rat-traps.
   I've been reading Milton, Pope, Burns, Blake, Wordsworth,
Coleridge, Keats and Shelley. And I've secretly concluded that if
men of supposed taste are ever sufficiently mature and composed,
none of those will be so valued as one of my contemporaries who
has too much humor to be comprehended by the unimaginatively
serious, now supposed to be the men of taste.
   Don't stay in below zero territory too long.

                                         Affectionately
                                         Sidney

[A partly typed, partly handwritten, unsigned poem, "An Abandoned Schoolhouse, To the Right Person, Fourteen Lines," was included with this letter. The
poem is the same here as in *The Poetry of Robert Frost*, with the exception that,
in the final version, the title is simply "To the Right Person." Above the date Frost
had handwritten a note: "Maybe I'll write you out one or two more or have Kay
type them as a more special favor. R."]

ALS, 2 pp.

## 124.

                                    29 August 1946   Ripton

              An Abandoned Schoolhouse
                To the Right Person
                Fourteen Lines

          In the one state of ours that is a shire
          There is a District Schoolhouse I admire—

As much as anything for situation.
There are few institutions standing higher
This side the Rockies in my estimation—
Two thousand feet above the ocean level.
It has two entries for co-education.
But there's a tight-shut look to either door
And to the windows of its fenestration
As if to say mere knowledge was the devil,
And this school wasn't keeping any more
Unless for penitents who took their seat
Upon its doorsteps as at Mercy's feet
To make up for a lack of meditation.

Dear Sidney:

I've been giving new poems to comparatively new friends—
newer to me than they are to you. I know some of them through
you. I musn't forget that you liked me in manuscript before you or
anyone else had seen me in print, and musn't be forgotten in my
present mood of wanting my new things to be read. The above is
as it got copied the first time and then corrected to go with my talk
on The Constant Symbol I reduced to writing for my *Collected
Poems* in the Modern Library (due sometime this year.) Ted Weeks
heard of my talk essay or preface and politely asked for it for the
*Atlantic.*\* Such affluence of publication would make me ashamed
except that I suffered such stringency more or less patiently for so
many years to begin with. You wont think I am too much pleased
with myself. I am only trying to entertain you a little where you
are in Dick's House. What you been doing? Taking too much on
yourself all day and every day all the year round I suspect. Charles
Bolté says so.† I've wondered at you and the way you give the
hours to the young in their aspirations (not to say ambitions). A
little of that drives me nervous. I saw four in four hours Tuesday
afternoon as my contribution to the Writers Conference, and
though two of them were good (one very good) I was keyed up to
fly by the time the dinner-bell rang. I didn't scream: I flew. Its the
sympathy that takes it out of the mentor. Isn't it splendid you have
such a self-sufficient good boy as Arthur and that I have such an
interesting independent daughter as Lesley?‡ I'm always hearing

great things about Arthur. Right on the ball in tennis and in the State Department. Children like them don't need anybody's shoulder to weep on. Not that they may not have to take their knocks. They expect to take them without us for cushion. They have lots to tell us rather than ask us when they come home. "Rich, are they not, in wonders seen." Full of life politics and philosophy. Thank God there are some to cheer us. Surely we can enjoy them without danger of being punished for overweening pride. We below bumbling in other quarters. I dont know whether you do or not. I know I do. You are probably under orders not to answer me. [Peace and rest?][5]

R.

*Edward Augustus Weeks (b. 1898): editor of the *Atlantic Monthly*, 1938–1966.
†Charles Guy Bolté (b. 1920): Dartmouth '41, writer, journalist, a student of Cox's and Frost's. He left college to fight in World War II as a British officer.
‡Lesley Frost served as cultural officer and director of the United States Information Library in Spain, 1945–1947. Arthur Macy Cox became an official in the CIA and the State Department and published *The Politics of Détente* in 1976.
§Frost's brackets

ALS, 1 p.

## 125.

Dear Robert                    9 September 1946    Hanover
    You get the first letter in my own hand; I was that grateful for the poem and letter. I am amused again at the way you keep insisting that you have no duplicity about you—it's strictly height above sea-level that you're concerned with. I could make a whole book about education out of "The Abandoned School House", though I suppose I shouldn't do it with your degree of abandon.
    I am a lucky duffer. My coronary thrombosis didn't come on until I was through a good six weeks at Cummington—the official eve of closing, and not until I was all-but fifty-seven. (My first hospitalization and the only serious illness I can remember. No need to look for perversity of mine, in giving time to people that I like, to account for signs of wear and tear after all these years.) And when it did come I took it for a strange form of indigestion in-

duced by devouring an excess of cucumbers. And I stayed around at Cummington for the Trustee's meeting, and saw the school into the formost lodgement for growth it's ever had. There was never any severe pain, never any spectacular collapse. And now I'm comfortable in a nice room for six weeks—four more. I read, have delightful visits from Alice and, for a few days, from Arthur and his admirable and charming fiancée, and get along famously with good nurses and one of the best of doctors. Beginning today I can have other visitors. Wendell is out for football, but I've had two entertaining calls from him.

It was nice to get from Knopf good-looking sample pages of *Indirections*. Speaking of humiliations, one of mine has been my five foot shelf of unpublishable works. This summer *The Atlantic* turned down an essay cut from *Winking at the Sphinx*. The which is one of the most readable and searching philosophical essays. It must be a book some day. It's deep enough to win assent from adherents of the modernism of the year. It's that this year.

Very affectionately<br>Sidney

ALS, 1 p.

## 126.

Dear Sidney:                    19 January 1947    Hanover

You didnt get much help out of me in Florida. Mrs Kirk at Key West failed me so I failed you. She must have been clear out of the state somewhere. Lillian [LaBatt Frost] had nothing to report in Coconut Grove or South Miami. But you came out all right on the other side of the peninsula. I'm no good at such things. My lack of intensity may be to blame. I never paw the ground, steam at the nostrils, froth at the mouth or gore fences do I? It has to be conceeded. Not getting too conscious of my deficiencies is probably what keeps me still going so late in the day. Remember me to Stockdale and thank him for his favor.* Tell him from me I wish he would like Cincinnati or wherever he finds himself. He will do his nation so much more good if he only will. He is one of the surest things I know. You sound well—and sure too.

Ever yours<br>R.F.

You shall have the set of booklets right off. I expect to get to South Miami on the 24th of Jan. for a stay of three or four weeks—a short one this year owing to relativity troubles. My address there: Box 100 Route 2 corner of Davis and Schoolhouse Roads South Miami Fla. Come over.

* William (Bill) Stockdale (b. 1919): a student of Cox's, Dartmouth '42, is a college educator in Minnesota.

TLS, 3 pp.

## 127.

Hanover

Dear Robert                                        [31 March 1947]

Please write to me before Lawrance Thompson arrives on April 11, bent on getting from me what I know and think about "Frost's 'pilgrim's progress' in the realm of spiritual matters." He sounds to me as if he were going to make a conventional academic biography, and wanted to use me to supply the comprehension of what is nearest to the secret, central you (which nobody quite knows?). I need to know whether or not you approve of my having the use of the material that Professor Newdick had gathered and written, and of my writing a biography. If I have definite assurance, it will help me to be kind without being wasteful when Mr. Thompson gets here. I want his book to be good, of its kind. But he is too much a product of the academic rolling and stamping mill to be able even briefly to fold himself to anything like your solid, protean shape. (He cannot think in such paradoxes: you must be on any particular day *either* solid *or* protean, and he will think his problem is to explain your inconsistency, instead of to grasp your flexible firmness of form.) He is talking disgustingly in terms of "Yankee background", "Scotch background", etc. I hate to distress you. It isn't *very* bad, and some Ph. D. is sure to do it, if he doesn't. But there is a place too for my effort; and if I last I shall make it, in some form. Now I am asking you: shall the form be biography-portrait, or shall it be just portrait?

INDIRECTIONS, shrouded in secrecy, sold 2200 the first month. I get some gratifying responses from a few old friends and a few strangers. No one in the English department has read it yet, and only four or five have made any reference to it in my presence. Nat Goodrich [Dartmouth College librarian] walked clear over to my study to tell me that he picked it up with no intention of reading it, could not put it down until he had finished it, and liked it.

Sam Morse writes, "The new Frost poems in the April *Atlantic* are wicked and wonderful." *

I have had a fine time teaching, and I seem to be doing ok as far as health goes. This vacation I shall work on an article the American Mercury editor asked for, after reading INDIRECTIONS, and on the book I aim to finish before I start a new and better book on R. F. I had one within two chapters of done two years ago. But I decided against it.

Hope you will enjoy California, stay well and be here in fine fettle before long.

Yours<br>Sidney

* The poems are "Etherealizing," "An Importer," "No Holy Wars for Them," and "But He Meant It," which became "The Broken Drought" in *The Poetry of Robert Frost.*

TLS, 4 pp.

## 128.

Dear Robert                    27 June 1947    Hanover

Alice and I had a pleasant drive over to Durham, Tuesday, to inquire about pottery prospects. We found that the Scheiers are giving a course at N. H. State this summer. But when we got there we found that the maximum enrollment had been reached. We could have sent to Lillian [LaBatt Frost] a blank on which to apply for a dormitory room and for inclusion in the waiting list, but we didn't think the chances looked good enough.

A few days earlier I had received from Dr. Gambrill, acting director of Cummington this summer, a catalog and a letter to be forwarded to Lillian, in very long delayed reply to her inquiry. The pottery teacher had been sent by his father to Italy to see if he could persuade an ex-prisoner of war who had become engaged to the pottery teacher's sister to do right by her. Meanwhile the pottery teacher's wife had relayed Lillian's inquiry. If she is still willing to give Cummington a chance I think many things about it, especially the location, will please her.

I had a friendly letter today from Max Baym, in which he says, "Is Robert Frost still in Hanover? How is he? I am still thinking of that memorable evening I spent at 13 Brewster Street (The scholar is not so accurate this time.), on my way back from Hanover to Brooklyn and of the sort of figures we cut in the early morning when Robert and his nephew (There's that mystery I once spoke of.) —also Robert's dog—escorted me to Harvard Square. Come to think of it, Sidney, there are four individuals I have ever had completely satisfactory conversations with: my father, Frost, Stieglitz, and You." He's a funny man but friendly and pretty genuine. He says he is responsible for at least a dozen sales of INDIRECTIONS.

So am I a funny man. I've been seeing myself in a perspective thirty years long as I read some of the letters I wrote Alice then. On the contrary, reading some of her letters surprises me; I am amazed to discover what unqualified feelings she overtly expressed. I guess I always have taken her teasing without quite the right kind and quantity of salt. Anyway she was a lovely girl, and I think that time has given more than it's taken.

Hope you're enjoying the "rare" good "day" or so "in June", and not minding the wet, dark, cold ones too much.

Alice bought me [Robert Lowell's] "Lord Weary's Castle" and Mary Webb's "Poems and The Spring of Joy" for Father's day. I like quirks and mocking or fierce runs of syllables in Lowell's poems, but I haven't found one yet that doesn't baffle me a little on several readings. And I don't believe his total feeling and intention is valuable enough to really wrack my brain. But he does seem to have humor and not to be riding all the contemporary gray mares.

Alice has been picking bushels of field strawberries to freeze and make into jam. I've hulled by the hour and picked, too, twice.

Hence these white spots on both arms—something like kalomine lotion to quiet the poison ivy sting and dry up the pustules. Not bad, thanks be.

I'll be writing again about the middle of August to ask if we can come and accept your invitation. Till then

Affectionately
Sidney

TLS, 2 pp.

## 129.

Dear Robert                    24 November 1947    Hanover

I'm pleased by a letter that came from Bill Stockdale this morning, and I'm going to quote a little of it.

"Indications are that Robert Frost will write his best poetry when he's older than Shaw now is. I've read the *Masque of Mercy* in *The Atlantic*. It's the wisest, teasingest thing I've ever struck. . . . he's America's best so far and can play first string on the All-World, All-Time Team. Not even Shakespeare ever wrote better blank verse lines than those which end the masque. And he (S) never spoke a greater Truth."

Too bad he's not advisor to the Nobel prize committee. And it's too bad that most of those who are most articulate about poets and writers have to make sure what somebody in England or France or Cloud-cuckoo Land thinks before they can pick their favorites. If we learned to perceive excellence instead of to consult authorities for it, then there would be enough voices like Bill Stockdale's to drown out the shriller pipes. It isn't the poor judges I object to most: it's the people who do not judge at all but quote the poor judges. At Dartmouth the shame is the critics that are taken seriously by those who haven't time for such matters. I don't object so much to Alec Laing and Philip Wheelwright as to the people who mistake lifelong schoolboys for either scholars or wise men.* I guess you have to have a mind yourself to recognize mind. And that makes it tough for the professional recognizers. They get parroted—a little while.

Anyway, here's to you, with affection,

Sidney

---

*Alexander Laing (1903–1976): poet, novelist, editor, teacher, assistant librarian, and director of the Public Affairs Laboratory at Dartmouth in 1947. Philip Wheelwright (1901–1970): philosopher and poet; Dartmouth professor of philosophy in 1947.

[This unfinished two-page letter, unsigned, written on yellow-legal-pad paper, is torn off on both pages; the first page is torn where there is handwriting; the second page after the writing has stopped. We do not know if Cox received this letter. On August 3, 1948, (ALS) Cox wrote to William Bronk: "My Frost book, finished, has been in the hands of Mrs. Morrison, Robert's secretary, to make sure that it contains no cause of irrelevant discomfort for acquaintances of Robert's and to get the needful permissions, for more than a month. No chirp from her. No peep from me."]

## 130.

Dear Sidney                                    [c. August 1948]
    Part of my reason for taking this cheerfully bright yellow paper is to help me reassure you about your dread book. Go ahead and publish it on me if you think you must, all things considered. I am at your mercy. As Alice says and you agree I am unwilling to recognize myself in your description. I am such a free wild animal that being defined is as hateful to me as being trapped and caged. But never mind my niceness. All I need do is keep from knowing what you make of me. Maybe it is only my work poem by poem and in detail you are attempting and not me personally. Better that I should control my curiosity and not ask to know. I must stay as unselfconscious as possible in the time that is left to me and for anything that remains [torn off] could have wished you had stuck [torn off] wait for publication till [torn off] [second page:] to the teachers at Springfield. I admire it greatly and I particularly like it for delimiting your style of teaching and distinguishing it from mine. You are a psychologist every minute of the class.

TLS, 3 pp.

131.

Dear Robert                8 January 1949    Hanover
Have you yet seen the December number of WHAT'S NEW?* It
is here at last, and if the poem, *From Plane to Plane* on page 10 is
not by you there is another great poet living who has been thinking some of the identical thoughts I have heard you utter within
the last eighteen months and whose ways are not to be distinguished from yours. Since it repeats at the end, on the second of
the two pages, your thought of last August about escaping thanks
I can't say how much I like it.
My former student, Joseph Dunham has certainly made for the
Abbott Laboratories a sumptuous confection, as some say: cover
painting by Utrillo; reproductions of paintings by Per Rom, Geor-
ges Roualt [Rouault], Doris Lee, Clara Klinghoffer, Lawrence Beall
Smith; decorations in color by several including Joe Jones, Paul
Sample and James Chapin; and lithographs by Joseph Hirsch and
Pablo Picasso. The colors are wonderfully good. Oh, yes, and
there is a two page spread with an original musical composition
from the suite *Materia Medica*. Most of the editors are apparently
doctors of medicine; two are the other kind, Ph. Ds. And the articles are on such topics as "Rutin in the Treatment of Frostbite,"
and "Ascorbic Acid: Natural vs. Synthetic." There are two stories
and two poems in this "special Christmas edition." All I mildly
protest at is that George Ratkai who painted the cornfield with
two men in it to accompany the poem didn't put the doctor's foot
on the dashboard, in the distance. That is, I shall have no other
objection unless you tell me that Joe had no right to print the
poem. I'd like to hear about that.
A good year of good health to you.

Affectionately
Sidney

*The house organ of the pharmaceutical firm, Abbott Laboratories, edited by Joseph
Dunham.

ALS, 2 pp.

## 132.

Dear Robert                    8 August [1949]    Hanover
     Something I just wrote at the bottom of page seventy-two made
me think of you. That brought back a vivid dream I had never
thought of in waking hours. In the dream you were distressed in a
way I never saw you and never shall see you, I'm sure. But the rec-
ollection sets me to writing to you.
     I hear of you from Phil Booth. And I read about you with no
small delight from the pen of Mark Van Doren, and with considerable pleasure from a variety of less illumined writers.*
     I hope you are going strong and that the great affection of old
friends sometimes is felt.
     I'm having grand mornings with my pencil and good times often
with returning students and congenial people such as it would be
silly to expect to find. We are expecting visits from a whole flock
of children and grandchildren in about three weeks.
     I am not the only one who is a little melancholy at the thought
that your visits will be at Amherst and not Dartmouth next year.
You must come to see us at least once.
     Keep well!

                                        Yours affectionately
                                        Sidney

     *Philip Booth (b. 1925): Dartmouth '47, poet, author of several volumes of poetry, in-
cluding *Syracuse Poems* (1970, 1973) and *Available Light* (1976). Van Doren's "Our Great
Poet, Whom We Read and Love: In His *Collected Poems* Robert Frost Again Speaks to Us
All" appeared on the front page of *The New York Herald-Tribune Weekly Book Review*
May 29, 1949.

TLS, 2 pp.

## 133.

Dear Robert                    3 May 1950    Hanover
     James Wheatley is the boy who wrote the excellent account in
the *Dartmouth* about his talk with you.* He is incidentally one of

the three maturest and subtlest men in my two writing classes, and one of the finest. The other day I found that he is supplementing his income by writing English briefs for the downtown Dartmouth Tutoring Bureau, and by lecturing to those who come round to them for aid just before exams. I was surprised, and at the same time assured that he was exerting himself to make his work real teaching, not just helping the discouraged to pass. Then, a week or so ago, I learned that he was going to write something about you. I was much pleased. I knew it would go much deeper than most of the English department is able to go, and be good. Now I have seen it I am even better pleased with it than I had dared to anticipate. And for once I promise that you will find little or nothing to object to, and more that you will like than you would normally expect.

I am glad we are to see each other next summer. Your last, that is to say, latest appearance here was so packed with excellence that it was, for its length, as good as could be.

Yours sincerely<br/>Sidney Cox

P.S. Peter Viereck gives me comfort among the younger poets, as I read him in Louis Untermeyer. All have humor and none claims to possess the absolute. They sing.

S.C.

---

*James Holbrook Wheatley (b. 1929): Dartmouth '51, class poet, editor of the student newspaper, *The Dartmouth*; now an English professor at Trinity College, Hartford, Connecticut.

TLS, 3 pp.

## 134.

Dear Robert                          22 September 1951    Hanover

We got home from my sabbatical yesterday afternoon, both of us well and still solvent, and full of good and varied memories. This morning I learn that in my absence you had an operation over here, and I am glad to guess that the trouble is all over now. Alice had a similar operation on her nose about eight or nine years ago, and has had no more difficulty.*

I don't know yet what will come of our trip, but I do know that we saw a lot and met a variety of interesting people. And what happened was unplanned and unschemed. For instance it was no doing of either one of us that we were selected to sit at the captain's table on the return voyage. The only prearrangement was my writing to John Kelleher who teaches Irish culture at Harvard and getting from him a list of people in Ireland to see and of places to go. The rest of the time, and much of the time in Ireland, I was not a professor but was instead merely Alice Cox's husband just seeing what was there to be seen.

In five days my college work commences. I'll be glad to be teaching again. I'll get hold of The Atlantic in a day or two and read the poem I heard of, merely, while I was in England. I was luckier with "How Hard it is Not To Be King When It's in You and in the Situation." Somebody sent me that. It is fun to see (after the fact) a poem growing and then to see the poem. It's great to have evidence how much of living and how long thinking combines (in you, chiefly) with such frivolous-seeming jokes and sly innuendoes. Again I see how those who hold poetry sacredly apart from every day living must be condemned to miss the greatest poet of their day.

But you are right and wise in the long run. And I guess that is best.

Yours sincerely<br>Sidney

---

* Frost was operated on for a cancerous lesion near his right eye in the summer of 1951 at the Mary Hitchcock Memorial Hospital in Hanover, New Hampshire.

## PART SIX

# Coda
## 1952−1957

*I just couldn't sell Sidney's friendship with you.*

ALICE COX *to* ROBERT FROST
*10 January 1953*

SIDNEY COX died on January 3, 1952, at age sixty-two. On a chill Sunday afternoon, January 6, the shocked Dartmouth community gathered for a memorial service in Rollins Chapel. There was no religious ceremony. Cox, the son of a minister, had left the institutional church years before. As Dartmouth professor Stearns Morse said, "The outward forms of Christianity he sloughed off in his later life; but what is essential in it remained—the burning individualism, the moral intensity." Robert Frost came up from Cambridge, Massachusetts—not an easy trip in the dead of winter for a seventy-seven-year-old man. He read Cox's favorite Frost poem, "Come In," "a call to come in / To the dark and lament." Morse saw tears in the old man's eyes. But Frost kept the service from becoming lugubrious: he made harmless little jokes to comfort Alice Cox.

Morse, giving the eulogy, spoke gracefully, compassionately, truthfully of his close friend. Cox burned with "a hard gem-like flame," not for "the moment's sake, but for the illumination of his life with meaning." The intensity, the high voltage of his work, had extinguished him early. Of his hundreds of students—the dull, the mediocre, the keen, the brilliant—none could forget him. He still lived for those who had tramped with him over the hills, those who had attended his Sunday nights, those who had sat in his classes, those who had "attained the reputation as writers he failed to attain." [1]

The Dartmouth Faculty Council Resolution—written by Cox's colleagues Hewette Joyce, Henry Williams, and Harry Schultz—assessed the magnitude of the loss: "Perhaps few men in the history of the College have influenced students so powerfully and variously as Sidney Cox." The Resolution stated: "his very intensity stirred antagonism in natures equally intense, yet no one would be with him without being stirred and quickened." The teacher "spent himself with the prodigality of the great artist. . . . He felt his responsibility to the human being in every one of his students, and it was to that human being he appealed, offering himself with a courage few possess." Cox "was in the great tradition of liberal education, which has always set itself the task of cultivating that which is noblest in men. . . . Generations of Dartmouth graduates are better men for having known Sidney Cox." [2]

Cox's greatest memorial was his life, the Resolution concluded; but students and alumni joined together to create another one: the Sidney Cox Memorial Prize, to be awarded each year to the undergraduate whose creative writing fulfilled Cox's "broad, flexible, but uncompromising definition of literature." The honorary chairmen of the committee were Robert Frost and A. B. Guthrie; the chairman was Budd Schulberg, who wrote to prospective donors: "For Sidney Cox there were no false barriers between life and literature. His teaching and his presence on the Dartmouth campus were an exciting spur to honest writing and creative thinking. One left his classes with a desire—if not a compulsion—to reach just a little more deeply into himself, to disdain easy formula, to struggle for meaningful form." [3]

Reshaping her life—she was now sixty—Alice Cox lived on a considerably reduced income. She moved to the third-floor "attic" apartment of her house, renting out the two lower floors. Sorting the letters Frost had written to her husband over four decades, she felt that, despite her financial needs, she could not turn the letters to profit: "I just couldn't sell Sidney's friendship with you," she told Frost. She gave the entire correspondence and Cox's first editions of Frost to the Dartmouth College Library. Then she looked about for employment. Answering an advertisement in *The Saturday Review of Literature*, she was hired as cook-housekeeper for a retired executive, the owner of an extensive ranch in Penablanca, New Mexico.

One thing remained—to publish, if she could, what Cox had wanted to say publicly about his friend. She submitted *A Swinger of Birches: A Portrait of Robert Frost* to several publishers, who rejected the manuscript. Undaunted, she persisted. In September 1954 she sent the book to Wilson Follett, an urbane, masterful editor at New York University Press. As an editor at Alfred A. Knopf in the late forties, he had had a hand in publishing Cox's *Indirections*; and he recognized the value of Cox's study. Follett accepted the manuscript, and he initiated a series of letters to the poet, inviting him to write an introduction to the volume. The vigorous exchanges between the two men were punctuated by long silences on Frost's part. One letter, of June 23, 1955, is lost, but Follett's quotations from it, in his letter of April 25, 1956, make it clear that Frost found the invitation dreadful, unthinkable. The editor was Frost's equal in shaping wily, agile, persuasive prose, but Frost complied by writing only "a grudging" introduction—until he learned that Alice Cox, unwilling to be dependent on her children, needed the royalties her husband's book would bring. Taking back his essay, Frost wrote a new one, which differs considerably from the original introduction. It is the second version that is printed in the opening pages of *A Swinger of Birches*, published in 1957, five years after Cox's death. The original one is printed here, with Letter 140.

In that small volume, Cox recounts the anecdotes, observations, and reflections he had wanted to disclose in print for twenty-five years. Frost, who had virtually silenced his friend in life, was powerless to silence him in death. The book says nothing derogatory about Frost. Praising him, it gives Frost's views on sex, love, poetry, and education. Favorably received, it sold well, probably because Cox captures the poet's mind at work, shaping, creating, ordering poetry, as well as the universe. Cox's study contributed to Frost's image as the kindly, quirkily brilliant New England sage. The book stands as an inimitable testament by someone who knew Frost—so the poet enigmatically said—better than he knew himself. Cox, who may well have embodied Frost's ideal of the teacher, was described by the poet as "at his best in his free letters. Yes, and of course in his teaching. A great teacher." Ironically enough, Frost wrote, "I wish I had kept some of the great letters he wrote me but I am no curator of letters or anything else."[4]

Through the years, Frost and Cox had confided in each other. Their friendship had deep roots; despite strains, it endured. Frost recognized Cox's rare gifts of complete sincerity and frankness, his sensitivity and total commitment to poetry. No mindless chitchat, no malicious gossip mar the Frost-Cox letters. Though undeniably a hero worshiper, Cox evoked much of what was truly noble in Frost. Cox had recognized Frost's genius when he read the early poems in manuscript. At that Plymouth, New Hampshire, dance and on the street the next day, Frost sensed trustworthiness, loyalty in Cox. The older man succeeded in "taking" the young teacher, and he kept a place for him throughout his crowded life.

Alice Cox felt her husband had substituted the poet for the god his New England forebears had worshiped. Writing in December 1956 from New Mexico, she had the final word in this strange, eventful relationship, in a letter of thanks for the introduction to *A Swinger of Birches* to a Frost she refused to worship.

Nature's first green may have been hard for the two men to hold, but it was gold. And, unlike the spring gold in Frost's poem, this gold stayed.

## NOTES

1. "In Memoriam: Sidney Cox," *Dartmouth Alumni Magazine*, 44 (February 1952):15.
2. Dartmouth College Faculty Council Resolution on the Death of Professor Sidney Cox, n.d.
3. 1 October 1952.
4. Introduction, p. vii.

TLS, 1 p.

# 135.

Dear Robert:                              10 January 1953   Hanover

We were very sorry not to hear you and see you when you were here in December. Barbie and her husband and her middle little boy (she has five children now) were spending five weeks with me. Val had gone down to Lexington, Kentucky, to buy horses for the Panama Jockey Club and was flying back the day you spoke. When we got to the airport, we found that he had missed the plane because of bad weather, and wanted us to go down to Manchester to get him there. So we didn't get back to Hanover until long after you had finished your reading.

I decided to stay on in Hanover. After living here twenty-seven years, I couldn't think of any place where I would belong, where people would know me when I walked along the street. It is too late to start a brand new life. So I moved up in the third floor apartment—the attic apartment—of the same house where Sidney and I lived. It is a place of my own.

Sidney left it to me to decide what to do with the letters you wrote him and the books and Christmas cards you sent him. He wanted to leave them to the Dartmouth Library, but he thought that I might need the money they might bring, to live on. I'll get along all right, so the other day Harold Rugg and I went over everything, and I gave the library—in Sidney's name—everything they did not have. I just couldn't sell Sidney's friendship with you.

Affectionately
Alice Cox

TLS, 2 pp.

# 136.

Dear Robert:                              28 July [1954]   Hanover

My first tomato was really ripe today. I feel rather smug about it, because two other families in this house bought plants from the same place and planted them within a few feet of mine, and theirs are barely colored.

I am having a very good time this summer taking care of Harold Rugg's garden while he is in Europe. It is a real adventure. I have planted seeds from India that have sprouted, coddled a poor little dried-up Manchurian apricot from North Dakota so that it is flourishing, and done the same to a quantity of plants that Harold gathered in the French Alps that arrived in sad condition. The only trouble is that the garden is so big, and all this rain encourages the weeds as well as the legitimate plants, and I never can catch up.

I have been meaning to write to you ever since I took out a volume of Gertrude Bell's letters from the Howe Library, and found that the last person to read them was not one of the usual patrons of the library who all have cards that are numbered but "Frost", way back in the early 40's; and I wondered if it was you.* Just now, I am reading Sarah Orne Jewett; she bears rereading. I like to read myself to sleep. I always used to read to Sidney until he fell asleep. Plattsburg means Bleak House.

A little while ago I had a nice little note from Irma—wondering if she had given me the right directions to The Ranch way back in November. I wrote her assuring her that she did.

The telegram that you sent at the time we presented the prize in Sidney's memory did not arrive until the day I was leaving for six weeks in Panama. Perhaps some one has written you telling about what a good time we had. The boys enjoyed it, too.

This afternoon I had a nice visit with Ruby Daggett down at the bookstore. Apparently both she and I are off your Christmas card list. She says that this year's card is reported to be about Gillie [Frost's collie]. We are fond of Gillie—and you. Please, mayn't we have one?

I am sorry that I am usually out of town when you are here. There are ten grandchildren now, Arthur has four, Barbie five, and Wumps one and a half.

I hope that you are feeling well and having fun.

Affectionately,
Alice Cox

* Gertrude Bell (1868–1926): English travel writer, expert on Arabia; her *Letters* were published in 1927.

TLS, 2 pp.

137.

Dear Mr. Frost:                    20 October 1954   New York

A September letter from Alice Cox tells me that Sidney Cox had just finished revising *A Swinger of Birches* when he died; also that Sidney when he had completed the first draft, sent the manuscript to you to find out if there were anything in it that you disapproved. Both are points of some importance to me, because, by an arrangement largely of my making, this Press is going to have the gratification of publishing *A Swinger of Birches* in the spring, and I should feel much less comfortable in my mind if either assurance were lacking. I hope you will think that few happier transactions could have been brought off behind your back while you were in South America.

There is only one thing missing from Cox's very fine portrait—he calls the little book a portrait in his subtitle—and that is something about Cox; about what he was in himself and about what he was (and, I suppose, is) to you. His pages are a saturation with Robert Frost, but Sidney Cox is almost totally ignored in them. Self-evidently, there will have to be some sort of introduction by someone who can speak knowledgeably about the facts of his long association with you. I have thought and thought, I have asked and asked, and I can neither think nor hear of anyone alive who is fit to say the right things in the right way, except—Robert Frost. Will you do that? The more I have thought of the possibility, the more I have inclined to see it as something that you could do with great gladness, and perhaps could hardly bear not to do. For that reason I find it an easy and not a hard thing to ask.

The idea, I should add, is all my own. It has grown on me in many sessions with the manuscript, until I have become pretty well incapable of reading Cox on Frost without the besetting conviction that it was meant and is destined to be also Frost on Cox.

It is, of course, not possible to have such an idea without the awareness that your introduction would do a great deal for the book—would make it easier to distribute more copies faster, would add a material leverage. And I don't see that that would be a bad thing, either, or even a bad motive. Nevertheless it is not my motive, and I should not be writing this letter if I were thinking first of merchandise. (I guess you will recall that I put up a fairly obstinate struggle for *Indirections*, and certainly no one can ever have imagined that *that* was a fight for merchandise.) We are going to be proud to publish *A Swinger of Birches*, whether or no. It is my belief that such words as you can give it will make the book more perfectly and completely itself. If you can see it so, I for one shall be very happy.

And, introduction or no, if for any reason you would like to see the revised manuscript, I shall take pleasure in sending it to you at once or whenever you say.

Yours sincerely,
Wilson Follett

TLS, 1 p.

## 138.

Dear Mr. Frost:                        10 May 1955   New York
Is it not possible for you to take a moment to acknowledge a fairly long-standing invitation to contribute some word of your own to Sidney Cox's *Swinger of Birches*, a book written with great devotion to you and to truth as Cox saw it? In a letter to you of last October I stated the reasons for hoping that you would do this and for believing that you would want to; if you have forgotten or mislaid the letter and would now consider what it said, I shall be glad to send you a copy. Whether you do or do not wish to do what was asked, it seems as if Cox's forty years of self-forgetful devotion ought to be worth at least a Yes or a No to a man who was also Cox's friend and who has been an inveterate and out-spoken friend of your work from *North of Boston*.

Let me add that, as I said last October, I shall be glad to show you the completed and revised text of *A Swinger of Birches* if you wish to see it. My information, which I have no reason not to trust, is that when you saw it in an earlier draft you thought well of it and felt grateful for it.

Yours sincerely,
Wilson Follett

TLS, 2 pp.

# 139.

Dear Mr. Frost:                    April 25, 1956    New York

It has taken me quite a while to digest a letter that you wrote last June 23—one that, apart from all practical considerations, was a nearly unassimilable shock. I have now got, I believe, where I can make a just commentary without dragging in a lot of emotional detritus, and I think it necessary to make it.

". . . I have to stand on my principles of a lifetime. I have never read anything about myself in manuscript. . . ." Sidney Cox believed, and died believing, that you had read in manuscript (unrevised version) this little book of his; may you not, then, have made one exception that has slipped your memory? In the book you found, he also believed, nothing to provoke an objection. He was a man of too much delicacy to print such an analysis of a living person—even if the person had not been Robert Frost—without making sure whether any of it went against the grain of the subject.

"I had rather not regard our support of each other as an exchange of favors as in politics (so-called)." If that means you and Sidney, he clearly wasn't trying to confer a favor on anybody but his public readers; he was trying to tell some truths that had lived themselves in him. If the sentence means you and me—heavens above, I have no spirit of either giving or asking favors, let alone swapping them. It seemed up to me to provide a chance that you might well have hated being deprived of.

". . . I am not going to be caught praising my praises if that is what Sidney has been writing and I can pretty safely assume he has for the friendship he bore me." The assumption that I wanted praise of the book is as foreign to all I meant as to all I said. You were important to Sidney Cox for four decades; there must have been senses in which he was and is important to you; something, sometime, you will surely need to say about the facts of the association. Can there ever be a better, more natural context for saying it? The facts of the association—those are what, and all, I had in mind.—As for Sidney's praises of you—well, of course he was writing about what was important to him, as it is to many, and I suppose you could call that praise. He was also dissecting to the marrow of a writer and a man, and if there is praise in doing that, there is certainly no puffery. He gave none; he wanted none; I want nothing for him that he did not want.

The short of it is, I should be nearer to happy (as what Vermonter wouldn't?) if you declined—"in some unhappiness," as you put it—to do what I asked instead of declining to do something fairly remote from it in spirit. I should be happiest of all if you found it a natural, a simply inevitable thing to do and just contentedly did it. Please tell me with considerate promptness, in one line or one word, that you will or won't.

Yours faithfully,
Wilson Follett

[In the first draft of this letter, the final sentence read, "No offence, my dear man, no offence." This sentence was scratched out, and "All's well now?" was substituted, probably in Kathleen Morrison's handwriting. Enclosed with the letter was the original "Preface" to *A Swinger of Birches*, reprinted here.]

TLS, 1 p.

## 140.

Dear Mr. Follett:                              28 June 1956   Ripton
I am sorry if my letter gave you a hard time. I wonder if I couldn't bring you peace and end this small to-do by writing you a bookselling preface. I trust one can be a little unscrupulous without being corrupt. Unscrupulous merely means not sticking at trifles. I have decided I can go as far as the enclosed without messing things up any further. The last sentence in the preface is all too mournfully true. All's well now?

Sincerely yours
Robert Frost

This is a book I am asked to introduce because it is about me and by a lifelong faithful friend. Our intimacy was a curious blend of differences that if properly handled might prove an almost literary curiosity. That much might be gathered I should think from my letters to him as I remember them. Are they not on deposit in the Dartmouth College Library for anybody to read? If the book is a success in bringing out our protagonism, his character and mine, his as much as mine, I suppose I must as of obligation do what I can to give the book its chance. I have never really read it and have nothing but other people's word to rely on for what it is like. I drew back from one glimpse over the edge into the first part of it more or less out of inability to contemplate myself as others say in print they see me. I read enough to make out that his difficulty was the same as mine herein, that of striking the right tone about our relations. This may be getting too autobiographical, but I can't help relating that I was so abashed for him as well as for myself by what I found in the first chapter or two sent for approval years ago that I never approved of it and in fact never sent it back. My default I was willing to have taken as a *nihil obstat*. I find most attempts to describe me much too disturbing either for my pleasure or my discipline. I am assured and I assume from my knowledge of Sidney Cox that the book is one texture of honesty and as such I may concede it all the value you please, but be the responsibility of giving it to the world entirely on the head of others. An amusing situation I submit—me caught talking up anybody else's talk about me. We were a strange pair in our at-variances. We kept it up between us in a kind of magnanimity or high-minded tolerance of each other's taste. I remember how it began one evening in 1911 when we met as strangers looking on at a school dance at Plymouth, New Hampshire, where we were both teachers, he in one school and I in another. I didn't know who he was except that he looked very teasably young. He didn't know who I was except it seems I looked too old. By saying something flippant about the theme papers he had to hurry away to correct I angered him to the point of his inquiring behind my back if it was because of alcohol I had got no further up in the world at my age. I was thirty-seven. I was just teaching psychology in the Plymouth Normal School. He disdained to speak to me on the street for a while afterwards. But his seriousness piqued the mischief in me and I set myself to take him. He came round all right, but it wasn't the last time he had to make an effort to get over being bothered by me. He worked at it and I can well believe he may have got a real story out of it. He was a great, a triumphant teacher. He was all sincerity. He once wrote an article for the *New Republic* about my sincerity. I was very fond of him in my way. I really set my heart on his literary success.

TLS, 1 p.

## 141.

Dear Mr. Frost:                              3 July 1956   New York

My hard time is all over, thank you kindly. And, gratuitously I know, I am very happy for you—more so, if possible, than for us.

Your Henry Holt and Company are an outfit of amiable enough gentry and ladry in most ways, but they are slightly on the dog-in-a-manger side about anything attempted in your behalf under auspices not theirs. (My information is that they were once offered *A Swinger of Birches*.) Sidney's manuscript is, of course, well salted with quotations from you, for which they could, theoretically, exact from us flesh and blood and a few bones in addition to hide and hair. I imagine they would be decently forbearing if you were to suggest to them that most of the brief illustrative bits that Sidney has used should be seen as coming under the right of reasonable quotation. Should you care to do that? The quotations seldom go beyond two to four lines, and all the excerpts are so managed as to tantalize the casual sampler into becoming a reader. We are, of course, prepared to supply an exact inventory of everything used.

Yours faithfully,
Wilson Follett

[This one-page letter, probably dictated by Frost, was handwritten, presumably by Kathleen Morrison.]

## 142.

Dear Alice:                              21 August 1956   Ripton

I don't know whether you know what's been going on between me and Wilson Follett, the editor of N.Y. University Press. He has wrung out of me a preface to Sidney's book which I am not sure it was in good taste for me to write. The thing hasn't gone so far that it can't be stopped if I see more reasons against it than for it. To say the least it is very unusual for a man to be prefacing a book about himself. The deciding question is how you feel in the matter, what you want me to do, and what you think Sidney would want me to do. Really nothing else matters. I don't mind doing odd things merely because they are odd. You and I and Sidney are an odd lot. You must know I have barely looked at the book. I haven't really read it. I have never been able to go deeply into any thing, review or article, that concerned my life or my work for fear it would overwhelm me with self-consciousness. I trust this doesn't put you in too hard a position. I will cheerfully do anything you please.

Thinking of you out there in NM.

I'm ever yours<br>RF

TLS, 3 pp.

## 143.

Dear Robert:        25 August [1956]    Pena Blanca, New Mexico
About three years ago Wilson Follett asked me for the manuscript of "A Swinger of Birches". Sidney had just finished revising it for the third or fourth time the week before he died. Wilson and the other editors at the New York University Press were enthusiastic about it, but before they got around to publishing the book some one got the idea that it would be wonderful if you would write a little preface about Sidney. Wilson wanted me to ask you, but I refused because I felt that it was a sort of imposition. So, I am afraid that he has been hounding you.

I am sure that Sidney would have been very happy to have you write a little preface. It would have meant a very great deal to him to have something of yours along with his. I don't think you would find anything embarrassingly personal in the manuscript which will make a rather small book concerned mainly with

Sidney's interpretation of your ideas. As for me, I am glad that you have written the preface for two reasons—it will mean that the book that Sidney worked at most of his leisure time after his first heart attack will have a much wider circulation. And I'll be frank—it will mean more money for me. So far I have been able to get along without asking anything from the children, but, until I got this job, it looked as if I would have to have a bit of help from them soon.

Since you have my address, you have probably heard of my adventure. Just for fun one cold grey day in January, I answered an advertisement in The Saturday Review. I tried to see if I could make somebody else see me as I see myself—out of over sixty applicants I was offered the position because I was "the only one perceptive enough to see that the real issue was personality". So I drove across the country to be cook and a sort of glorified housekeeper in this beautiful luxurious place at the mouth of Cochiti Canyon, twelve miles on a dirt road from the little tumble-down Spanish town of Pena Blanca. Our nearest neighbors are the Indians at the Cochiti Pueblo, eight miles away. Most of the time there is no one here but Mr. Young and Marianita, the Indian girl who does all the cleaning, dish washing, etc. I am very fond of her and am happy to be accepted as a friend by her many relatives at the pueblo. Once a week I drive the 45 miles up to Santa Fe to do the shopping.

Mr. Young is 71, was vice president of the J. Walter Thompson Company (the largest advertising agency in the world) and is now senior consultant. He is a really cultivated man and treats me as an equal, and we get along fine. This ranch was his summer place until his wife died four years ago when he decided to give up his New York apartment and make this his home. As a sort of hobby he raises apples; last year he sold 35,000 bushels. Besides, we have cherries and peaches and plums—and a Jersey cow. There is a small vegetable garden and flowers for us to work at. The ranch manager and his wife and two boys are the only other white people on the place. My life here is different from anything I ever experienced before, and I am willing to try it for a year.

I had a nice letter from Irma a while ago that I meant to answer at once, but somehow this country has infected me with mañanaitis. I haven't even written my children for weeks; we have breakfast at 7, and we are usually asleep by 9. Every day we hope for rain, and watch the clouds gather up the canyon. There is usually considerable thunder, but the rain falls somewhere else. Most of the wells have dried up, and the trees are really suffering. The birds here are wonderful and Marianita and I not only feed them but spend time looking for them in the bird books. We have been putting out food for a couple of grey foxes and watching them come down the mesa. And there are the deer that we look for in the orchard. Later, they say there is usually a bear or two there, and wild turkeys.

This is what always happens when I start a letter nowadays— I spend pages describing the ranch and this strange beautiful country and the Indian dances that I have been to, and the life at the pueblo that Marianita tells me about. Tonight, Mr. Young is in New York and Marianita is home, and there is absolute quiet. The stars seem much closer than in New England. It is all quite wonderful.

Affectionately and gratefully,
Alice Cox

TLS, 1 p.

## 144.

Dear Mr. Follett:                    14 September 1956   Ripton

A letter from Alice Cox puts our situation in an entirely new light. She doesn't share my hesitation about the preface at all. She wants it and is sure Sidney would want it. That's all I ask and should have asked from the first. It doesn't matter to me now about this slight discomfort I may still feel in prefacing my own praises. If it is not too late I should like another chance at the preface to touch it up a little and perhaps make it sound a little less grudging. This is partly for my own sake; if I've got to do the unusual thing I don't want to be ungraceful or ungenerous. Sidney and I were great friends and stayed so in spite of the bullying he often got from me in my letters people tell me who have read them where they are on deposit at the Dartmouth College Library. Sometimes his evangelicality made me talk to him much like a Nestor. So if you will let me have my copy to do my relenting with. Which is the way the thing usually winds up with me.

Of course I'm not going to take pay for doing this.

Ever yours
Robert Frost

TLS, 1 p.

## 145.

Dear Mrs. Morrison:            13 December 1956   New York

This note acknowledges with thanks the introduction to *A Swinger of Birches* received some two hours ago. (It is going to be called Introduction rather than Preface if no one demurs: a preface, to my mind, is the author's preamble, not someone else's. And Mr. Frost's name will be at the end of it.)

Here's a small thing: In the sentence "I have stolen look enough over the edge of the book to see that what went on between is brought out much as in our correspondence," surely the intention was ". . . what went on between us"? I have, at a venture, put in the "us," and it stays unless you send me word to take it out.

I tried last week to get this establishment to telegraph Mr. Frost "Wilson Follett is suffering" instead of what actually went, but no one would do it; they said it was *infra dig*. My idea was that it would give a good laugh to a man who likes to laugh.

Everybody is deeply grateful to him for having, so to say, de-Frosted the earlier version of his two pages.

Yours sincerely,
Wilson Follett

TLS, 2 pp.

## 146.

Dear Robert:                16 December [1956]    Pena Blanca
    Thank you. The little introduction is exactly right for a 177 page book that starts—

"Robert Frost never let his head get caught in a halo. He never stood still for admirers to pull a laurel wreath down over his eyes. He kept free to exchange a taunt and a you-and-I-both wink with rogues and the repressed rascal in nearly all of us. He has let nothing come between him and the funny world."

I still feel that the publishers should not have burdened you with the job. I know how much you dislike writing something to order, and this must have been especially hard. But I am grateful, and I am sure that Sidney would be happy with it.

As you probably felt as I did, it seemed to me for years that Sidney had substituted you for the God that his preacher forebears had worshipped, and the missionary spirit was rampant. I liked you and the poems you wrote and the things you said, but I wanted Sidney to stand on his own feet—not on yours. So it was hard all around. But it seemed to me that he was much more mellow and mature the last ten years or so of his life. He might have done more good writing if he had not burned himself up with his teaching, and his teaching came first with him.

When anything interesting happens to me I make carbons and send them around to the children, and you may be amused by the ones I am enclosing. The West is still a bit wild here. I am spending Christmas in Washington with Arthur and his family and then I am going to Hanover for ten days or so. I wish I could have been there when you read and talked a while ago.

    A happy Christmas to you, and a good new year,
                                        Affectionately,
                                        Alice Cox

# Index

Individuals listed here are American unless otherwise identified.